Practical Health Promotion

PRACTICAL
HEALTH
PROMOTION

John Hubley and June Copeman

polity

First published in 2008 by Polity Press
Reprinted with corrections 2010

Polity Press
65 Bridge Street
Cambridge CB2 1UR, UK

Polity Press
350 Main Street
Malden, MA 02148, USA

ISBN-13: 978-07456-3665-8
ISBN-13: 978-07456-3666-5 (pb)

A catalogue record for this book is available from the British Library.

Designed and typeset in 9.5 on 13pt Utopia
by Peter Ducker MISTD
Printed in Italy by Rotolito Lombarda

The publisher has used its best endeavours to ensure that the URLs for external websites referred to
in this book are correct and active at the time of going to press. However, the publisher has no
responsibility for the websites and can make no guarantee that a site will remain live or that the
content is or will remain appropriate.

Every effort has been made to trace all copyright holders, but if any have been inadvertently
overlooked the publisher will be pleased to include any necessary credits
in any subsequent reprint or edition.

For further information on Polity, visit our website: www.polity.co.uk

Contents

Detailed chapter contents

About the authors

John Hubley and June Copeman worked together for many years at Leeds Metropolitan University, teaching health promotion to a wide range of health and social care professionals, at pre- and post-registration levels, from across the world. This textbook is the culmination of their many years of teaching together, and their recognition of the need for a really accessible book that would help students to integrate health promotion theory with their day-to-day professional practice.

John Hubley died very suddenly after completing work on this book. As well as being a Principal Lecturer at Leeds Metropolitan University, he was involved with training, consultancy and research activities in more than twenty-five countries. He worked with a wide variety of organizations in the planning, implementation and evaluation of health promotion projects. Many of the photographs in the book were taken by John, some during his international health promotion work. His previous books include *The AIDS Handbook* (2005) and *Communicating Health* (2004). To quote a former student, who later became a colleague on international projects: 'John is remembered for his devotion to health promotion research and for his warmth and wit. He was a man who took everything he did seriously.'

June Copeman is the Head of Nutrition and Dietetics at Leeds Metropolitan University. She is also a registered dietitian, with ongoing links to the NHS. Although she is interested in a wide range of issues related to food and eating, her main area of expertise is the nutritional needs of older people. Her previous publications include *Nutritional Care for Older People* (1999).

Please visit the webpage that accompanies this book at:

www.polity.co.uk/healthpromotion

Hubley & Copeman - Practical Health Promotion

Polity is pleased to announce...

... the publication of *Practical Health Promotion* in April 2008. You can see a sample chapter of the text – packed with photos, diagrams, activities and student-friendly features – by clicking to the right (don't worry if you spot any errors or typos in this – it hasn't been proofread yet). Alongside this comprehensive and accessible overview of health promotion, John Hubley and June Copeman have worked hard to provide additional materials on this supporting website. For students, there are multiple choice questions to accompany each chapter, five case studies and exercises covering various themes in the book, useful internet links and a searchable glossary. On the instructor side of the site you can find PowerPoint presentations to use in teaching as well as a worksheet for each chapter.

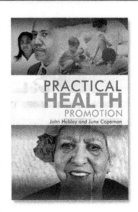

PRACTICAL
HEALTH
PROMOTION
John Hubley and June Copeman

Together, the website and textbook offer a complete package for students needing a beginners' practical guide to health promotion today in all its various forms. We hope you find this website a useful addition to the book and enjoy using the two together as a toolkit to help you gain the skills necessary for health promotion in the twenty-first century.

Click here for a sample chapter

The site includes:

For students:
- Multiple choice questions for each chapter
- Case studies
- Extra exercises
- Internet links
- A searchable glossary

For lecturers:
- PowerPoint presentations to use in teaching
- Worksheets to use with your students

Introduction

How to use this book

Health promotion:
The process of enabling people to increase control over, and to improve their health. (WHO, 1998)

Health promotion is a core component of public health and combines health education directed at individuals and communities, service improvements to make them more appropriate and acceptable, and advocacy directed at influencing policies that affect health. Health promotion is an essential part of the work of most health and community workers, including nurses, doctors, allied health workers, rehabilitation therapists, community workers, and environmental and public health practitioners.

With illustrations, case studies, guidelines, and checklists with step-by-step 'how-tos', this book provides:

- a practical introduction to the discipline of health promotion, the debates and ethical issues involved in promoting health and encouraging healthy lifestyles, reorienting services, developing community action on health and tackling social and economic determinants of health and influencing policy
- links to some key competencies/skills in public health, communication for health and health promotion identified in the Department of Health Skills for Health Programme and National Occupational Standards
- a guide to the promotion of health in the community, workplace, education, primary care, hospital and other health settings
- a starting point for further studies in health promotion. At the end of each chapter we include suggestions for further reading and in the final chapter provide an overview of sources of literature in health promotion. In the website that accompanies this book we provide a comprehensive and regularly updated set of links to relevant websites containing information on health promotion, powerpoint presentations linked to the content of each chapter, and some additional resource material.

Organization of the book

This book is organized around the iterative health promotion planning cycle shown in figure 1 and introduced in chapter 1. The process that we put forward is a cycle because, no matter how much time and effort you put into planning your health promotion, what is really important is how much impact you have achieved and what lessons you can learn for the future. Health promotion planning is a continuous – 'iterative' – process of analysis, intervention and evaluation/reflection, followed by further action.

Figure 1 The iterative health promotion planning cycle

The structure of the book is show in figure 2.

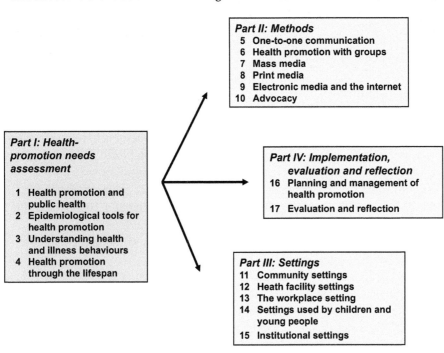

Figure 2 The structure of the book

Health Promotion Needs Assessment

Part I of the book introduces health promotion, the use of epidemiology in analysis of needs/influences on health, and the role of behavioural models in understanding human motivation, and explores how an understanding of lifespan processes can be used in interventions tailored to the needs of people at different stages of the life course.

Defining Health Promotion Strategy – Methods and Settings

Part II (chapters 5–10) and Part III (chapters 11–15) introduce core health promotion methods and settings. Each chapter presents an overview of the method or setting in health promotion with case studies and 'how to' checklists giving practical guidelines on action.

Implementation, Evaluation and Reflection

Chapter 16 in Part IV presents a basic guide to management skills for health promotion, including setting objectives, managing people, developing training programmes and promoting organizational change and improvements in services.

Chapter 17 reviews the evaluation of health promotion and the skills that enable a practitioner to reflect on their practices and learn from experience. Basic concepts in evaluation and evidence-based practice are introduced alongside guidelines on evaluating evidence for impact of health promotion.

Each chapter ends with suggested further reading. The final chapter also explores ways of learning more about health promotion through health promotion research literature and other routes.

PART I

Health Promotion Needs Assessment

1 Health Promotion and Public Health

Contents

1 Health Promotion and Public Health

Key issues within this chapter:

- Health promotion is a key element of public health practice.
- Health promotion involves a combination of health education, service improvement and advocacy.
- Many health workers, professional groups, community-based workers and volunteers have a role in health promotion.
- Health promotion is an evolving discipline with many ongoing debates concerning principles and practice, including the balance between health education and legislation, the role of individualistic and structuralist approaches, the levels at which to operate, the nature of the core values/ethical principles, and the balance between coercive, persuasive and health empowerment approaches.
- A systematic approach to planning health promotion needs to take into account assessment of needs and influences on health, and involves decisions on target groups, methods, settings and timing of activities.

By the end of this chapter you should be able to:

- understand the history of prevention, public health and the evolution of health promotion
- define health promotion and its component parts – health education, service improvement and advocacy
- have considered the debates in health promotion, including approaches and core values/ethical principles, and assessed your own personal approach
- apply principles of health promotion to planning a health promotion intervention.

What is health promotion?

The starting point for any discussion of health promotion is the Ottawa Charter, which in 1986 set out the concept of health promotion (WHO, 1986). Alongside the five key areas of action, summarized in box 1.1, the Ottawa Charter also reaffirmed the importance of community participation and introduced the goal of empowerment – a concept of which we will say more later in this book.

Box 1.1 Extracts from the Ottawa Charter for Health Promotion

Health promotion is the process of enabling people to increase control over, and to improve, their health. To reach a state of complete physical, mental and social wellbeing, an individual or group must be able to identify and to realize aspirations, to satisfy needs, and to change or cope with the environment. Health is, therefore, seen as a resource for everyday life, not the objective of living. Health is a positive concept emphasizing social and personal resources, as well as physical capacities. Therefore, health promotion is not just the responsibility of the health sector, but goes beyond healthy life-styles to wellbeing.

HEALTH PROMOTION ACTION MEANS:
Building Healthy Public Policy – Health promotion goes beyond health care. It puts health on the agenda of policy makers in all sectors and at all levels. It directs policy makers to be aware of the health consequences of their decisions and accept their responsibilities for health.

Health promotion policy combines diverse but complementary approaches including legislation, fiscal measures, taxation and organizational change. It is coordinated action that leads to health, income and social policies that foster greater equity. Joint action contributes to ensuring safer and healthier goods and services, healthier public services, and cleaner, more enjoyable environments.

Health promotion policy requires the identification of obstacles to the adoption of healthy public policies in non-health sectors, and ways of removing them. The aim must be to make the healthier choice the easier choice.

Creating Supportive Environments – Health promotion generates living and working conditions that are safe, stimulating, satisfying and enjoyable. Systematic assessment of the health impact of a rapidly changing environment – particularly in areas of technology, work, energy production and urbanization – is essential and must be followed by action to ensure positive benefit to the health of the public. The protection of the natural and built environments and the conservation of natural resources must be addressed in any health promotion strategy.

Strengthening Community Action – At the heart of this process is the empowerment of communities, their ownership and control of their own endeavours and destinies. Community development draws on existing human and material resources in the community to enhance self-help and social support, and to develop flexible systems for strengthening public participation and direction of health matters.

Developing Personal Skills – Health promotion supports personal and social development through providing information, education for health and enhancing life skills. By so doing, it increases the options available to people to exercise more control over their health and environment, and to make choices conducive to health. Enabling people to learn throughout life, to prepare themselves for all of its stages and to cope with chronic illness and injuries is essential. This has to be facilitated in school, home, work and community settings. Action is required through educational, professional, commercial and voluntary bodies, and within the institutions themselves.

Reorienting Health Services – The responsibility for health promotion in health services is shared among individuals, community groups, health professionals, health service institutions and governments. They must work together towards a health-care system that contributes to the pursuit of health. Reorienting health services also requires stronger attention to health research as well as changes in professional education and training. This must lead to a change of attitude and organization of health services, which refocuses on the total needs of the individual as a whole person.

Health education:'
A process with intellectual, psychological and social dimensions relating to activities that increase the abilities of people to make informed decisions affecting their personal, family and community well-being. This process, based on scientific principles, facilitates learning and behavioural change in both health personnel and consumers, including children and youth.
(Ross and Mico, 1997)

Service improvement:
Promoting change in services to make them more effective, accessible or acceptable to the community.

Advocacy: Activities directed at changing policy of organizations or governments.

Putting health promotion into practice – regrouping the five dimensions of the Ottawa Charter

Two of the action areas in the Ottawa Charter's concept of health promotion (box 1.1) – *Developing personal skills* and *Strengthening community action* – can be seen as different dimensions of health education. The action area *Reorienting health services* can be broadened to encompass other sectors such as schools, environmental services, community development and social services. *Building healthy public policy* and *Creating supportive environments* both involve advocacy. A practical approach to health promotion is to regroup the five components in the Ottawa Charter into the three areas of action: *h*ealth *e*ducation, *s*ervice *i*mprovement and *ad*vocacy for policy

Activity 1.1

For one of the following, or a health topic of your own choice, apply the HESIAD approach and suggest contributions of health education, service improvement and advocacy: reduction of injuries among children from road traffic; promotion of measles immunization; prevention of falls in elderly people; reduction of sexually transmitted infections among young people; promotion of breast cancer screening among Asian women.

changes (HESIAD) (see figure.1.1). In box 1.2 we show how the HESIAD framework can be applied to different health topics.

Figure 1.1 The HESIAD framework for health promotion

Health education	**Service improvement**	**Advocacy**
Communication directed at individuals, families and communities to influence:	*Improvements in quality and quantity of services:*	*Agenda setting and advocacy for healthy public policy*
Awareness/knowledge Decision-making Beliefs/attitudes Empowerment Individual and community action/behaviour change Community participation	Accessibility Case management Counselling Patient education Outreach Social marketing	Policies for health Income generation Removal of obstacles Discrimination Inequalities Gender barriers

A wide variety of professionals and volunteers are involved in health promotion, each with an important role to play. Inter-professional working is often a key aspect of planning and implementing health promotion activities.

Box 1.2   Examples of application of HESIAD

Health topic	Three components of a comprehensive health promotion strategy		
	Health education	Service improvement	Advocacy
Physical exercise	Promotion of benefits of exercise, understanding of the kinds of exercise that will improve health and skills in specific exercise methods	Improved leisure/exercise facilities, exercise promotion within primary care – e.g. provision of personalized tailored advice on exercise, GP exercise referral schemes to local gyms or exercise programmes targeted to specific groups (middle aged or elderly people within day care and institutions etc.)	Develop local policies for exercise facilities especially for socially excluded groups, subsidies for exercise programmes, partnerships to increase exercise opportunities etc.
Tobacco smoking	Promotion of increased awareness of the risks of smoking, the benefits of quitting and practical skills in resisting peer pressure, refusing cigarettes and different ways of stopping smoking	Developing anti-smoking within primary care, stop-smoking clinics, availability of stop-smoking aids (e.g. nicotine patches)	Enforcement of controls on tobacco promotion, sales to young people and smoking in public places; subsidies for stop-smoking aids
Alcohol abuse	Directed at young people, young adults and other age groups on appropriate alcohol use, self-monitoring of alcohol consumption, resisting peer pressure etc.	Development of services for helping persons with chronic dependency	The initiation of public policies affecting the pricing and availability of alcohol to different age groups; extending licensing laws in the hope of reducing the pressure to binge drink
Nutrition – promotion of fruit and vegetable consumption	Using schools and mass media to promote awareness of the health benefits of eating fruit and vegetables	Ensuring that schools and workplace canteens provide fruit and vegetables; collaborating with shops in deprived housing estates to increase stocks of fruit and vegetables	Subsidies for farmers to grow fruit and vegetables; actions to reduce sales prices of fruit and vegetables (e.g. subsidies for shops, transport costs); guidelines on meals provided in schools, institutions, etc.

Health promotion as a multi-disciplinary activity

Health promotion is a core part of the work of many different groups inside and outside health services – see box 1.3.

Box 1.3 Who does health promotion?

Health services
Nurses
School health nurses
Health visitors
Community public health nurses
Midwives
General practitioners
Doctors
Physiotherapists
Occupational therapists
Dietitians
Exercise counsellors
Pharmacists
Opticians/optometrists
Speech and language therapists
Ambulance services

Local Authorities and non-statutory agencies
Youth workers
Teachers
Play workers
Community workers
Social workers
Environmental health officers
Prison workers

Private sector and voluntary agencies
Occupational health doctors and nurses
Trade union safety representatives
Pressure groups, e.g. Action on Smoking and Health
    (ASH), the Royal Society for the Prevention of
    Accidents (RoSPA)

Media
Health correspondents

Most health authorities in the United Kingdom have specialist public health/health promotion services located within primary care organizations to provide a support role to the health promotion work carried out by the field staff listed above. Many universities offer post graduate diplomas or masters degrees in health promotion or public health or similar courses, which are recognized qualifications for specialist public health/health promotion personnel. The role of these specialist support services is in a state of change; in some areas the name health promotion is still used, while in others the more generic term public health is used, with a strong focus on health promotion in their expected roles.

The funding and provision of continuing professional development (CPD) is also changing, being more fragmented and diverse, with in-service and self-reflective study becoming more common than formal higher education qualifications.

National bodies provide strategic support for health promotion. In England during 2000 the Health Education Authority evolved into the Health Development Agency, and in 2005 this became absorbed into the National Institute for Clinical Excellence. In Scotland the main national body was the Health Education Board for Scotland, which in 2005 was absorbed into NHS Health Scotland with the status of a special health board. Strategic support for health promotion is provided at the national level in Wales by the Health Promotion Division and in Northern Ireland by the Health Promotion Agency.

The scope for prevention of ill health and rationale for the promotion of health

The rationale for health promotion comes from the scope to prevent ill health through the promotion of health and healthy living. In 2005 the World Heath Organization reviewed global health and produced the breakdown of the causes of deaths for the UK, shown in figure 1.2.

Figure 1.2
Projected deaths in the United Kingdom, by cause, for all ages, 2005 (WHO, 2005)

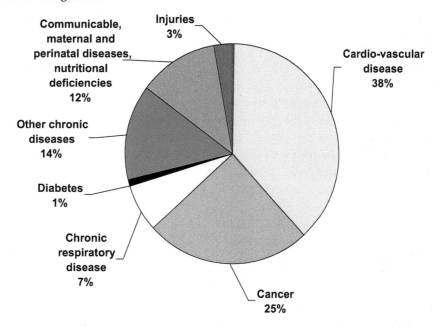

The quality of life of individuals and the burden on health service provision and resources is compromised by a range of health issues, such as chronic illnesses, injuries, mental illness, oral health and substance abuse. These represent a considerable burden both on individuals and on the cost of treatment for health services. The application of epidemiology to the study of causes of ill health shows that much of the current burden of disease can be prevented or alleviated by appropriate action. The promotion of healthy lifestyle has become a key element of health policy, as indicated in *Saving Lives: Our Healthier Nation* and equivalent documents in Scotland and Wales in 1999 (box 1.4).

Box 1.4 *Saving Lives: Our Healthier Nation* (1999)

This White Paper from the Department of Health for England set the agenda for health policy for the next decade. Lifestyle and human behaviour was given a prominent role through its 'Ten Tips for Better Health'.

1 Don't smoke. If you can, stop. If you can't, cut down.
2 Follow a balanced diet with plenty of fruit and vegetables.
3 Keep physically active.
4 Manage stress by, for example, talking things through and making time to relax.
5 If you drink alcohol, do so in moderation.
6 Cover up in the sun, and protect children from sunburn.
7 Practise safer sex.
8 Take up cancer screening opportunities.
9 Be safe on the roads: follow the Highway Code.
10 Learn the First Aid ABC – airways, breathing, circulation

(Department of Health, 1999)

Historical overview of health promotion

The setting up in the United Kingdom of the National Health Service in 1947 was a time of great hope. The general assumption was that, with universal and accessible health care, the health of the population would improve, thereby reducing the need for health services.

By the 1970s it had become evident that this approach with its faith in medical science and technology was naïve, that many health problems persisted, and that there was a need to 'refocus upstream' (see box 1.5).

Box 1.5 Refocusing upstream

I am standing by the shore of a swiftly flowing river and hear the cry of a drowning man. I jump into the cold waters. I fight against the strong current and force my way to the struggling man. I hold on hard and gradually pull him to shore. I lay him out on the bank and revive him with artificial respiration. Just when he begins to breathe, I hear another cry for help.

I jump into the cold waters. I fight against the strong current, and swim forcefully to the struggling woman. I grab hold and gradually pull her to shore. I lift her out on the bank beside the man and work to revive her with artificial respiration. Just when she begins to breathe, I hear another cry for help. I jump into the cold waters. Fighting again against the strong current, I force my way to the struggling man. I am getting tired, so with great effort I eventually pull him to shore. I lay him out on the bank and try to revive him with artificial respiration. Just when he begins to breathe, I hear another cry for help. Near exhaustion, it occurs to me that I'm so busy jumping in, pulling them to shore, applying artificial respiration that I have no time to see who is upstream pushing them all in ....

(A story told by Irving Zola, but used in McKinlay, 1981)

Of considerable influence was the publication in 1973 of the report *A New Perspective on the Health of the Canadians,* by the then prime minister of Canada, Marc Lalonde. Central to this report was the health field model. This argued that – far from being determined by health services – health was determined by human biology or genetic endowment, environment and human behaviour (see figure 1.3). The term *lifestyle* entered the discourse as a key determinant of health.

Lifestyle: The sum total of behaviours that make up the way people live. including leisure and work.

Figure 1.3 The health field model (Lalonde, 1973)

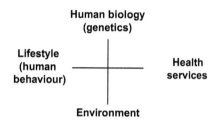

Health field model

Activity 1.2

Apply the health field model and suggest possible human biology, health services, environment and lifestyle influences for one of the following: coronary heart disease, diabetes, breast cancer, road traffic injuries. Which of the four components do you feel have the most influence on the health topic you have chosen?

In the UK in 1976 a discussion paper, *Prevention and Health, Everybody's Business,* and a White Paper *Prevention and Health,* were published and resulted in an expansion of health education services throughout the United Kingdom. On the international stage in 1977 the World Health Organization convened its meeting of the World Health Assembly in Alma Ata (then in the USSR, now in Kazakhstan) which issued its landmark declaration on primary health care. This declaration affirmed the importance of prevention but at the same time introduced other key concepts: social justice, tackling poverty, appropriate technology, community participation, and the need for economic and social action to address the determinants of health.

Criticisms of health education and the emergence of health promotion

By the early 1980s there was increasing disquiet among the health community. While accepting the importance of lifestyle, many felt that not enough attention was being given to the social and economic factors that influenced it. In England, Sir Douglas Black produced a damning report that highlighted the persistence of inequalities in health. In Scotland, similar inequalities were documented by one of the present

Box 1.6   A timeline of important events affecting the development of health promotion in the United Kingdom

1948   WHO constitution, with its definition of health as a complete state of physical, mental and social wellbeing

1965   Publication of McKeown, *Medicine in Modern Society*

1971   Publication of Cochrane, *Effectiveness and Efficiency*

1973   Lalonde Report, *A New Perspective on the Health of the Canadians*

1976   Publication of Illich, *Medical Nemesis: The Expropriation of Health*

1976   Publication by DHSS of discussion paper *Prevention and Health, Everybody's Business* and White Paper *Prevention and Health*

1977   World Health Assembly issues Alma Ata Declaration on Primary Health Care

1979   Launch of journal *Radical Community Medicine* (later to become *Critical Public Health*)

1980   Black, *Inequalities in Health: Report of a Research Working Group* (DHSS)

1981   Publication of McKinley, 'A case for refocussing upstream'

1983   *Scotland, the Real Divide* – review of poverty in Scotland (Brown and Cook)

1984   *Radical Community Medicine* publishes special issue on public health

1985   European region of World Health Organization sets targets for Health for All by the year 2000

1986   *Ottawa Charter for Health Promotion* produced at the WHO's first International Congress for Health Promotion

1988   Publication of the Acheson report *Public Health in England*
          Publication of Ashton and Seymour, *The New Public Health*

1992   *The Health of the Nation* report (DHSS)

1998   Publication of the Acheson Report *Independent Inquiry into Inequalities in Health*

1998   Society of Public Health Medicine opens membership to non-medical practitioners and changes name to Society of Public Health

1998   *Better Health: Better Wales* (Welsh Office)

1999   *Saving Lives: Our Healthier Nation,* White Paper (Department of Health, England)

1999   *Towards a Healthier Scotland: a White Paper on Health* (Scottish Office)

2003   *Improving Health in Scotland* (Scottish Executive)

2004   *Choosing Health* (Department of Health, England)

authors in a chapter in Gordon Brown and Robin Cook's book *Scotland, the Real Divide* (see Hubley, 1983), the editors of which later became key figures in the New Labour government.

Many health educators became critical of what they saw as an over-reliance on a medical model of health and a 'victim blaming' approach which put most effort into persuading individuals to change, while ignoring powerful influences in the family, the community and society. They saw a need for political action to influence local and national governments to introduce policies that promoted health. The early 1980s had also seen an unprecedented global mobilization to introduce international guidelines to limit the marketing of infant formulas in poor countries, which included actions such as consumer boycotts of Nestlé. Particularly aggressive programmes in Australia were pushing conventional health education to the limits, with hard-hitting anti-smoking television advertising which challenged commercial interests. Pressure groups such as ASH in the UK and street action movements such as BUGA UP in Australia were challenging the tobacco industry through pressure group techniques and direct action.

These concerns about the limitations of health education led to the conference in 1986 in Ottawa which set out the concept of health promotion discussed earlier in this chapter.

> **Victim blaming:** An approach to health education which emphasizes individual action and does not address external forces that influence the individual person.

> **Social exclusion:** A term to describe the structures and dynamic processes of inequality among groups in society. Social exclusion refers to the inability of certain groups or individuals to participate fully in life due to structural inequalities in access to social, economic, political and cultural resources. These inequalities arise out of oppression related to race, class, gender, disability, sexual orientation, immigrant status and religion. (Definition adapted from Galabuzi, 2002)

Inequalities in health

One of the most important criticisms was that health education approaches, based mainly on behaviour change of individuals, were failing to address inequalities in health. Figure 1.4 shows that anti-smoking programmes in the 1960s had successfully reduced levels of smoking in Great Britain. But the decline had been greater in the professional groups, leading to a widening of the gap between rich and poor. Health education, as it was then being practised, was reaching mainly better-off groups in society. It was conclusions such as this for smoking and other health problems that led to a rethinking of health education and the emergence of the broader notion of health promotion.

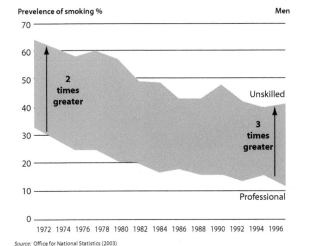

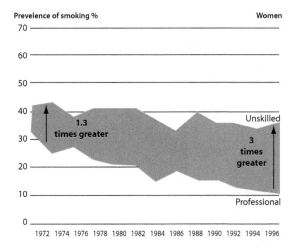

Source: Office for National Statistics (2003)

Figure 1.4 Increasing inequalities in smoking in Great Britain (men and women aged sixteen and over)

The issue of inequalities in health and social exclusion became a central feature of the health policy of the New Labour government that came into power in 1997. A series of reports exposed the inequalities in health between geographic regions, social classes and ethnic groups. The most significant of these was the Acheson Report in 1998, which drew on the 'rainbow model' of Dahlgren and Whitehead (1991) (figure 1.5) to show that inequalities were a result of an interaction of many factors in society and called for the following actions to tackle inequalities:

- breaking the cycle of inequalities
- tackling the major killer diseases
- improving access to services
- strengthening disadvantaged communities
- targeted interventions for specific groups.

The main determinants of health

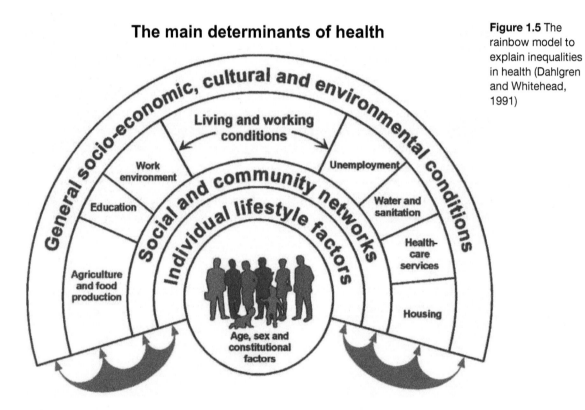

Figure 1.5 The rainbow model to explain inequalities in health (Dahlgren and Whitehead, 1991)

The chain of events by which structural factors in society influence health is shown in Jason's story, reproduced in box 1.7

Box 1.7 What makes Jason unhealthy?

The extract below appeared in the opening pages of the report *Toward a Healthy Future: Second Report on the Health of Canadians* (1999), prepared by the Federal, Provincial and Territorial Advisory Committee on Population Health. It challenged the readers to consider how determinants of health issues are rooted in the structure of society.

Why is Jason in the hospital?
   Because he has a bad infection in his leg.
But why does he have an infection?
   Because he has a cut on his leg and it got infected.
But why does he have a cut on his leg?
   Because he was playing in the junk yard next to his apartment building and there was some sharp, jagged steel there that he fell on.
But why was he playing in a junk yard?
   Because his neighbourhood is kind of run down. A lot of kids play there and there is no one to supervise them.
But why does he live in that neighbourhood?
   Because his parents can't afford a nicer place to live.

But why can't his parents afford a nicer place to live?
   Because his Dad is unemployed and his Mom is sick.
But why is his Dad unemployed?
   Because he doesn't have much education and he can't find a job.
But why ...?

(Federal, Provincial and Territorial Advisory Committee on Population Health, 1999)

The determinants of health are rooted in the structure of society. For example, healthy foods such as fresh fruit and vegetables are often priced out of the reach of the poorest families.

Activity 1.3

Choose a health problem in a person and use the *But why?* approach to prepare a similar story to that of Jason which brings out the social determinants of health.

The New Public Health

Public health: The science and art of preventing disease, prolonging life and promoting health through the organized efforts of society. (Department of Health 1999)

Health promotion is a major component of public health. The New Public Health movement promoted the idea of a campaigning approach to public health that championed the cause of prevention and tackling the social determinants of ill health. Many of these ideas were brought out in a special issue on public health of the journal *Radical Community Medicine*, and the term was used as the title of a textbook by Ashton and Seymour that was published by the Open University in 1988. One of the mouthpieces of this movement – the journal *Critical Public Health* – emerged. The Faculty of Public Health Medicine opened its doors in 1998 to non-medical persons and in 2002 the NHS started to employ non-medical persons as directors of public health. In 2003 the faculty dropped the word 'medicine' from its title to adopt the broader and more representative title Faculty of Public Health and set up a voluntary register of public health specialists. The ten core competences required for acceptance of practitioners onto the voluntary register are listed in box 1.8. These link to the National Occupational Standards and National Workforce Competencies integral to the Public Health Careers Framework being developed as part of the Skills for Health programme for use across the health sector.

Box 1.8 The ten areas of competencies in public health

1 Surveillance and assessment of the population's health and wellbeing
2 Promoting and protecting its health and wellbeing
3 Developing quality and risk management within an evaluative culture
4 Collaborative working for health
5 Developing health programmes and services and reducing inequalities
6 Policy and strategy development and implementation to improve health
7 Working with – and for – communities to improve health and wellbeing
8 Strategic leadership
9 Research and development to improve health and wellbeing
10 Ethically managing self, people and resources to improve health/wellbeing

---

Much of the original discussion surrounding these ten competencies centred on identifying the skill requirements of public health specialists and health promotion personnel wishing to become part of the newly formed voluntary register of public health specialists. However, this list of competencies is increasingly being used to identify the contribution to public health of nurses, environmental officers and the many other health related professional groups listed in box 1.3 who carry out health promotion.

Activity 1.4

Examine the list of ten areas of competencies in box 1.8. How important are each of these to your own area of work? Rate each on a scale of 1 to 5 and compare your rating with those of your colleagues. What skills do you need to carry out each of these ten?

Debates in health promotion

Health promotion is an evolving discipline and there is continuing debate on key practice issues (see box 1.9).

Box 1.9 Areas of debates in health promotion practice

- The relevance of medical or social models of health and disease
- Individual and structural approaches
- Levels of health promotion practice
- Core values of health promotion
- Coercion, persuasion and health empowerment approaches
- Ethics of health promotion
- Principles of health promotion practice

The relevance of medical and social models of health and disease

Holistic approach: An approach that addresses all of the dimensions of health (physical, mental, emotional, spiritual, vocational, social).

The medical model of health emphasizes disease rather than health, and sees people as machines which break down and require medical technology to repair them. While the medical model recognizes that individual behaviour can be a risk factor, it sees behaviour change as something that is in the power of the individual. In contrast, the social model takes a more holistic view of health, which it sees as influenced by culture, social class, economic position and environment.

Individual and structural approaches

Figure 1.6
Structuralistic and individualistic approaches in health promotion (Midha and Sullivan, 1998)

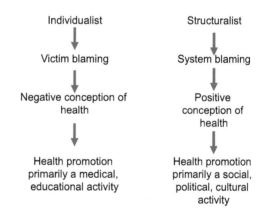

Tension between individualistic and structuralistic approaches remains a source of lively debate and discussion within current health promotion practice. A simple either/or polarization of individualistic and structuralistic approaches such as in figure 1.6 is useful but simplifies what are in fact a range of options for approaches to working with people, assumptions about causes of ill health, points of intervention and values.

In many situations these approaches need to be combined. It is possible to deal with the individual but locate the problem within a wider context. For example, faced with a man who has borderline hypertension, and drawing on evidence from systematic reviews that he can reduce his blood pressure by losing some weight and taking exercise, it would seem appropriate to advise him to change his behaviour. But even so, the advice would have to take into account the influences of food availability, affordability and income.

Levels of health promotion practice

An alternative to an individual/structural approach is one which sees health promotion as operating from the individual, the family and the community through to the international level (see figure 1.7).

Such a framework is useful because it recognizes that influences on our actions can operate at different levels and that accordingly our health promotion activities need to be carried out at different levels. Examples of health promotion actions at different levels to address tobacco consumption are provided in box 1.10.

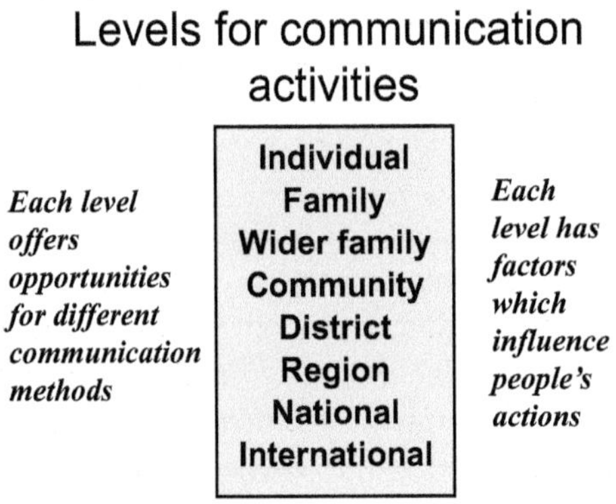

Levels for communication activities

Each level offers opportunities for different communication methods

| Individual |
| Family |
| Wider family |
| Community |
| District |
| Region |
| National |
| International |

Each level has factors which influence people's actions

Figure 1.7 Levels for health promotion

Core values of health promotion

Values are attributes that are held in high regard by individuals, communities, societies and social movements. The principles of health promotion are made up of the body of knowledge, conceptual tools and theory derived from evidence-based practice. However, implementation of these

Values: Statements about what is right, what is good and what is to be done, what ought to be.

Activity 1.5

Drawing on the example of box 1.10, produce a table of health promotion activities at different levels for one of the following health topics: breastfeeding promotion, reduction of sexually transmitted infections, reduction of road traffic injuries. Which levels have the most influence for the health topic you have chosen?

Equity in health: Equity means fairness. Equity in health means that people's needs guide the distribution of opportunities for wellbeing.
(WHO, 1996)

Box 1.10 Examples of health promotion activities at different levels for smoking/tobacco controls

Level	Example of health promotion activity at that level
Individual	Individual counselling on smoking cessation
Family	Inviting both partners to come to a smoking group
Community	Working with imams and other religious leaders to introduce tobacco education in the Asian community in a town; introduction of a stop-smoking clinic into a community
District	Working with district councils to encourage adherence to the smoking ban in public places
Region	A regional television advertising campaign to promote a non-smoking norm
National	Lobbying government to control sponsorship of events by tobacco companies
International	Introduction by World Health Organization of Tobacco Framework Convention Treaty for control of smoking

principles will reflect the underlying values of the practitioner. One distinction between values and principles is that, while theory and principles can be proven through evaluation and evidence, in contrast, values are beliefs that are held. That view is challenged by others who argue that concepts of proof and evidence themselves reflect values about the nature of the world – so nothing is value-free!

Are there values that are universally applicable and provide core principles for health promotion? A King's Fund project on public health and public values (New, 1998) suggested the following to be essential for public health:

- **fairness and equality** – these relate to measures to minimize disparities and inequalities in health.
- **efficiency and health** – the importance of promoting interventions that are of proven effectiveness and also those which are of the least cost.
- **autonomy and security** – this influences the balance between an individual's right to choose and society's right to make an individual conform in order to protect others.
- **democracy** – this value gives authority to the state to intervene to promote public health.

A good example of how values can affect the practice of health promotion is in the concept of health itself. In its charter the World Health Organization defined health as 'Not merely the absence of disease but a complete state of physical, mental and social wellbeing'. While this definition has been criticized for lack of precision and near impossibility of attainment, it does make an important distinction between health as a positive state compared to disease. The UK Society of Health Education and Promotion argues that preventing illness is a narrow goal compared with the wider one of promoting the general health and wellbeing of people and recommends that health promoters should:

- not think of health as just the absence of illness
- acknowledge that health is not an objective state but a subjective process and that the meanings of 'health' will shift and change depending on communities, circumstances and culture
- focus not on determinants of illness but on elements that strengthen and maintain health
- develop epidemiologies and indicators of health.

We will be exploring many of these values in other parts of this book, especially in discussions of approaches and ethics of health promotion.

Activity 1.6

Look at the four values identified by the King's Fund (New, 1998) in the list above. Do you agree with them? Do your colleagues feel the same way? Are there any values that you would like to add to their list?

Coercion	Persuasion	Health empowerment
Use of laws, regulations, legal sanctions and pricing to force people to act in a particular way even if they do not want to	Seeking to influence people to adopt particular health actions – however, the individual has the right to decline	Focus on developing decision-making skills and the confidence to bring about change; the decision on which health actions to adopt is left to the individual/community

Figure 1.8 The coercion/persuasion /health empowerment continuum in health promotion

---

Coercion, persuasion or health empowerment approaches

Health promotion involves a continuum of activities, summarized in figure 1.8.

Coercion The use of legal sanctions and threat of fines or imprisonment or the manipulation of prices is controversial as it involves forcing individuals to act against their will. However, most people would support this in some cases – for example, actions such as legislation on the wearing of seat belts, against selling cigarettes to persons under the age of sixteen or regulations on safety of electrical and gas appliances. Others raise concern about the intrusive nature of health promotion, which they see as paternalistic, interfering with rights and freedoms and imposing a 'nanny state' where the government tells people what to do.

Persuasion The persuasive approach places strong emphasis on influencing individuals or communities to change their behaviour through explanations, advice and argument. The decisions on which behaviour to change usually arise from epidemiological research and recommendations of national expert groups. In applying this strategy, extensive use is made of social, psychological and communication models of behaviour change to identify arguments that could be used to convince people. Critics of the persuasive approach argue that, by focusing our efforts on influencing people to act in a specific way, we are in fact denying choice. In multicultural Britain, with its rich and diverse communities, there is a real risk of one culture imposing its values on another. However, advocates of persuasive approaches argue that, in situations where the evidence of a beneficial effect of adopting the advice is very strong, persuasion is justified. They also point out that persuasion is not coercion, and the public can refuse to comply. Persuasion does not necessarily imply an individualistic approach, as communications to individuals to change their behaviour can be combined with improvements in health services and social conditions which facilitate healthy choices.

Health empowerment This approach seeks to develop the capacity of individuals and communities to make informed decisions. It draws upon counselling, community development, and social learning theory, and is mainly undertaken person to person. There is a strong emphasis on participatory learning methods.

  Health empowerment can usefully be considered as being made up of two components: self-efficacy – the belief that a person has concerning their ability to change their surroundings – and health literacy, which can be seen as the intellectual and social capacity to make informed decisions on health matters.

Health empowerment	=	self-efficacy	+	health literacy
		Affective/cognitive		Cognitive/communication
		High self-esteem		Understanding of health and disease
		Feeling of power and control		Decision-making skills
		Confidence to take action		Ability to communicate health issues
		Beliefs about ability to change situation		

The concepts of self-efficacy (and its derivation from social learning theory) and health literacy are discussed in chapters 3 and 8.

  A health empowerment approach puts an emphasis on the involvement of individuals and communities as active participants in the process of defining the goals for

Critics argue that coercive and persuasive approaches to health promotion can have a negative effect. In a multicultural society, there is a danger of one culture imposing its values on another.

change and strengthening their capacity to make informed choice about their health. The adoption of such an approach resolves some of the ethical dilemmas about the use of coercion and persuasion. However, it does raise other problems. What happens if the decisions of one individual or community are at the expense of another? Is it realistic to expect people to make informed decisions on issues such as the risk of infection with bovine spongiform encephalopathy (BSE) or the safety of the combined vaccine against measles, mumps and rubella (MMR), which require the understanding of complex epidemiological processes? Can individuals – no matter how health empowered they are – stand up against the national and international forces in globalized societies? Also, in the case of emergencies and disease outbreaks, such as severe acute respiratory syndrome (SARS) and bird flu (caused by an influenza virus, some strains of which are serious, e.g. the highly pathogenic H5N1), a rapid response is required – and many people feel that a short intensive campaign using persuasion and coercion is justified.

To some people a decision whether to adopt coercive, persuasive or health empowerment approaches is determined by individual and professional values. For example, the code of ethics of the Society of Public Health Education in the United States calls for 'change by choice and not by coercion'. Others take a more pragmatic approach and base their choice on the nature of the issue, the seriousness and urgency for action, the strength of evidence that adopting a particular behaviour change would lead to real improvements, and the presence or absence of the national and international forces that constrain individuals to act in certain ways.

> ### Activity 1.7
>
> Consider the following heath topics. Describe what would be involved in a coercive, persuasive and health empowerment response. Which of these three approaches would you take for each topic?
>
> - Advising a family whether to allow their child to have an MMR immunization
> - Advising a teenage girl who has just discovered that she is pregnant
> - Advising a middle-aged man, who has just been diagnosed as having hypertension, on what to eat
> - Working in a community in which some children have recently been injured in road traffic accidents
> - Advising a family who has just discovered that their unborn child has sickle cell anaemia

Ethics of health promotion

Ethics is the study of morals, duties, values and virtues. Ethics can also be a code of rules and understandings that has been worked out by the members of a profession to govern their own practice. Values and ethical principles lead to moral imperatives – judgements about what should or should not be done.

A good starting point for ethics is the framework suggested by Beachamp and Childress (1994), which articulates four key principles:

- autonomy (respect for persons and individual rights, acceptance of differences)
- beneficence (doing good, optimizing benefits over burdens, preventing harm)
- maleficence (not doing harm)
- justice (a fair distribution of benefits, risks and costs).

Justice involves confronting issues of equity, inequalities in health and social exclusion. In practice, beneficence and maleficence involve answering the following questions:

- How serious is the health problem?
- To what extent can the individuals and communities affected take action to improve their situation?
- To what extent do the communities affected recognize the problem and how far are they willing to take action?
- What evidence is there that taking action will lead to significant improvements?
- What is the likelihood of taking action leading to a worsening of the situation?
- What would be the impact – either positive or negative – of the proposed action on health inequalities?

Of course such questions raise issues about what is meant by terms such as 'serious', 'evidence of effectiveness' and 'health inequalities', and more on these will be provided in later chapters. However, you can see how your approach to change might be different according to the health topic. If a problem is serious (e.g. road traffic injuries) and the individuals affected (e.g. pre-school children) are unable to take action, you might feel it ethically justifiable to pass legislation about the use of child safety belts. In situations where an individual has the means to change his or her life and the problem is serious (e.g. adult obesity) you might feel that a persuasive approach based on promotion of exercise and diet might be appropriate. In a situation in which a number of options are possible, you might wish to take a health empowerment approach to promote informed decision-making. Whatever strategy you choose, it is important to implement it to the best of your ability and to evaluate in order to determine what impact – positive or negative – it is having on the community.

Activity 1.8

Consider the following health promotion activities. What ethical issues would you have to take into account in deciding whether to carry them out?

- Increasing the licensing hours for public houses
- Setting up a sexual health clinic for adolescents under sixteen years old
- Encouraging the general public to come for HIV screening
- Advising a person with hypertension to reduce their salt intake
- Introducing regulations to lower the salt content of foods
- Persuading a pregnant woman to stop smoking

Principles of health promotion practice

The Society for Health Education and Promotion Specialists has outlined a set of principles of practice, shown in box 1.11, which address some of these ethical issues.

Box 1.11 Principles and practice of health promotion

Members of the Society for Health Education and Promotion Specialists (SHEPS) adhere to a set of principles of practice and an associated code of conduct. These key principles of practice are:

- adequate needs assessment
- promoting self-esteem and autonomy
- valuing others
- relevance and sensitivity to client group
- acting on social, economic and environmental determinants of health
- empowering people to exercise informed choice and influence structures and systems
- setting activity into its appropriate context
- sustainability of interventions
- reducing or eliminating inequalities in health at local, national and international levels

- using research and undertaking evaluation and dissemination
- providing accurate and appropriate information
- keeping knowledge of health promotion developments up to date
- having due regard to confidentiality and the requirements of the law
- encouraging others to develop their potential to promote health
- using methods and processes that are health promoting.

Health promotion planning process

In planning a health promotion intervention, a number of decisions are involved that are summarized in figure 1.9. Embedded in those decisions are the debates considered in the previous section. By adopting an approach based on needs assessment, experiment and evaluation, health promotion becomes an evidence-based pragmatic iterative approach involving analysis and reflection.

Define health-promotion strategy
- *Mix of health education, service improvement and advocacy?*
- *Health education approach?*
- *Methods?*
- *Settings?*
- *Persons/groups involved in delivery?*
- *Timing?*
- *Targets?*

Health-promotion needs/situation analysis
- *Current situation?*
- *Health needs?*
- *Influences on health?*
- *Influences on health actions?*
- *Target groups?*

Health promotion planning cycle

Implement
- *How to put it all together?*
- *How do we overcome barriers?*
- *How to monitor activities?*

Evaluate, reflect, learn
- *Were our targets achieved?*
- *What lessons were learnt?*
- *How can we make our programmes better?*

Figure 1.9 The iterative health promotion planning cycle

Needs/situation analysis

The first stage of the health promotion planning cycle involves assessing the present situation and deciding whether there is a need for change and a role for health promotion. Making a situation assessment involves not only analysing the present situation but asking questions: why that situation arose, what factors contribute to its continuation and what contribution health promotion could make to improve the situation.

Health needs The concept of needs is a heavily loaded one (see chapter 2), which is why some people prefer the more neutral term 'situation' analysis. Underlying the question 'How do we decide what changes are needed?' is a more fundamental one: 'What right have we to intervene and make changes? – or, to put it more bluntly: 'What right have we to interfere in people's lives?' This involves considering the values and ethics of health promotion which we discussed in the previous section.

You need to decide whether to focus on a specific health topic/disease or to take a broader approach that concentrates on health in general. For example, with school-children or elderly people, rather than taking one health topic such as injury preven-tion, you may want to take a broad approach and promote a healthy lifestyle that includes a range of issues that affect their general health. Even in situations when a person comes to you with a very specific problem, e.g. a middle-aged man with raised blood pressure, you could focus on the blood pressure or take a broader approach that looks at the lifestyle of that person and their general health. However, there will also be situations when a disease-focused approach may be highly appropriate, especially when there are clear and effective actions that would deal with the problem. For example, if there is a very specific issue in a community (e.g. carbon monoxide poisoning, injuries from broken glass in play areas, a family with child who has been diagnosed with diabetes, a workplace with a noise problem), you might wish to focus on that single topic and resolve it.

Influences on health As part of the situation assessment you will need to find out the specific influences on health in the community. This might involve identifying the contribution of the four components of the health field model (figure 1.3) – human biology, health services, the environment and lifestyle/behaviour – or applying the rainbow model of Dahlgren and Whitehead (1991) shown in figure 1.5.

In chapter 2 we introduce some epidemiological tools that are helpful in under-standing health needs, influences on health and the scope for health promotion.

Influences on health actions In seeking to understand the influences on health actions or behaviour, health promoters have developed models drawing on various disciplines, including politics, sociology, anthropology and psychology. In chapter 3 we review some of these models which have been found useful in understanding influences on the actions of individuals, families and communities.

At-risk group: The section of the population in a community that has the greatest health need.

Target groups The term target group refers to the section of the commu-nity at which the health promotion activities are directed. These might be the people in the community with the greatest risk of disease (e.g. the schoolchild or elderly person) or those who have influence over the health of others (i.e. the 'gatekeepers', such as parents, teachers, community lead-ers and politicians). It is useful to consider the separate ethnic, cultural, income and age groups in a community, as each will have distinct needs

Target group: The section of the community to whom health promotion activities should be directed in order to improve the health of the at-risk group.

Even when dealing with a very specific health problem – for example, diabetes – it is important not just to take a narrow focus on blood sugar levels, but also to consider broader issues such as a balanced diet and healthy lifestyle.

that need to be addressed in a 'tailored' approach. Both needs and opportunities for health promotion also change during life, and in chapter 4 we examine how an understanding of the life course can be used in planning health promotion.

Defining the health promotion strategy

The second step in the health promotion planning cycle is to decide your strategy by considering the alternative methods and settings that will enable you to reach your target audience.

Approach You will need to decide what position you adopt in the coercion/persuasion/health empowerment continuum in figure 1.8. For some, this decision is a matter of ideology and values. We take the view, however, that choice of approach would depend on the context of the health issue and the community.

Methods Health promotion methods fall into two broad groups (box 1.12). Person-to-person methods are all those activities where you are in direct contact with the target group. Mass-media methods include all those where communication takes place through electronic and print media without direct face-to-face contact. Further information on each of these methods is provided in the chapters in part II.

Box 1.12 Methods in health promotion

	Examples of methods
Person-to-person	Counselling One-to-one Peer education Lobbying of politicians Group discussion/group meeting Self-help group Public meeting Community development/organization
Mass-media	Radio Television Magazines and newspapers Leaflets and direct mail Billboards Multi-media, e.g. CD-ROM Internet-based – websites and discussion groups

Settings A key decision when using person-to-person methods is which setting you should use in order to reach the intended target group. When the concept of health promotion was first introduced, the adoption of a 'settings approach' became a core feature. A settings approach seeks to maximize the health promotion potential of a setting through the adoption of quality standards. There are international movements for 'healthy cities', 'health promoting schools' and 'health promoting hospitals'. These are loose federations of institutions who have agreed to follow quality standards for health promotion and exchange information and to support each other. In part III we discuss some of the settings used most widely for health promotion: community; health facilities; the workplace; schools; and institutional settings, e.g. care homes and prisons.

> **Setting:** A specific context/location from which to carry out health promotion. Common settings are health facilities, the workplace, schools, the community and institutions.

When planning health promotion it is important to bear in mind the distinct needs of the target group and the setting in which the activities are to take place. If working with schoolchildren, for example, it would be important to gain the cooperation of gatekeepers, such as the head teacher and parents.

Implementation/evaluation, reflection and learning

The third step in the health promotion planning cycle involves the setting up, organizing, management and monitoring of activities which are considered in chapter 16. The final stage of evaluation, reflection and learning forms the basis for chapter 17.

> **Activity 1.9**
>
> Apply the planning cycle described in figure 1.9 to a health promotion issue of your own choice and briefly list the decisions you have made at each step.

Some concluding remarks on health promotion

Health promotion is a vital part of public health programmes. Applying the systematic problem-solving approach shown in figure 1.9 will allow you to set up health promotion programmes that are rooted in community needs. In the following chapters we present practical guidelines on assessing needs, understanding health and illness behaviours, and how to use a range of interpersonal- and media-based methods in many settings. As will become clear, there are a range of applications and practice levels to be taken into account.

As we review each method and setting, we will revisit the debates raised in this chapter: the role of medical and social models, individualistic and structuralistic approaches, the contribution of different levels of operation, values, ethics, and the coercion/persuasion/empowerment continuum. As in all good debates, there are no right or wrong answers. Rather it is a question of taking a flexible pragmatic approach based on the specific context, tailoring programmes to meet local needs, involving communities in planning and implementation, and being prepared to modify and change in response to the evaluation of results achieved.

Further reading

For a more detailed discussion of ethical issues in health promotion, see:
- Cribb, A., and Duncan, P. (2002). *Health Promotion and Professional Ethics.* Oxford: Blackwell Science.

For a multi-disciplinary perspective on behaviour change and health promotion, see:
- Kerr, J. et al. (2004). *The ABC of Behaviour Change: a Guide to Successful Disease Prevention and Health Promotion.* London: Churchill Livingstone.

For a detailed overview of health promotion concepts, see:
- Tones, K., and Green, J. (2004). *Health Promotion: Planning and Strategies.* Thousand Oaks, CA: Sage Publications.

CHAPTER 2
Epidemiological Tools for Health Promotion

Contents

2 Epidemiological Tools for Health Promotion

Key issues within this chapter:

- Epidemiology provides the scientific basis for determining the distribution and determinants of health and disease in communities and the scope for promotion of health.

- Assessment of health promotion needs involves assessing the extent of the health and disease in a community, and the trends, seriousness, and feasibility for prevention and control.

- Prevention can be done at three levels – primary, secondary and tertiary.

- Primary prevention requires an understanding of causes of ill health, which comes from the application of analytical epidemiology and the assessment of evidence for causality.

- Secondary prevention involves understanding the scope for early detection of disease and the appropriateness of initiating screening programmes.

- Tertiary prevention involves actions taken once the disease has become serious.

By the end of this chapter you should be able to:

- use epidemiological tools to describe the health situation in communities and determine health promotion needs

- understand the methods used to determine the cause and risk factors for a health issue and the scope for prevention

- understand the contribution of health promotion in screening programmes.

What is epidemiology?

This chapter will introduce some key epidemiological tools that we use to assess health promotion needs and to understand the scope for prevention and control of disease and the promotion of health. Epidemiology is split into two main approaches – descriptive and analytic (see figure 2.1).

> **Epidemiology:** The study of the distribution and determinant of health related states or events in specified populations, and the application of this study to control health problems.
> (Last et al. 2000)

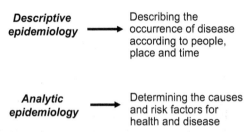

Figure 2.1 The role of epidemiology

The first approach is to ask questions to establish the health problem and the three key elements – people, place and time:

- What are the health promotion needs?
- What are the health problems?
- How many people are affected? (people)
- Who is affected? (people)
- Which communities are affected? (place)
- What are the trends? (changes over time)

The second approach is mainly centred on answering the question *Why did it happen?* This involves making comparisons between groups with and without a disease and between groups exposed and not exposed to a possible causal factor.

Assessing health promotion needs

Assessing health promotion needs is an important first step in planning health promotion activities. However, the concept of need is not straight-forward and consists of two elements:

> **Health needs assessment**
> A systematic method for reviewing the health issues facing a population, leading to agreed priorities and resource allocation that will improve health and reduce inequalities.
> (Department of Health, 2005)

- **Health service-determined needs** – These are needs as identified by health and other services. Typically these focus on the main concern of health services, which is the allocation of effort and resources, and are based on distribution of indicators of health and disease. They include

  - normative criteria: What is the situation here compared with the average for the community, city, region or country?

- comparative criteria: What is the situation in this location compared to other communities?
- time-based trends: Is the problem increasing?

● **Community-determined needs or 'wants'**

- expressed needs: covering issues that individuals and communities have already brought to the attention of the authorities, through their contacts with health services, politicians, letters to newspapers, etc.
- felt needs: covering individual and community concerns, including those which have not been drawn to the attention of the authorities.

Figure 2.2 shows the relationship between these two groups of needs. There may be areas of overlap but there are also needs that differ between health services and communities. Indeed, it is possible that there are hidden needs of which neither the community nor health services are aware. It is important to identify felt and expressed needs because these are issues which are priorities for communities and which they are more likely to act upon. You can find out expressed needs by talking to health workers, local leaders and politicians, exploring back issues of local newspapers and reading minutes of local government meetings. Identifying felt needs involves going into communities and talking with individuals and community groups about their concerns.

Figure 2.2 Health service- and community-determined needs

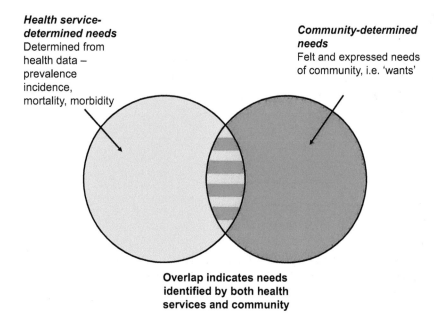

Health service-determined needs
Determined from health data – prevalence incidence, mortality, morbidity

Community-determined needs
Felt and expressed needs of community, i.e. 'wants'

Overlap indicates needs identified by both health services and community

Assessing priorities

The classic epidemiological approach to setting priorities involves asking the following questions.

- *What is the size of the health problem?* The prevalence of the problem is the number of people affected.
- *Is the problem increasing, i.e. what are the trends?* To what extent is the incidence increasing and is it affecting a particular group or geographical area? When the incidence has increased past a predetermined threshold we might use the term epidemic.
- *How serious is the health problem?* What impact is it having on death rates, sickness and quality of life? Is there a cure? Does it result in permanent disability?
- *How feasible would it be to prevent and control the problem?* How feasible is it to tackle the problem? Answering this question involves considering both epidemiological and social factors.

> **Prevalence:** Total number of persons in a population with a disease at a given date (point prevalence) or in a given period (period prevalence).

> **Incidence:** Number of new cases of disease in a given time period (per year, month, week, etc).

> **Epidemic:** An increase in the number of cases over past experience for a given population.

Epidemiological questions are:

- Are causes known?
- Can it be prevented?
- Will early detection improve treatment outcome?

Social factors to be considered are:

- Is there public support for action?
- Is the topic something that the community feels strongly about and would therefore become actively involved in taking preventive actions?
- Are resources – staff, finance and time – available for tackling the problem?

Activity 2.1

Choose a health topic in your community. Apply the criteria for establishing priorities described above to examine whether it should be a priority.

Indicators for health and disease

An indicator is something that can be measured, is easy to obtain and can provide a meaningful indication of the level of health. Typically indicators have been constructed for

- **health** and **wellbeing**
- **death** (mortality)
- **sickness** (morbidity)

- **birth** rate
- **factors in the environment** that put people at risk, such as exposure to air pollution, access to sport facilities, parks, etc.
- **behaviours by the community**, such as uptake of health services and actions that protect their health (e.g. exercise), as well as those that put them at risk, such as smoking, unhealthy diet or excessive alcohol consumption.

Examples of common indicators used in planning health promotion are given in box 2.1.

Box 2.1 Some common indicators used for measuring disease in a population

Vital statistics
- Crude birth rate – number of live births per 1,000 total population per year
- Crude death rate – number of deaths occurring per 1,000 total population per year
- General fertility rate – number of live births per 1,000 women of child-bearing age (between the ages of 15 and 44) per year

Age-specific death rates
- Infant mortality rate – number of deaths in a year of children less than 1 year old per 1,000 live births in the same year
- Perinatal deaths after 28 weeks pregnancy to one week of life per 1,000 live births in the same year

Disease-specific death rates – e.g. suicides per year per 100,000 population

Disease-specific sickness rates – e.g. number of cases of measles notified

Standardized mortality ratios (SMR) – a measure of health that is adjusted for the age distribution in a community. An SMR of 100 indicates that the death rate adjusted for age differences is the same as the national or regional average (depending which has been chosen as the standard). SMRs greater or lower than 100 indicate that the age-adjusted death rates are greater or lower than the national or regional average.

Subjective wellbeing

A criticism of many health indicators is that they reinforce a medical model by measuring disease rather than health. Various attempts have been made to define indicators to measure a person's 'quality of life', 'wellbeing' and happiness (see for example box 2.2). Inevitably such indicators represent subjective decisions as to what constitutes quality of life and reflect cultural assumptions and values. With those reservations in mind, the search for an alternative to indicators of disease is important in health promotion as it focuses attention on the fact that health is more than just the absence of disease.

Subjective wellbeing:
An individual's personal assessment of their state of wellbeing.

It is important to take into account individuals' assessments of their wellbeing and quality of life, rather than just focusing on measuring disease.

Box 2.2 Subjective wellbeing and older people

In constructing its report *Opportunity Age,* the English Longitudinal Study of Aging created the *c*ontrol *a*utonomy, *s*elf-realization, *p*leasure (CASP-19) scale with the following nineteen statements to measure the quality of life of older persons.

 1 My age prevents me from doing the things I would like to do.
 2 I feel that what happens to me is out of my control.
 3 I feel free to plan for the future.
 4 I feel left out of things.
 5 I can do the things that I want to do.
 6 Family responsibilities prevent me from doing what I want to do.
 7 I feel that I can please myself what I do.
 8 My health stops me from doing things I want to do.
 9 Shortage of money stops me from doing the things I want to do.
10 I look forward to each day.
11 I feel that my life has meaning.
12 I enjoy the things that I do.
13 I enjoy being in the company of others.
14 On balance, I look back on my life with a sense of happiness.
15 I feel full of energy these days.
16 I choose to do things that I have never done before.
17 I feel satisfied with the way my life has turned out.
18 I feel that life is full of opportunities.
19 I feel that the future looks good for me.

> ### Activity 2.2
>
> Suggest a list of questions that could be asked to a twenty-year-old (or another age category of your own choice) to measure subjective wellbeing.

International classification of diseases (ICD)

The World Health Organization maintains a statistical classification of diseases, injuries and causes of death, which is internationally recognized and used. Each disease and cause of death is given an ICD number, so it is possible to compare health data from different countries using a standard classification. For example, cancers are recorded as ICD-9, and there are sub-codes for different kinds of cancers ranging from 140 to 208 inclusive.

Where do we get data on health and disease?

Some common sources of health data are summarised in box 2.3.

> ### Box 2.3 Common sources of health data
>
> *Death certificates* – When deaths are registered, the death certificate includes information on who has died, their age, and the cause of death as diagnosed by the doctor.
>
> *Notifications* – These are notifiable diseases that are required by law to be reported by health services, e.g. tuberculosis, food poisoning.
>
> *Surveillance* – Special programmes are used to monitor the occurrence of certain diseases, for example the anonymous testing of blood from pregnant women for HIV from sentinel sites.
>
> *Health records* – These include records of hospitals, GPs, police and other services.
>
> *Surveys – ongoing* – Surveys that the government carries out on an annual basis, for example the General Household Survey, the Health Survey.
>
> *Surveys – ad hoc* – Surveys carried out on special occasions: from time to time the government commissions a survey of the health and behaviours of particular population groups.

Health data from routinely collected surveys and records are easiest to obtain but not always useful. Existing data may not include the information you need. In particular, routinely collected data have a strong orientation to disease rather than health. There are issues of confidentiality to take into account and ethical clearance will be needed from health services to retrieve health data from records. The illnesses that come to the attention of health services are usually the 'tip of the iceberg', and illness episodes managed through self-care, self-medication and consultation with practitioners of complementary medicine do not appear in NHS records. Getting information involves a trade-off. The information that is the easiest to obtain – from routinely collected surveys – may not be very useful. The most useful information comes from specifically designed surveys which require the most expense and effort to carry out.

Analysing health data – 'people'

Health data are analysed according to who is affected – age, gender, ethnicity and deprivation.

Box 2.4 Social class

Reports on inequalities in health in the United Kingdom make heavy use of the concept of social class. The five-point social-class classification was the principal classification of socio-economic status used in the UK when it first appeared in the Registrar General's Annual Report for 1911. Analysis using this classification has consistently shown social gradients for a wide range of health indicators, with social classes IV and V having a disproportionate amount of ill health. From 2001, the Registrar General's classification of social class was replaced in all UK official statistics by the new National Statistics Socio-Economic Classification (NSSEC). These socio-economic classifications are based on occupation, in combination with employment status and, in some circumstances, size of workplace. The five social-class groups in the Registrar General's classification are shown below, as well as the five-part and simplified three-part classification of the new system.

Poverty: A state of low income. Poverty can be measured according to whether or not a person has an income that is below half the national average (relative poverty) or is eligible to claim mean-tested social benefits (absolute poverty).

Social class: A measure of a person's position in society.

Registrar General's Classification	
Social class	Occupation
I Professional	Accountants, engineers, doctors
II Managerial technical Intermediate	Marketing and sales managers, teachers, journalists, nurses
III Non-manual skilled	Clerks, shop assistants, cashiers
IIIM Manual skilled	Carpenters, goods van drivers, joiners, cooks
IV Partly skilled	Security guards, machine tool operators, farm workers
V Unskilled	Building and civil engineering labourers, other labourers, cleaners

National Statistics Socio-Economic Classification			
	Five-class version		Three-class version
1	Managerial and professional occupations	1	Managerial and professional occupations
2	Intermediate occupations	2	Intermediate occupations
3	Small employers and own-account workers		
4	Lower supervisory and technical occupations		
5	Semi-routine and routine occupations	3	Routine occupations
	Never worked and long-term unemployed		Never worked and long-term unemployed

Advertising and marketing companies use a similar but slightly different system of social grading which employs letters A, B and C according to occupation, with A being the higher and D the lower end of the scale.

Analysing health data – 'place'

Analysing data by place shows which communities are affected. This is helpful both to allocate resources to the places in greatest need and to identify local factors which may impact on the health of the community.

Health data are often aggregated at district, regional or national level, but you may want information for a particular community. Small area statistics are data that can be retrieved and analysed for small geographical areas and have been particularly useful for identifying pockets of social deprivation and special need. The main source of information for small area statistics has been the census that takes place every ten years and the smaller-scale mid-term census every five years. Obtaining these statistics used to be very difficult and involved costly surveys. With the linking of data on census and health service records to postal codes, and with the use of computers, it is becoming easier to obtain information on local communities. However, boundary areas for different services such as health, education, police, social services and local government are often quite different, which adds further complications to obtaining data.

Prevention

Prevention takes place at three levels (figure 2.3).

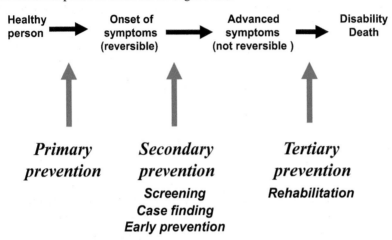

Figure 2.3 Levels of prevention

Primary prevention consists of actions that keep people healthy and free from disease. This might involve measures such as immunization, or the encouragement of healthy lifestyles such as sensible diet and adequate exercise/physical activity.

Secondary prevention involves actions to identify disease when it is at an early stage. This might mean encouraging people to go for treatment at the first signs of a health problem. Moles that might be early skin cancer, a cough that might be the first sign of tuberculosis, fever that may be an early sign of meningitis are all examples of health symptoms where it is important that people have sufficient understanding of their bodies in order to make an informed decision. GPs often complain that people reporting trivial symptoms waste their time. However, this is balanced by people delaying coming for treatment because they do not realize a problem is serious.

For some conditions it can be too late to wait until symptoms become observable. Screening is the name given to the process of testing people for hidden ('sub-clinical') disease. This testing can be opportunistic (e.g. when a woman comes for antenatal care she may be routinely tested for various conditions) or be an active process of asking people to come for screening. The role of health promotion is to encourage people to attend for screening and provide the understanding to help them make informed decisions on the actions to take once they have received the results of the screening. Examples of the role of health promotion to support current screening programmes are provided in box 2.5.

Not all health issues are suitable for screening, and a decision to launch a large-scale screening programme involves medical, ethical and practical considerations. An important advocacy function for health promotion is to encourage informed debate among the public and decision-makers on policies for large-scale screening programmes.

> **Screening:** The organized attempt to detect, among apparently healthy people in the community, disorders or risk factors of which they were unaware.

Box 2.5 Examples of some current screening programmes and implications for health promotion

Category of screening programme	Examples of screening programmes	Implications for health promotion
Large-scale screening offered to sections of the community falling within defined risk categories (mass or targeted screening)	*Screening programmes currently operating in the UK* ● Chlamydia testing directed at young persons ● Mammography for women over 50 ● Cervical smear test for women aged 20 to 64 years ● Sickle cell anaemia test for babies born to African Caribbean families ● Testing of newborn infants for hypothyroidism and phenylketonuria ● Testing for bladder cancer for persons working in chemicals and dyestuffs industries *Under consideration but not approved for large-scale screening programmes:* ● Colo-rectal cancer ● Prostate cancer	**Health education** directed at the target populations to promote uptake of screening, understanding of screening tests and informed decision-making about the implication of test results **Service improvement** to ensure that screening services are accessible, acceptable, confidential and effective and that staff have communication skills to promote informed decision-making **Advocacy** to promote informed public debate about the ethics and effectiveness of screening programmes and the benefits of increasing the number of diseases for large-scale screening programmes are to be actively promoted.
Screening offered: ● opportunistically to people coming to health care services ● as part of clinical diagnostic procedures ● for persons attending well-person clinics ● to sections of the community at risk through genetic or lifestyle factors	● Blood-pressure testing ● Cholesterol screening ● Genetic tests for BRCA (breast cancer gene) ● HIV testing ● Glaucoma testing for persons having eye tests ● Retinal screening of persons with diabetes	**Health education** of the general public to promote awareness of these tests and their availability; information to patients before and after the test to explain the purpose of the testing, to obtain informed consent, and on the implications of the test results **Service improvement** to improve communication skills of staff so that they can promote informed decision-making by patients **Advocacy** to promote informed public debate about the availability and quality of screening services offered within primary care and the extent to which the screening facility should be actively promoted to the surrounding community.

Box 2.6 Promoting the uptake of Chlamydia screening among young people in Bradford

Chlamydia is a sexually transmitted infection that affects over 10 per cent of sexually active young people in the UK under the age of 25. Most people who have chlamydia have no symptoms, allowing it to be passed on unknowingly from one person to another. If left untreated, chlamydia can lead to chronic pelvic pain, ectopic pregnancies and infertility.

The chlamydia screening programme was set up by the Department of Health in 2006 to raise awareness about and provide screening and free treatment for the infection to all young people under 25. The screening simply involves taking a sample of urine for testing. Treatment is a free, single dose antibiotic tablet.

In Bradford and the Airedale district the screening and treatment service was established in GP surgeries, clinics and other community venues. In support of their screening activities, health promotion specialists designed advertising material to appeal to young persons for buses and local radio and a website. This built on a pilot study two years earlier which had found that radio campaigns were the most effective, with 177 of a total of 361 respondents stating this to be in the medium they remembered. This was followed by posters on buses, with 109 respondents, TV and magazines with 85 and 80 respectively, and only 53 noticing adverts from leaflets. The advertisements were well received and the survey revealed that a high level of knowledge about chlamydia had been generated.

Tertiary prevention involves actions taken once a disease has become serious. The aim is to promote recovery, minimize further disability and restore functioning to as high a level as possible.

Health promotion at this stage focuses mainly on rehabilitation, helping to speed recovery and reach maximum functioning. This usually involves working with the patients and their families over time and advising on appropriate use of medicines, recommending lifestyle changes (e.g. diet and exercise) and providing counselling and social support to develop a positive approach to the changed circumstances.

Activity 2.3

Suggest which actions – if any – might be taken as part of primary, secondary and tertiary prevention of the following: lung cancer, heart disease, obesity, cycle injuries, osteoporosis and elderly people, skin cancer, breast cancer, growth faltering among infants.

Establishing causes

Cause: Any factor that can directly lead to disease, e.g. chemicals, radiation, micro-organisms, environment, lifestyle/behaviour.

Risk factor: Something which can increase the likelihood of disease but on its own is insufficient to cause disease, e.g. age, sex, family history, low income.

Health promotion involves addressing the determinants of health – whether in society, the environment, the community or the individual. An understanding of the issues involved with causality is essential to ensure that our efforts are directed at addressing the true causes of disease, including any barriers to good health.

Primary prevention is only possible if we understand the causes of a health problem. For example, primary prevention is possible for lung cancer because we know that the disease is caused by smoking tobacco. However, primary prevention is not yet possible for breast cancer because the causes are not known (except for the small percentage of cases that are due to the BRCA gene). Cervical cancer is an example of a disease which, until quite recently, was considered suitable only for secondary prevention through cervical screening. However, we now know that it is a sexually transmitted disease spread by the human papilloma virus – so primary prevention has become an option.

An important question is what causes the cause? As you saw in 'What makes Jason unhealthy?' in box 1.7, there can be a whole chain of causes. Causal factors can be at the individual, family, community, national and international level. Some can be changed or modified, others are fixed.

There are many factors, such as age, gender, previous illness, housing and ethnicity, that may predispose a person to become susceptible to a particular disease but may not on their own be sufficient to cause disease, and these are called risk factors. For example, increasing age is a risk factor for cataract, and breast and prostate cancers. Persons from Africa are more likely to have the genetic mutation that causes sickle cell anaemia. Young adult men are more likely than older men to get testicular cancer.

Confounding factors

One of the main challenges in epidemiology is to distinguish true causes from factors that might be associated but not causal – the so-called confounding factors. An example of a confounding factor is the apparent link between coffee drinking and pancreatic cancer found in a case control study by MacMahon et al. (1981). However, closer examination showed that the real causal relationship was between pancreatic cancer and smoking. It just happened that the heavy smokers involved in the studies were also heavy coffee drinkers – hence the apparent association.

> **Confounding factors:** Factors which appear to be associated with a disease but in fact are not causal.

The branch of epidemiology that is involved with establishing causal influences on health is called analytical epidemiology. The study designs fall into two broad groups.

Group one analytical epidemiology study designs

These study designs are useful for suggesting possible causes but do not have the power to prove causal relationships because they only measure associations.

Ecological studies These compare disease in one community with others – for example, studies comparing the dental health of people in some communities and not others provided the first clues that fluoride in water might protect from dental decay.

Cross-sectional studies These are surveys of samples of the population at a single point in time. Information from such surveys might show that people with high levels of disease also share characteristics – for example, diet, housing, exposure to environmental hazards.

Case control studies These compare a sample of people with the disease or condition under study with a control sample of people without the disease. The probability that the people with the disease are more likely to have a particular characteristic (e.g. a lifestyle factor) or exposure is compared with the control and called the odds ratio. An odds ratio greater than 1 suggests that the characteristic is more likely to be found

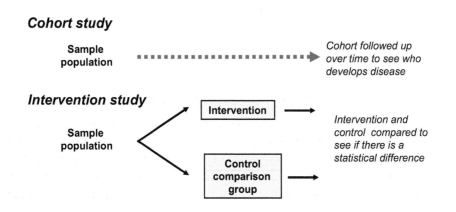

Figure 2.4 Cohort and intervention studies

in the people with the disease. Case control studies are particularly useful for study-ing rare diseases or when information is needed very quickly, such as when a new health problem has arisen. The quality of case control studies depends heavily on the selection of controls and people's ability to recall events which may have happened a long time in the past.

Group two analytical study designs

These are stronger designs which can provide evidence for causal relationships.

Cohort studies – also called prospective or longitudinal studies A sample of people is followed over time and their lifestyle and their exposure to potential hazards, as well as the incidence of disease, is monitored. These studies can measure relative risk and provide powerful evidence for causal links. However, they are expensive to carry out because of the time and effort involved in follow-up. They are not suitable for rare diseases because of the large sample sizes needed to include enough cases. The most famous example of the use of this approach was the British doctors' cohort study of the 1950s. Sir Richard Doll and his colleagues recruited 40,000 British male doctors in 1951 and followed them for fifty years. The results showed that many more doctors who smoked went on to develop lung cancer than those who did not smoke (see figure 2.5) and provided clear evidence for a causal link between smoking and lung cancer. (Doll and Hill, 1954).

Figure 2.5
Correlation between smoking and cancer found in the cohort study of UK doctors carried out by Sir Richard Doll

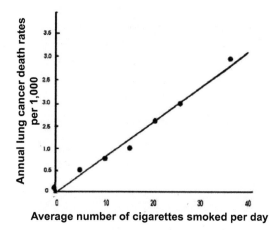

Death rates from lung cancer (per 1,000) by number of cigarettes smoked, British doctors, 1951–61

Intervention study or randomized trial This involves exposing a group of people to an intervention such as a health promotion programme to modify lifestyle. After a suitable interval a follow-up study is carried out to find out if the intervention offers significantly more benefits compared to that of a similar group who had not received the intervention. In randomized control trials (also called experimental designs) the intervention and control groups are selected at random, and this is considered the 'gold standard' of evidence-based practice. In community interventions randomization is more difficult, and an alternative approach (called quasi-experimental) is used which compares the impact on one community with that on other similar communities matched for key variables such as ethnicity, income, age distribution, etc. The quality of the evidence generated in community intervention trials depends heavily on the selection of controls.

Relative and attributable risk Relative risk provides a measure of the strength of a causal relationship. The higher the relative risk, the more likely it is that there is a causal relationship. Attributable risk answers the question that politicians and policy-makers often ask when faced with public health decisions – how much disease could be prevented and how many lives be saved if we were to remove that causal factor?

Making a decision about cause is not easy and involves weighing up a body of evidence and applying the criteria in box 2.7, which have become the *de facto* standard for assessing causality.

Statistical significance: A statistical test can determine the likelihood or probability that the results of an intervention reflect a true effect or are due to chance. The p value (probability) is the likelihood that the result is due to chance. If the p value is, for example, less than (<) 0.05, then there is less than a 5 per cent probability that the result is due to chance. The highest p value accepted in most research as evidence of significance is 0.05. If the p value is greater than 0.05 there is a good chance that any apparent benefit of an intervention is a statistical fluke and will have to be disregarded.

Box 2.7 Criteria for causality – adapted from Bradford-Hill (1965)

Temporal sequence – Did exposure to the factor take place before the occurrence of disease? For example, you would need to establish that a worker was exposed to asbestos before he or she developed mesothelioma. If exposure was only after the disease developed, you would have to discount asbestos as a possible cause.

Strength – The stronger the association between the disease and the factor (i.e. the relative risk or odds ratio), the more likely it is that the relationship is causal.

Dose response relationship – If the likelihood of disease increases with greater exposure to the factor, this provides support for a causal relationship.

Replication of findings – Is the association also found when others repeat the study in different settings?

Biological plausibility – Does the cause–effect relationship fit in with what we already know about biology and disease? For example, studies on the effect of radon gas on cancer are supported by laboratory demonstrations that radiation can damage DNA.

Consideration of alternative explanations – Have all the possible alternative causes been considered and is there evidence to rule them out?

Experiment – What evidence is there from intervention trials that the removal of the causal factor (e.g. reduction in smoking, high salt diet, high sugar consumption) can lead to improved health?

Coherence with established facts – Does the association fit in with existing theory and knowledge? While in most cases this applies, it is important to bear in mind that occasionally a discovery might be made that is so radical and revolutionary that it overturns conventional wisdom.

Systematic review: A systematic process of searching out published evaluations of interventions and critically appraising the findings and drawing conclusions on the effectiveness of the methodology under study. Systematic reviews are normally carried out on intervention studies or randomized control trials.

Meta-analysis: A study of the research literature on a particular issue or topic. A statistical analysis is carried out of the data presented in the various studies under examination and an overview is presented of the findings.

Systematic reviews

In a systematic review the research literature is surveyed to identify all the relevant published studies. Priority is given to studies which have strong designs, especially randomized control trials of interventions. Each research study chosen is usually reviewed by more than one person, using a set of criteria which include study objectives, sampling, research design, results, and quality of statistical analysis. The review then draws conclusions about the weight of evidence for or against a particular intervention having an impact on health.

Systematic reviews are powerful tools for showing the causes of health problems. A starting point for planning health promotion on a particular health topic is to look at internet websites such as that of the Cochrane Library to see if there have been any systematic reviews carried out that provide an evidence base for effective action. However, the ability of a systematic review to come to conclusions depends on the quality of the available studies. This process is most suited to medical interventions using randomized control trials. It is less suited to health promotion because it can be difficult to randomize communities, and outputs such as behaviour change, informed decision-making and health empowerment are more difficult to measure.

Epidemiology and health promotion debates

Epidemiology is a valuable tool but needs to be seen in the context of the debates in health promotion discussed in chapter 1. There is a risk of epidemiology emphasizing prevention and disease and reinforcing the medical model. One of the challenges is to develop further the social epidemiology of health and subjective wellbeing.

However, even with its limitations, epidemiology is a key discipline in health promotion. Unless we understand the specific factors that influence a given health problem we cannot take action to prevent it and promote health. We could waste time and effort (and the good will of the community) carrying out actions that will not have an impact. Just as there is a strong ethical imperative that our actions should not harm people, equally it is imperative that our actions should actually provide some kind of benefit. Epidemiology is therefore important in the ethics of heath promotion.

This poses challenges for health promotion. Given that, even after applying the criteria in box 2.7, we rarely have 100 per cent certainty, how definite about a cause should we be in order to take action? For a public health measure such as reducing smoking the evidence linking that behaviour to lung cancer is very strong. But a disease such as coronary heart disease is multi-factorial, involving many different causal factors including diet, exercise, smoking and raised blood pressure. We have to base our health promotion on the best available knowledge, but at the same time must accept that we will make mistakes and, as our understanding of health and disease improves, will need constantly to revise our health promotion efforts.

Another problem comes with the fact that epidemiology is a study of populations. While epidemiology might produce generalizations about how much in the way of vitamins and minerals, and how much exercise an average person needs, we are often dealing with individuals whose needs might be different from the average, either due to their lifestyle or because of their genetic history. This poses difficulties for health promotion. There is strong pressure to take findings from epidemiology and turn them into clear and simple advice, such as "Eat five portions of vegetables or fruit a day', 'Reduce your salt intake', 'Walk for 20 minutes a day', 'Brush your teeth after every meal'. Such generalized messages highlight the weaknesses of persuasive approaches to health promotion because they represent an oversimplification. We need to find ways of tailoring messages to each individual's unique and specific needs and move towards health empowerment approaches.

Epidemiology can involve complex research designs and elaborate statistical calculations. If you find such studies in journals difficult to understand (we certainly do!), think about what the community must feel. Faced with apparently conflicting advice from doctors, mass-media advertising, and reports in newspapers of the latest 'miracle cure' or 'research finding', it is not surprising that those in the community often shrug their shoulders and either do nothing or choose a course of action that to them seems the most sensible. The drop in immunization rates following the MMR autism

Despite pressure to take more exercise, many people continue to make short journeys by car when they could easily walk or jog.

media scare in 2003 shows that the public are concerned about health and pay attention to what they read or hear in the media – and they do not always trust government 'experts'. Health promotion has a vital role to play through schools, the mass media and the community in the development of a public who are health literate and able to interpret and apply health information to their decision-making.

Epidemiology has achieved notable success in explaining links between asbestos and cancer, smoking and lung cancer, and sugar and dental health. However, it cannot explain the underlying reasons why these destructive practices persist – even in the face of sustained health promotion. For that we need to apply other disciplines, such as economics, politics, sociology, anthropology and psychology which are explored in other chapters of this book.

Further reading

For a general guide to epidemiology, see:
- Beaglehole, R., Bonita, R., and Kjellström, T. (2006). *Basic Epidemiology*. 2nd edn, Geneva: World Health Organization.

For a useful guide to interpreting epidemiological research, see:
- Greenhaigh, T. (2006). *How to Read a Paper: The Basics of Evidence-Based Medicine.* Oxford: Blackwell.

For an overview of epidemiology and public health in international settings, see:
- Walley, J., Wright J., and Hubley, J. (2001). *Public Health – An Action Guide to Improving Health in Developing Countries.* Oxford: Oxford University Press.

3 Understanding Health and Illness Behaviours

Contents

3 Understanding Health and Illness Behaviours

Key issues within this chapter:

- An understanding of influences on health and illness behaviour is necessary in order to plan effective health promotion interventions.
- Influences on behaviour operate at the level of the individual, family and friends, community, and nation and society.
- A range of models can be applied to understanding influences on behaviour and health decision-making.
- Social and ethnographic research is necessary to ensure that health promotion interventions are tailored to the specific needs and situation of individuals and communities.

By the end of this chapter you should be able to:

- apply models of behaviour to understand factors at the level of the individual, family and friends, community, and nation and society that influence health actions
- identify the contribution of social research to health promotion planning
- draw on models of health and illness behaviour to plan tailored health promotion interventions.

Introduction

An understanding of human behaviour is central to health promotion. If we want to help people to take power and make decisions about their health, to take action to tackle the forces that control their lives, we need to have such an understanding of what influences behaviour and promotes health action. We need to appreciate how people make decisions about their lives and the forces that influence those decisions.

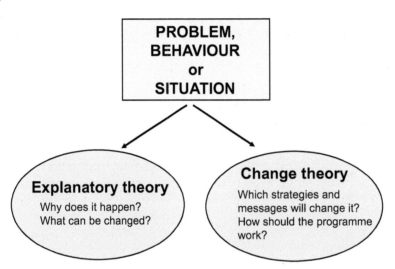

Figure 3.1 What models do

In this book we use the term 'theory' to refer to broad concepts and principles and the term 'models' for specific frameworks that can be applied to understand health behaviours. A model will often draw upon one or more theories.

In seeking to understand behaviour, researchers draw from a wide range of disciplines including psychology, sociology, economics and anthropology. Many different models have been proposed which fall into two groups. The first group are called *explanatory models* and the second *change models* (see figure 3.1). This chapter will discuss some theories and introduce a range of models that we have found helpful in health promotion.

Behaviour: A word used to describe specific acts that a person carries out. The terms actions and practices are functionally equivalent.

What are behaviours?

Some behaviours are more easily changed than others, so it is helpful to distinguish different kinds of behaviour.

- **Decision-based behaviour** – where a person goes through a conscious decision-making process before deciding to perform (or not to perform) the behaviour – e.g. a person's decision to start taking regular exercise.

Motivations: Internal factors within a person that influence their actions. While behaviours can be directly observed, motivations are based on thought processes such as beliefs, attitudes, values and drives, which can only be determined indirectly through processes such as questioning.

- **One-time behaviour** – a behaviour that a person is likely to carry out only a few times in their life – e.g. take their child for immunization, install a smoke alarm in their house, have a vasectomy.
- **Routine behaviour or habit** – an action that people do regularly – usually without a conscious decision, such as washing hands after going to the toilet.
- **Addictive behaviour** – when there is some reinforcement of the behaviour through a biological or psychological adaptation leading to dependency on a substance – e.g. cigarettes, drugs, alcohol.
- **Custom** (also called a behavioural norm) – a behaviour shared by a group of people which forms part of the culture of the community – e.g. the diets of ethnic minorities, body piercing among young people.
- **Tradition** – behaviour passed down over time by sections of society – e.g. circumcision, avoidance of certain foods.
- **Lifestyle** – a collection of behaviours that make up a person's way of life – e.g. patterns of eating, exercise, leisure, clothing, etc.

These categories overlap. What may start as a decision, such as to put on a seatbelt or start to take regular exercise, might become a routine. Health promotion with individuals in a community to encourage them not to smoke might lead to a norm not to smoke. A decision to start smoking might lead to a biological dependency, i.e. an addiction.

> **Activity 3.1**
>
> Suggest an example of a health related behaviour for each of the categories of behaviours listed above. Which behaviours do you think might be easier to change?

Illness behaviour – the medical anthropology perspective

Health behaviour: Behaviours carried out by healthy people to keep themselves healthy. Primary prevention involves the promotion of health behaviours.

There is a long tradition (Young, 2004) of research into illness behaviour – how people act when they perceive symptoms and take steps to deal with them (figure 3.2).

Feeling something is wrong

Illness behaviours: Behaviours carried out by people when they perceive themselves to have symptoms of illness. Secondary prevention involves encouraging appropriate illness behaviours.

What do people perceive to be symptoms? What is seen to be abnormal and needs action?

A symptom is something that people experience. For example, you might have some pain or feel unwell, and this prompts you to go for help. How you respond will depend on your interpretation of those symptoms. This will be determined by your understanding of health and illness; it is socially defined and affected by culture and gender

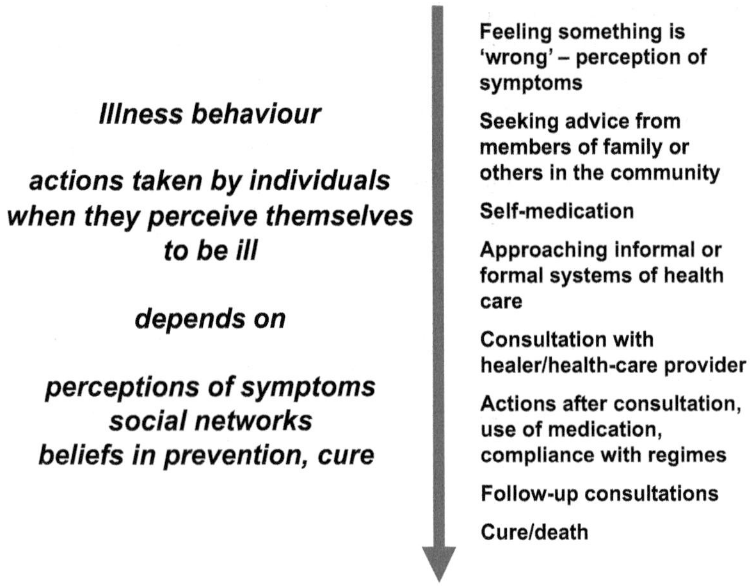

Illness behaviour

actions taken by individuals when they perceive themselves to be ill

depends on

*perceptions of symptoms
social networks
beliefs in prevention, cure*

Feeling something is 'wrong' – perception of symptoms

Seeking advice from members of family or others in the community

Self-medication

Approaching informal or formal systems of health care

Consultation with healer/health-care provider

Actions after consultation, use of medication, compliance with regimes

Follow-up consultations

Cure/death

Figure 3.2 Illness behaviour

Seeking advice from others

Often the first step when we feel that something is wrong with our health is to tell someone else. The sociologist Talcott Parsons (Parsons, 1951) developed a construct called the sick role. According to Parsons, a person's illness needs to be legitimized by others in order for them to be able to adopt a sick role. As part of this sick role a person might be excused certain obligations, such as attendance at work or school, but would also have to take specific actions to get better, such as consult a doctor. Another sociologist, Eliot Freidson (1970), introduced the concept of the *lay referral system* to describe the involvements of social networks such as family and friends in the process of consultation and advice-seeking.

Self-medication

The first line of action is often to take home remedies, herbal remedies or non-prescription 'over-the-counter' medicines purchased from the pharmacist.

Consultation with a health-care provider

If the problem persists, people may consult a health-care provider, who may be a pharmacist, a GP or a practitioner of complementary medicine or traditional medicine serving an ethnic minority community.

There has been considerable research about health worker–patient communication, including the length of the consultation, the quality of communication, the understanding of the information provided, and the extent to which the patient is able to ask questions. The general consensus is that communication is often inadequate. This is partly a result of the lack of training of health-care providers in communication skills and the differing cultural, education and social backgrounds that often exist between them and their patients. We will return to this in our discussion of one-to-one communication in chapter 5 and patient education in chapter 12.

After the consultation

After the consultation the person may collect medicines from the pharmacist. At this stage there are further opportunities for interaction and discussion about the medicines provided. Another focus for research is on the use of medicines by patients (see chapter 12).

Models of behaviour

In this chapter we will draw on the concept of levels of influence introduced in chapter 1 and consider models of behaviour that operate at each level (see box 3.1).

Box 3.1 Models for health and illness behaviour

Level of theory	Model or theory	Integrative models that combine elements of more than one model
Individual	Biological models Motivation theory Cognitive dissonance theory Health belief model Stages of change model	Ecological model Health action model
Family/friends	Social learning theory Theory of reasoned action Social network theory	
Community	Social capital theory Communication of innovations theory	
Nation/society	Normative models Culture-based models Economic/legal models	

Before seeking advice from a health-care provider, most people take medicines at home and consult friends and family.

Individual level

Biological models Many aspects of our behaviour are influenced by our biology and genetic make-up. These include

- drives such as hunger, thirst and sex
- physiological dependencies that are caused by exposure to additive substances e.g. nicotine, alcohol and drugs
- genetic factors.

Social and psychological factors influence the decision to initiate smoking, start taking drugs and drink alcohol. However, once those decisions have been taken a range of biological processes come into play. Addictive substances cause changes in the body, including biochemical dependency with unpleasant withdrawal symptoms. An immediate practical implication is that whenever addictive behaviours are involved it is not enough just to rely on exhortations to people to quit. You have to address the dependency that their body has developed for that substance and consider *how* they will give it up. This might involve providing stop-smoking clinics, nicotine patches and alcohol or drug rehabilitation centres. These are not always successful, reinforcing the view that our main priority should be to focus health promotion efforts on the initial decisions to experiment with drugs or on maintaining alcohol consumption within safe limits.

In animals the term *instinct* is used to describe genetically programmed behaviours such as migration and feeding patterns. In recent years our understanding of the human genome and the way it affects our health has vastly increased. One of the big questions is: How much of our behaviour is determined by our genes and therefore out of our control?

Motivation theory Our biological and evolutionary make-up ensures that hunger, thirst and sex remain basic drives that have a profound influence on our actions – but their effects are mediated by society and culture. The humanist psychologist Abraham Maslow (1943) suggested that people have hierarchies of needs. He pointed out that you need to deal with people's basic security needs such as housing, food and clothing before you could think about other needs. He went on to propose the existence of 'higher' needs, such as love and personal fulfilment, which he called 'self-actualization'. The theory is useful for reminding us that we need first to address people's basic needs before we can expect them to consider others. However, Maslow's suggestions for so-called higher-order needs are more controversial, as constructs such as self-actualization are highly culture-specific and value laden.

Cognitive dissonance theory A common approach in health promotion is to try to change behaviour by raising awareness of harmful consequences, e.g. that smoking causes lung cancer. This approach forms the basis of cognitive dissonance theory, proposed by Leon Festinger (1957). According to this theory, uncomfortable information causes a 'dissonance' or a clash, rather like two adjacent notes on a piano. In the same way that dissonance in music is resolved through 'consonance', we expect the person to resolve the conflict between the incoming information on health risks and their lifestyle by changing their own attitudes and practices, e.g. by giving up smoking.

However, this approach breaks down because people do not always resolve the dissonance by changing their behaviour. According to cognitive dissonance theory, they can also resolve the dissonance by disregarding any information that makes them feel uncomfortable.

One of the best examples of the use of cognitive dissonance is that of fear appeals. By giving people information on the dangers of smoking or casual sex, and showing pictures of diseased lungs or people dying, it is hoped to create a dissonance which will then be resolved by the person changing their behaviour. However, the reverse may happen. Faced with uncomfortable information, a common reaction is to shrug it off, deny and disbelieve it. The use of fear or shock appeals in mass-media campaigns is discussed further in chapter 7.

Activity 3.2

Suggest some examples where you might try to discourage someone from unhealthy behaviours using cognitive dissonance. How do you think people might respond – through denial, or through acceptance and change?

Health belief model The health belief model is the first of two 'value expectancy theories' that we describe (Janz and Becker, 1984; Strecher and Rosenstock, 1997).

According to value expectancy theory, a person will weigh up the costs and benefits – 'pros and cons' – of taking action and will choose the approach which appears to provide the greatest benefits. However, what is important is the person's own perception of benefits. Exchange theory, which looks at the costs a consumer has to pay for a product, is similar to value expectancy theory and is a part of the social marketing approach to health promotion discussed in chapter 7.

The health belief model was first introduced by M. H. Becker to explain utilization of health services and has been widely applied to other health-related behaviours. The model tries to explain health actions through the interaction of three sets of beliefs:

- perceived susceptibility
- perceived seriousness
- perceived benefits and disadvantages.

Health belief model

Figure 3.3 The health belief model

For a person to take action he/she must:

 believe they are susceptible

 believe the health problem is serious

 believe that the advantages of taking action outweigh the disadvantages.

> A trigger may be needed to encourage the person to act.

The model helps to explain why, even after receiving health education, people may not take action.

- They may accept a disease is serious but do not believe they are at risk.
- They may accept that they are at risk but not believe the problem is serious.
- They may believe that the effort of taking action is not worth the potential benefits.

The health belief model provides a useful checklist of issues that need to be addressed in a health education campaign. A major weakness is that it sees behaviour change in a highly individualistic way and does not take into account social influences.

Stages of change model This model, also called the transtheoretical model (Prochaska and DiClemente 1982), proposes that an individual goes through the following stages before taking action:

- **pre-contemplation** – the person is unaware of the behaviour and not interested in changing
- **contemplation** – the person has heard of the practice and is thinking of change

- **trial** – the person is ready for change and willing to try it out
- **maintenance** – the person incorporates the change into their life style
- **relapse** – the person tries it out but then returns to original practices.

The model is useful because it explains how, in a given community, people may be at different stages in the adoption of a behaviour, and you will need to adapt your approach accordingly. In figure 3.4 we provide an example of how the model can be used in health promotion on smoking. The starting point is to ask questions concerning their feelings about giving up smoking. The health promotion response is tailored to the stage they are at.

Figure 3.4 Using the stages of change model to develop tailored advice on smoking

How do you feel about smoking?

Not interested (pre-contemplation)	Thinking about quitting (contemplation)	Ready to quit (trial)
Encourage the client to think about quitting	**Trigger the decision to quit**	**Encourage client to take the first step**
• Focus on providing information on the benefits of stopping smoking and the support available so the smoker can make an informed decision	• Give them a chance to discuss their concerns about smoking • Provide motivational advice and support • Refer for health check, e.g. on lung function	• Praise them for reaching that decision • Reinforce their decision to stop • Help them decide the best strategy for stopping smoking • Advise on available services, e.g. stop-smoking clinics

---

Activity 3.3

Apply the health belief model and stages of change model to one of the following behaviours:

- bringing a child for MMR immunization
- taking exercise to prevent heart disease
- wearing eye protection goggles in a workplace.

What kinds of health promotion actions does each model suggest you should apply? Which model do you think is the most useful for your health topic?

Family/friends level

This group of theories considers the individual in the context of others around them and recognizes that people do not act in isolation from others.

Social learning theory Social learning theory, also called social cognitive theory, was developed by Albert Bandura (Bandura, 1986). He disagreed with earlier 'behaviourist' ideas that saw learning only as a result of external influences, and instead put forward the view that people learn through their own experiences – by observing the actions of others. He suggested that each individual has a self-system and that human action is an interplay between the self-system and the environment. Bandura proposed that human activity has four special characteristics: the ability to symbolize tone's experiences, to learn from others, to regulate one's own behaviour, and to reflect on one's own situation.

In this interaction between the individual and the environment, Bandura argues that it is people's beliefs about the world around them that have the most influence on their actions. Beliefs are 'an individual's representation of reality that has enough personal validity and credibility to guide behaviour and thought'. Beliefs affect human perception, interpretation and behaviour and are therefore the source of motivation. According to Bandura's theory an important influence on belief is observing the actions of others – a process he called 'modelling'.

Of particular importance are beliefs about oneself – the self-concept and the concepts of self-efficacy and self-esteem. According to social learning theory, people with low self-esteem are more likely to be persuaded by others to perform harmful behaviours such as smoking, drinking and taking drugs. People with high self-esteem are more able to resist pressures and have the self-efficacy to do what they feel is right.

> **Self-efficacy:** Belief in one's capabilities to organize and execute the actions required to manage prospective situations.

Social learning theory has been widely adopted in health promotion because it emphasizes the importance of understanding individuals within their social context. Many people feel that the promotion of self-esteem is an important health promotion goal in its own right – especially in school health education and in work with disadvantaged and socially excluded groups. The concept of self-efficacy is especially useful and is a key part of the health empowerment approach to promotion we introduced in chapter 1.

> **Self-esteem:** The extent to which a person regards him- or herself to be of value.

Images and modelling One of the implications of social learning theory is that we learn by modelling our behaviour on others. Such 'role models' may have positive or negative influences, e.g. when a presenter of a children's TV programme or a rock star is exposed for taking drugs. A common strategy in health promotion is to promote positive role models, such as by publicizing examples of a celebrity showing a positive attribute, e.g. being a good father or living a healthy life.

In chapter 7 we discuss how the world of advertising makes heavy use of modelling. Advertisers try to make their product stand out by giving it a distinct image. Images of 'being cool', glamorous professions, risk taking, cowboys in the open countryside, the use of products by celebrities are all employed to associate products with desirable attributes.

Theory of Reasoned Action This theory (Fishbein and Ajzen, 1975) is the second model we present based on value expectancy theory. While the health belief model focuses on the individual and his or her beliefs, the theory of reasoned action considers the individual and the influence of those around them. One of the strengths of the theory is that it fits very well with everyday experience. Sometimes we want to do something but do not because we feel that others would not approve of us doing it. On other occasions we may be pressurized by others to do things we may not want to do. Applying the theory involves initial research/questioning to find out:

- what consequences the person believes might follow if he or she adopts the behaviour and to what extent that person rates those consequences positively or negatively. If they believe that the overall consequences will be positive, then that person will have a favourable attitude to adopting that behaviour.
  - what the person believes that those around them would feel if they were to adopt that behaviour. If they believe that the people most important to them would be in favour of them adopting the behaviour, they would have a positive 'subjective norm'. If they believed that people around them would object, then they would have a negative subjective norm.

Subjective norm: A person's overall perception of whether the people in their network would approve or disapprove of them carrying out a particular action.

Figure 3.5 Theory of reasoned action

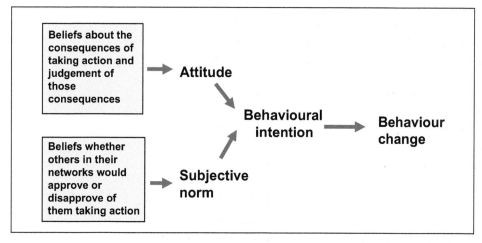

A useful feature of this theory is that it separates the intention of doing something from the action itself. Which of the two – the attitude or the subjective norm – will have the most influence on forming the intention will depend on the personal characteristics of the person, especially their self-confidence and self-esteem. Some people are strong willed enough to resist outside pressure, but others are highly susceptible.

The term 'enabling factors' was introduced by Lawrence Green to include factors such as money, resources, skills, specific relevant knowledge and accessible services. One of us (JH) has modified the theory of reasoned action by suggesting that enabling factors need to be in place before the intention is translated into action. This modification is called BASNEF – an acronym for *b*eliefs *a*ttitudes *s*ubjective *n*orms and *e*nabling *f*actors (Hubley, 2003). The theory of planned behaviour is another modification of the theory of reasoned action (Ajzen, 1988) and combines elements of social learning theory and includes beliefs about one's ability to bring about change – i.e. self-efficacy. The theory of planned behaviour has been applied to a wide variety of health behaviours, including diet, contraceptive use, substance use, attendance for health screening and road safety (see reviews by Stead et al., 2005).

> **Social networks:** That set of contacts with relatives, friends, neighbours etc. through which individuals maintain a social network and receive emotional support, material aid, services and information and develop new social contacts. (Walker et al.,1977)

Social Network Theory A weakness of many models of behaviour is that they see individual action in isolation from others. Social network theory seeks to understand individuals within the social context of their partners, family, friends and community (see box 3.2). Social networks provide channels for flows of information in communities, pressures to act in particular ways, and also the support for people with illnesses. Not only are they vital to understanding influences on health actions but they appear directly to influence health. A cohort study in Almeda county, California, found that survival rates from a heart attack improved with increasing level of social support. Socially isolated persons had three times the age-adjusted mortality rate of those with strong social networks (Berkman and Syme, 1979). The protective value of social

Numerous social networks can be found within a community, including families, friendship groups, church and voluntary organizations, and sports clubs

Box 3.2 How social networks influence health

Social networks as sources of information

- We find out information about health and other topics through our networks and we tend to believe information from the people that we trust (have high source credibility).

Social networks as source of pressure and influence

- Some people may have more influence than others, and in health promotion we need to find out who are the influences at family, peer and community level.

Social networks as sources of support

- When we have financial difficulties, are sick or have other problems we rely on our network of family and friends for emotional and practical support.

Significant other: The individual who has the most influence on our lives – usually a partner, parent, family member or close friend.

Source credibility: The term used to describe how much we trust particular persons or sources of information.

Opinion leader: A person in a community network who has influence over the way others in that community think and act.

Box 3.3 How to investigate social networks

Investigating social networks in a community involves obtaining information through observation and questioning to determine the following information:

- Who are the most influential people in the network?
- Are the relationships in the network one-way or two-way (reciprocal)?
- Are there different networks for different topics, e.g. health, legal problems, cars, home decorating, etc.?
- How important is family membership in community life? How are families and kinship groups typically organized within the culture?
- What roles do the father, mother, son, daughter, grandparents (or other persons typically part of the family within a certain culture) play within the family?
- Who generally makes health related decisions within the family (i.e. what to do when a member is sick, whether to take certain preventive measures, what the family will eat, what money can be allocated for health related expenses, whether a sick member may follow certain medical advice)?
- Who are the most influential people in the community? Are there informal leaders who are looked to for decisions although they remain in the background?

networks, including long-standing relationships such as marriage, has been repeatedly demonstrated in studies of mental illness (Walker et al., 1977) and other health topics (Berkman et al., 1992; House et al., 1988). In recent years the concept of social network has emerged as a key component of social capital. This will be discussed in more detail in the next section.

> **Activity 3.4**
>
> Draw a series of concentric circles. Write your name in the centre of the first circle. In the next circle put the names of the people in your social network who have the most influence on your life. In the next circle put people who have some influence, but are less important than those in the inner circle. What does this diagram say about the influences on your life and health related decisions? If you were to make a diagram like this for another person, how do you think you might be able to use it in heath promotion with that person?

Community-level theories

Social Capital Theory Social capital draws upon both nineteenth-century concepts of community and social network theory. In the nineteenth century, concern about the flow of people from rural areas to cities led the German sociologist Frederick Tönnies to introduce the terms *Gemeinschaft*, to describe close-knit rural communities based on interpersonal contact, and *Gesellschaft*, for the more organized and hierarchical urban societies (for a translation of his book, see Tönnies,1957). The French sociologist Emile Durkheim (1952) tried to explain higher suicide rates found among urban and unmarried persons by putting forward the concept of 'anomie' – a Greek work for lack of norms or social ties. Social capital theory considers social networks and cooperation between people to be beneficial, (Kawachi, 1997). This will be discussed further when we consider health promotion in community settings in chapter 11.

> **Social capital:** The networks, norms, relationships, values and informal sanctions that shape the quantity and cooperative quality of a society's social interactions. (Office of National Statistics 2003)

Communication of innovations theory Communication of innovations theory – also called diffusion theory – was developed by Everett Rogers to explain why some new ideas or 'innovations' spread faster than others. He studied the rate of adoption of different innovations such as health practices, new curricula in schools, improved farming crops, and the take-up of prescribing new medicines by doctors. The theory suggests that new ideas – whether health practices such as exercise or the latest mobile phone – spread in similar ways through social networks and that the rate of spread depends both on the nature of the innovation and the social system into which it has been introduced (Rogers and Shoemaker, 1983).

The theory predicts that the speed at which an innovation will spread will depend on the extent to which it satisfies the following conditions:

- **perceived relative advantage** – does the community perceive it to have any advantages over what its members are doing already?
- **trialability** – can people try it out?
- **observability** – are the benefits of the innovation clearly visible in the short term?
- **low complexity** – does it involve learning new skills?
- **high affordability** – is it low cost – in effort, in time and in money?
- **compatability** – does it fit into existing lifestyle and culture?

Communication of innovations theory suggests that innovations spread more rapidly when the idea for the innovation comes from the members of the organization or community rather than being imposed from outside. The theory highlights the culture of the community and its readiness to accept new ideas and the importance of opinion leaders spreading a new idea through their social networks. Communication of innovations is a useful theory because it forces us to examine exactly what we want to promote in a community and provides a simple tool to enable us to predict how easy it will be to persuade people to adopt the innovation (Green et al., 1987).

Activity 3.5

Apply communication of innovations theory to the introduction of one of the following into a community with which you are familiar. What predictions would the theory make about how easy or difficult it might be to introduce the practice?

- Installing smoke alarms in homes
- Children wearing cycle helmets
- Dog owners using 'poop and scoop' when walking their dogs
- Eating five portions of fruit or vegetables a day

Norms: Patterns of behaviour that are shared by a group of people at a regional or national level. Another word for a norm is a custom.

Models at the national level

Norms and customs A norm is a behaviour that is normal – most people do it. Norms can operate at different levels: a country or region, a local community, an ethnic group or a section of society such as young people. Customs is another word used to describe behaviours shared by groups of people.

Imagine you are asking someone to follow a particular action, e.g. going jogging or cooking a particular food. If no one else in their family or community is doing the same thing, you are actually asking them to go against what is current practice. That takes a lot of determination – some people thrive on being different from the crowd but the rest of us prefer to wait and see and then follow. So the influence of norms explains why health promotion directed at individuals often fails.

However, it is not just the norm itself that matters – it is also people's perceptions of what is the norm. For example, many young people (and adults!) mistakenly believe that everyone is having higher levels of sex than is actually the case. This, in turn, leads to them feeling they should conform to their mistaken perception of the prevailing norm.

One approach in health promotion is to focus on changing norms in society. A good example is the banning of smoking in public places – restaurants, offices, airplanes – in order to change norms about smoking. Another more controversial example is the extending of licensing hours in pubs in the hope that it will ease the pressure on drinking and influence norms of drinking.

Culture We can apply the concept of culture and subculture to any group of people:

regional groups, ethnic minorities, migrant communities, refugees, youth movements, etc.

The concept of culture combines all or some of the following elements:

- **norms**: shared characteristics of a group
- **traditions**: ideas, values and practices that have been held for a long time and passed on to the next generation
- **systems of thought and ideas**: reinforced by language, religion and systems of medicine.

Box 3.4 How to determine the role of culture on health

Is the health issue affected by any of the following?

- *Life course*: family structure, patterns of influence among family members, the role of women, children, rituals and roles surrounding birth, growing up, relations with other people, sex and marriage, family formation, work, growing old, death
- *Masculinity and femininity*: the roles of men and women in society, views of what makes a 'man' and 'woman', beauty and body image, gender stereotypes, divisions of roles and responsibilities between genders
- *Patterns of living and consumption*: clothing, housing, child-rearing, food production, storage and consumption, hygiene practices, sanitation
- *Health and illness behaviours*: concepts of health and illness, ideas about mental illness and handicap, care of sick people, traditional medicine systems, patterns of help seeking when ill, use of doctors and traditional healers, responses to pain, concepts about the biological workings of the body, growth, conception, pregnancy, birth, etc.
- *Patterns of communication*: language, verbal and non-verbal communication, taboos on public discussion of sensitive items, vocabulary of the language, oral traditions
- *Religion and 'world view'*: ideas about the meaning of life and death, rituals surrounding important life events, ideals about the possibility and desirability of change
- *Patterns of social influence, social networks and political organization*: influences in family and community, community leadership and authority, political structures, divisions and social inequalities
- *Economic patterns*: types of employment, home based or workplace, casual or permanent, self-employed, family concern or employee, financial interdependency within the extended family, access to capital funds to initiate new ventures.

If the answer is yes, then you will need to take the influence of culture into account in your health promotion. This will mean involving key members of that community in planning the intervention and promoting actions that are consistent with the cultural norms in that community.

The discipline of medical anthropology has drawn attention to the fascinating diversity of ideas about health and disease in different parts of the world (Helman, 2000). A historical perspective reminds us that the concept of diseases caused by germs is a relatively recent phenomenon in Europe. Before recent history, ideas about health were based on concepts such as the imbalance of humours and miasma or bad smells – ideas that dated back to ancient Greece. Today many different systems of health co-exist on our planet – Chinese medicine based on the duality of yin and yang and the Hindu Ayurvedic and Islamic Unani systems are only a few of the many different systems of health that are practised.

It is important to take the influence of culture into account when planning health promotion, be it related to ethnic diversity, generation differences, or other factors.

Activity 3.6

Choose a section of the community with its own distinct cultural identity. Describe their characteristics using the headings in box 3.4. How would you need to adjust your health promotion approach to meet the needs of that community?

Integrative models

Two models seek to integrate elements of models described above.

Ecological model Ken McElroy's ecological model provides a useful framework for looking at the individual in the context of his or her relationship with others and the general community (McElroy, 1988). It includes many elements from models discussed earlier and sets factors at the individual and community level in the context of those operating at the national level.

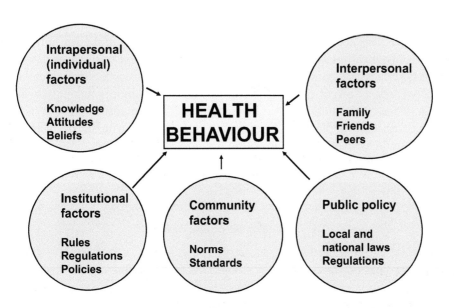

Figure 3.6 An ecological model for health promotion (McElroy, 1988)

Health action model The health action model developed by Keith Tones (Tones and Tilford, 2001) also brings together many features from models described above, including the roles of intention, beliefs, motivational factors, social-network influences, self-concept/self-esteem factors and enabling factors.

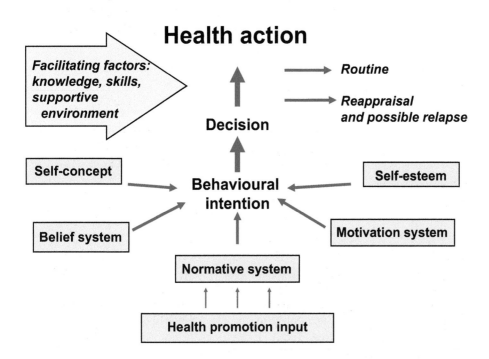

Figure 3.7 The health action model

Tailored communication: Any combination of information or change strategies intended to reach one specific person, based on characteristics that are unique to that person, that are related to the outcome of interest and have been derived from an individual assessment.
(Kreuter et al., 1999)

Tailored health promotion and the use of health promotion theories

Tailored communications – also called targeted communications – are those in which the message is specifically designed to meet a person's or community's needs. Preparing a tailored communication involves finding out information on the individual or community through some kind of information gathering, such as a survey, an interview or the completion of an online health risk appraisal (for more information on this last, see chapter 9).

Box 3.5 How to tailor a communication to influence a health action

1 Select the health actions you are interested in promoting based on an assessment of the needs of the person or community.
2 Develop and administer a questionnaire based on one or more health-promotion theories, e.g. health belief model or stages of change model, or social learning theory. The questions should seek to determine the presence or absence of the specific factors predicted by the model used.
3 List the understandings, beliefs and values that are held that have a positive impact on adoption of the health action and also those that have a negative impact.
4 Prepare and deliver a message that reinforces the positive factors you have identified and minimizes the negative aspects.
5 Evaluate the impact of the message on uptake of the health action. Based on the results of your evaluation, modify the message accordingly.

Box 3.6 Case study: Tailored communications – healthy birthdays

In a health promotion intervention carried out in the United States to encourage low-income African Americans to stop smoking, birthday cards and newsletters were individually tailored based upon ethnicity, gender, and the individual's readiness to change according to the stages of change model. Smokers received either prompting by health-care providers or tailored cards and newsletters. Thirty-three per cent of smokers who received only the tailored cards and letters quit smoking compared to 13 per cent of smokers who received prompting by health-care providers (statistical significance at $p < 0.05$). (Lipkus et al., 2000).

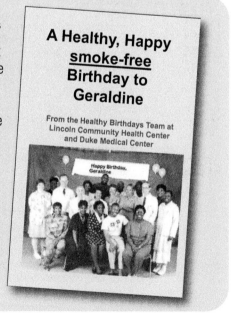

The role of research in understanding behaviour

In order to tailor health promotion you need to carry out some research to understand your community and the reasons why people act in a particular way. The history of health promotion is littered with programmes that failed because they were based on incorrect assumptions and inadequate research on the real situation in communities had not been carried out. The two main approaches to health promotion research are summarized in box 3.7. To some people the choice of quantitative or qualitative research is a matter of ideology, paradigm and value stance, and there is an ongoing debate about the relative merits of the two approaches. We take a pragmatic view that sees both methods playing complementary roles in generating different kinds of data – both of which are required in health promotion.

Box 3.7 Qualitative and quantitative research in health promotion

	Quantitative research	Qualitative research
Description	Emphasis on collection of information that can be quantified and subjected to statistical analysis	Also called ethnographic research – emphasis on the researcher seeking to understand the different factors that influence a given situation and to provide suggestions for further research or health promotion action
Main uses	Useful for providing data on the size of problem and also for setting priorities. Answers questions such as How many? Who is affected? Also provides information on characteristics of persons affected that might be useful for targeting health promotion interventions. Provides information for evaluation of programme impact.	Useful for answering questions such as why people carry out activities – i.e. underlying reasons for actions. Qualitative research is particularly useful at the early stages of understanding a problem when you want to keep an open mind, avoid preconceptions and understand the interaction of many different factors that influence a given situation.
Kinds of data collected	Information on educational, economic and social backgrounds of people in a community; numbers (i.e. norms); location of people who carry out specific behaviours, hold certain beliefs; relative importance of different sources of influence, e.g. family and community members, mass media, health services	For collection of information on ideas, perceptions, feelings, values in a community and the relation of these to culture, religion and wider world views of life. May be used to evaluate health promotion programmes, especially attempts to influence values, interests and factors behind behaviour change.

	Quantitative research	Qualitative research
Principal methods	Surveys on representative samples of the community, collecting data by analysis of records, direct observation, self-completed questionnaires and interviews. Questionnaires/schedules used to collect data that consist mainly of closed questions requiring specific responses in predetermined categories.	Observation, interviews or focus group discussions using unstructured or semi-structured questionnaires that allow people to explain in their own words their feelings and views.
Relationship with health promotion theory	The types of questions asked are often linked to categories of information highlighted by specific theories, e.g. health belief model and stages of change model.	Questions may be informed by theory, but the linkage is less rigid, as the aim is not to allow preconceptions to influence findings. Some researchers feel strongly that theory should not be used to generate questions but should arise out of the data (grounded theory approach).
Sampling	Statistical sampling methods are used to determine both the number of people sampled and how they are selected. Random, purposive and convenience sampling methods are employed.	Uses smaller samples, including members of the community under study and informants who are selected because of their understanding of the local situation.

Models, theories and debates in health promotion

The choice of models and theories is also a reflection of the debates in health promotion reviewed in chapter 1, especially those concerning medical and social models, individualistic compared to structuralistic approaches, levels of influence and the coercion/persuasion health empowerment continuum.

Some of the models have been criticized because they focus on exploring the determinants of behaviour and therefore reinforce individualist approaches to health promotion. Other models examine the individual in a social context or the influence of culture. A general weakness of many of them is that they draw on psychological, sociological and anthropological theory, and there is a need to include elements of political and economic theory. In the discussion of advocacy in chapter 10 we consider the role of political pressure groups in agenda-setting.

We do not take the view that there is such a thing as a single correct model. Models and theories are ways of trying to explain complex situations and suggest approaches to take – in particular they suggest the kinds of information that we need to obtain on our communities by research, e.g. the contribution of specific beliefs, norms, cultural factors and network influences. Once that information is available we can make the informed decisions that we outlined at the end of chapter 1, especially at whom to direct our health promotion efforts, what kinds of messages to promote, what channels to use and what level we need to work on. The right model is the one that helps us to design health promotion activities that are effective.

Further Reading

For a stimulating discussion of the influence of culture on health behaviour see:
- Helman, C. G. (2000). *Culture, Health and Illness*. London: Arnold.

For useful overviews of the theories of behaviour change, see:
- Glanz, K., Rimer, B. K., and Lewis, F. M. (eds) (2002). *Health Behavior and Health Education: Theory, Research and Practice*. San Francisco: Jossey-Bass.

For an authoritative discussion of recent developments in health promotion theory, see:
- DiClemente, R. J., Crosby, R. A., and Kegler, M. C. (eds) (2002). *Emerging Theories in Health Promotion Practice and Research: Strategies for Improving Public Health*. San Francisco: Jossey-Bass.

Health Promotion through the Lifespan

Contents

Health Promotion through the Lifespan

Key issues within this chapter:

- It is useful to take a lifespan approach to exploring health promotion needs and opportunities across the life course.
- Significant events in the life course vary according to the culture, ethnicity, class and the age cohort within which the person falls.
- Key influences on health, such as family, social networks, social support, relationships, employment/income, health beliefs, access to health care and access to health information, change during the life course.

By the end of this chapter you should be able to:

- identify the critical stages in the life course that influence health
- appreciate the diversity and changing nature of life courses in society
- recognize the opportunities that are presented for health promotion at different stages in the lifespan
- use considerations of lifespan and life course when planning health promotion interventions.

There are many ways of describing the human lifespan. The Seven Ages of Man of Shakespeare's *As You Like It* and the four *asramas* of Hindu society are only two of the many ways in which societies have organized social functions and needs and conceptualized the passage through life.

The approach we take in this book is based on the health promotion context in European society in the twenty-first century. Age in years is the obvious starting point for considering the lifespan but, on its own, is limited. Physical, social, health, development and cultural changes through life take place at different ages in different people. With those reservations, we will discuss health through the lifespan according to the age groups in box 4.1. Inevitably there is blurring between these age categories, and they should be considered as overlapping age bands – a rough guide rather than a blueprint.

Box 4.1 A basic framework for considering the lifespan

	Pre-conception to birth
0–4 years	Preschool child
5–9	Pre-pubescent school-aged child
10–17	Pubescent and adolescent school child
18–24	Young person
25–49	Middle adult
50–69	Older adult
70+	Elderly person

Critical issues affecting a lifespan approach

Approaches to the lifespan

The stages of a person's life course can be grouped by:

- **chronological age:** widely used but not always very meaningful
- **biological stages:** according to the biological changes in the human body, such as the emergence of adult teeth, puberty
- **educational criteria:** age of entrance to nursery school, primary school and secondary school, minimum school-leaving age
- **legal criteria:** legal definitions, e.g. age of consent for sex, age for voting, age for purchase of cigarettes and alcohol, age of responsibility for crimes
- **economic criteria:** the age at which people work and receive a pension
- **social and cultural significance:** the roles that people take on in society, with transition from one stage to another sometimes being marked by 'rites of passage' – initiation into adulthood, circumcision, first communion, marriage, retirement, etc. (Van Gennep, 1977)

Lifespan: The overall duration of a person's life determined by natural, environmental and social processes.

Life course: The social element of a lifespan, which may have fairly clear 'stages' or transitions but may also be marked by planned or unplanned life events. (Adapted from Hunt, 2005)

Activity 4.1

Write down what you consider to be the main stages that people go through in their lives and the age ranges that you think are most useful. How do your stages compare with the ranges used in this chapter? If yours are different, what made you choose your age ranges? (Remember that the ones we have used in this book are quite arbitrary and there is no universally right answer.)

Developmental milestones

Development: Changes in skill and capacity to function during life.

Development can include changes in thinking (cognitive development), emotions (emotional development), and interaction with others (social development). It depends in part on changes in the body – called maturation – determined largely by genetic potential and in part in response to the environment, including learning from others and the acquisition of knowledge and skills through the family and school.

Maturation: Changes in the body, including height, weight, and the size of organs and neurons in the brain.

Developmental screening is the name given to the process of detecting possible delays in development in order to initiate remedial action. Health services provide developmental screening soon after birth, as the preschool child is growing up, and on entering school.

Learning

Learning takes place throughout life through informal and formal processes. For the young child it takes place within the context of the family, and as a child gets older it comes from a wider range of sources, such as school, the media, books, magazines, television and the internet. Alongside mass media and the internet, adults have access to learning opportunities through their workplace, communities and social networks and contact with health services.

Cohort effects

The beliefs, values and attitudes towards work, leisure and health of today's children and adults will be different from those of previous years. Life course issues are constantly evolving in response to historical and social events and will be different for people born in the 1930s, the 1940s and later years. It is useful to consider the population as a series of cohorts working their way through their life course, each with their own set of values, issues and concerns. Terms such as 'baby boomers' for the people born in the post-Second World War period, 'Generation X' for those born from the mid-1960s to the mid-1970s, and the 'Millennial Generation' for those born in the mid-1970s onwards have been used to describe cohorts with their distinctive features.

1 Example of a self-report lifeline charting wellbeing through typical life events

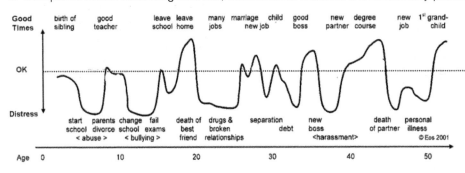

Figure 4.1
Examples of
lifelines (with thanks
to Dai Williams)

2 Composite lifeline illustrating traumas, unsuccessful transitions and recovery points

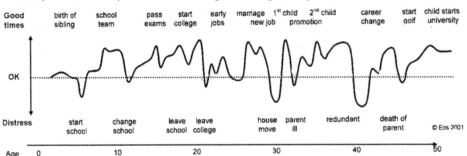

Life events and transition theory

The impact of life events on stress has been the driving force behind theories of transitions, lifespan and the life course. Life events fall into two broad groups. Universal life events are those which most people will experience at some stage in their life, such as adolescence, marriage, childbirth, menopause, retirement and death. Extraordinary life experiences – also called traumatic life events – are those which only some people experience, e.g. serious illness, an injury causing trauma, violent crime, the unexpected death of a loved one, divorce, natural and man-made disasters, domestic violence, unemployment, sexual abuse, etc. There has been considerable interest in the extent to which life events cause stress, which in turn leads to ill health, and the extent to which health can be promoted through providing coping skills. Figure 4.1, from the work of the occupational psychologist Dai Williams, shows two examples of the range of events that can happen during the life course. Holmes and Rahe (1967) produced the list of life events in box 4.2. Each life event was given a score ('life changing unit') for the amount of stress it might cause. An intriguing feature of this classification is that events which most people would consider positive, such as marriage, going on vacation and Christmas, may contribute to stress.

It is certainly useful to look at the way life events affect people, but the evidence for

> **Life events**: Important events that happen during a person's life course.

the impact of specific life events on stress and health is mixed. Many life events are part of everyday life, and responses such as grief are natural and normal. People respond to the same event in different ways depending on their personal characteristics and coping skills. Also important are their social networks (see chapter 2) – especially whether or not they are in a supportive relationship.

Box 4.2 A selection of life events used in the social readjustment rating scale (Holmes and Rahe, 1967)

Death of spouse	Major change in responsibilities at work
Divorce	Children leaving home
Prison term	Trouble with in-laws
Death of a close family member	Outstanding personal achievement
Personal injury or illness	Spouse begins or stops work
Marriage	Starting or ending school
Losing one's job	Change in living conditions
Retirement	Change in work hours, conditions
Change in health of family member	Change in residence
Pregnancy	Change in school
Sexual difficulties	Change in social activities
Addition of family member	Change in sleeping habits
Major change in financial state	Change in eating habits
Death of a close friend	Vacation
Changing to a different line of work	Christmas
Change in frequency of arguments with spouse	

Activity 4.2

Prepare a timeline of the most significant life events in your own life and display it in the same way as in Figure 4.1. Which events do you feel have had the most impact on you as a person? Do you agree with the importance of the items from the life events list of Holmes and Rahe in box 4.2? Is there anything you would like to add or remove?

The role of ceremonies in marking life transitions

Most societies mark transition through life's stages with rituals and ceremonies. Between the christening/naming ceremony and the funeral is an ever changing and rich range of rituals, including birthday parties, first communion, barmitzvahs, the eighteenth birthday, the graduation ceremony, the hen/stag party, the wedding, the retirement party, children's birthday parties, parties to mark the change of decade and – if you are lucky – the hundredth birthday, with a card from the queen! Such ceremonies provide an important social function – the public recognition of a person's transition from one stage of life to another.

Less obvious is the contribution of health service activities to life's ceremonies, including the first visit to the antenatal clinic, a baby's ultrasonic scan and the weighing of the baby at the clinic.

Health needs through life

Health promotion needs change through life for biological, environmental, social and lifestyle reasons. During the life course, our bodies change in shape, size and susceptibility to ill health and disease. At critical points, such as early childhood and during pregnancy, we have special needs and face additional health threats. Figure 4.2 shows how the prevalence of major accidents changes at different stages of life. Some health problems, mainly chronic degenerative diseases such as cancers, heart disease and arthritis, develop over a long period of time and so affect mainly older people.

At some stages in life we may be put in higher risk situations, e.g. when as a child we are considered old enough to go out on our own, when we are old enough legally to buy cigarettes and drink alcohol, when we start to drive, go to work, are old enough to serve in the armed forces, when we are most sexually active, etc. A good example of how health-risk behaviours can change through the life course is provided by a qualitative study by McDermott et al. (2006) of smoking by women in Australia. Smoking increased in their sample when the young women left their parental homes and was maintained at a steady level during the period when they were living a 'partying' mode of life as single women. For some of the sample, entering a long-term relationship with a non-smoker and/or the first pregnancy were life events that provided the trigger to stop smoking.

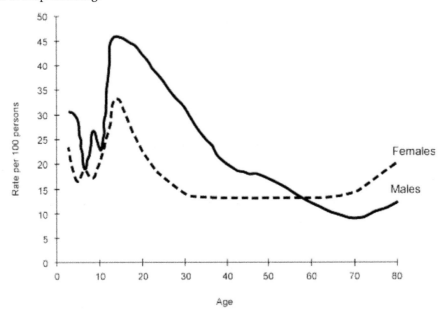

Figure 4.2
Prevalence of major accidents, by gender and age, England, 1996 (Acheson, 1998)

Changing demographic profile

The numbers of people in each stage of the life course is changing. Over the period 2000 to 2030 the number of persons in Europe aged over sixty-five is expected to increase from 15.5 to 24.3 per cent. This increase is a result of the decline in birth rate, the consequence of the baby boom that took place at the end of the Second World War and because people are living longer due to improvements in health. A fall in the number of working adults relative to the number of older persons (the elderly support ratio) will mean there will be fewer adults to provide informal care to older family members and friends. The numbers of people at different ages are shown in the population pyramid in figure 4.3, where each horizontal bar shows the cohort of people in an age range.

Figure 4.3
Population pyramid for the United Kingdom in the year 2005 (Office of National Statistics)

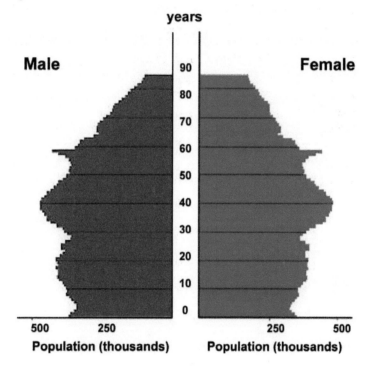

The elderly support ratio:
The number of persons aged ≥65 years per 100 persons compared to those aged 20 to 64 years.

Activity 4.3

Make a list of the main implications of an aging society and how this affects health promotion priorities.

Health promotion should take into consideration changing needs across the life course. Some health problems, for example, affect mainly older people.

The role of the family

We need to look at individuals in the context of their family and social network. The concept of the family goes well beyond the stereotypical nuclear family portrayed in advertisements and varies according to culture, country and community and changes throughout life. Families can consist of a heterosexual or same-sex couple, a single parent and children, a family with preschool children, with school-aged children, with adolescents, with children who go between two divorced parents, reconstituted families, families with older adults, and extended families with networks of relatives living nearby or separated by distance.

Families provide food, shelter, protection and the context in which a child acquires the values of the society. Families are the main care providers in our society for children, the sick and frail elderly people. At each stage of life the family changes, takes on new tasks, drops others. An important role for health promotion is to support and strengthen the capacity of families. Therefore you need to be sensitive to and understand the diverse and changing nature and role of families, what affects the capacity of families and what we can do to support them – in whatever form they exist.

Life courses in a multicultural society

Modern society is diverse and multicultural. Over the years our communities have been enriched by incoming migrants from Africa, Asia, the Caribbean and Europe. Each brings its own culture, way of life and conceptualization of the lifespan, including the roles of individuals, families, life events and transitions. We also have to recognize that the experience of an ethnic group in the United Kingdom is not always a positive one and that racism and discrimination can affect people's lives at every stage of the life course.

Inequalities and social exclusion

In chapter 1 we considered how persistence of inequalities in health have stimulated intensive debate on the nature of health promotion responses. The effects of social exclusion, poverty and inequalities can be seen at every stage of life, from the foetus to the grave. Many of the processes within the lifespan, such as child-rearing, school and work, reinforce inequalities and create a perpetuating 'cycle of poverty'. Children born to poor families face enormous difficulties breaking out from this cycle.

Box 4.3 Social exclusion, theories of poverty and the lifespan

Suggested explanations for the persistence of poverty include:

- *structural theories*: Inequalities in health are a reflection of inequalities in society and have their roots in an economic system through which the wealth and health of some can only be achieved at the expense of others.
- *local deprivation*: Inequalities are due to local geographical and social factors. Some localities are marginalized, with poorer services, schools, housing and environment combined with low employment/income-generating potential.
- *culture of poverty*: Poor and marginalized individuals and communities are disempowered and have developed coping mechanisms for survival, e.g. smoking, which are dysfunctional with regard to health.
- *cycle of deprivation*: The attitudes, behaviours and lifestyle factors that lead to poverty and ill health are passed from one generation to another through socialization, child-rearing and the family, thus perpetuating poverty.

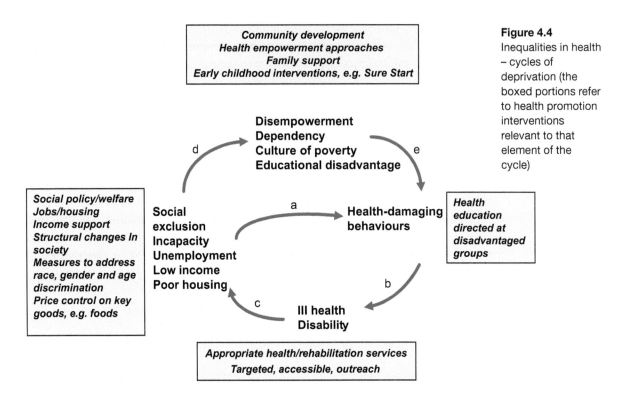

Figure 4.4
Inequalities in health – cycles of deprivation (the boxed portions refer to health promotion interventions relevant to that element of the cycle)

The factors which lead to and reinforce inequalities in health form two interlocking cycles, shown in figure 4.4. The first cycle shows social exclusion leading to the adoption of health damaging behaviour, ill health and disability, which in turn lead to further incapacity and disadvantage. The consequence is a culture of poverty, disempowerment, dependency and ill health. The second cycle highlights the perpetuation of this culture of poverty through the family (socialization and child-rearing) and schooling. The reinforcement of social inequalities from one generation to another means that an effective response must act at different points in the life course and include:

● social policies that address economic and social causes of deprivation and mitigate the effects of social·exclusion
● health services that meet the specific needs of disadvantaged groups
● health education targeted at disadvantaged groups using suitable channels and culturally sensitive approaches
● community and family-based health promotion approaches
● early childhood intervention programmes to support families.

Sexuality

The nature of sexuality in modern society is diversified, with heterosexual, gay and trans-gender communities, each with distinct health promotion needs. In recent years the rights of gay people have been recognized in law to bring them in line with those of heterosexual married and cohabiting couples, and provisions have been made for the legal contract of same-sex partnerships and adoption of children. The emergence of sexuality is an important stage of the human life course and one of the defining features of adolescence.

Pre-conception to birth

Events that take place before conception can have an important impact on the health of a child and its mother. The health of a baby is affected by the nutrition and health status of the mother at the time of conception – which in turn is dependent on the nutritional experience of the mother in her own childhood. An example of a health promotion response to pre-conceptual care is the Department of Health leaflet 'Thinking of having a baby', which seeks to persuade women to take folic acid as early as possible in order to reduce the risk of the baby developing spina bifida.

Conception may be a result of a conscious decision to have a child or be an unplanned and possibly unwelcome event. A decision to have a baby is of enormous significance and marks the transition from two people living together to their forming a family unit. One of the challenges for health promotion is to ensure that this transition is the result of informed decision-making.

Genome: The complete set of genetic information contained in a person's DNA.

Box 4.4 Human genetics and health

Programmes such as the human genome project have greatly increased our understanding of the role of genetics in health. Some illnesses, such as haemophilia, are sex linked, i.e. are carried on the X chromosome. As men only have one X chromosome they are vulnerable to sex-linked inherited disorders. Other inherited disorders, such as sickle cell anaemia, Huntington's chorea and spina bifida, affect both boys and girls. The BRCA1 gene can predispose women carriers to develop breast cancer. Genetic counselling is increasingly being made available to couples to assess the likely risk of inherited disorders. Counselling should take place before conception so that the couple are prepared for possible risks and can make an informed decision about the possibilities of giving birth to a child with a genetic disorder. Increasingly, tests are available that can be used on the foetus *in utero* to determine for

certain whether the child has actually acquired a genetic disorder. At that stage families need help to make a difficult decision about continuing with the pregnancy and the ethical and moral issues involved.

In the United States, the surgeon general has launched a programme of 'genomic awareness' in which families are encouraged to use social gatherings to find out about their family history of inherited disorders and diseases, such as diabetes, heart disease, hypertension and mental illness, and use this information to assess their family risk and take preventive actions. This is currently focused on adults assessing their risks and not directed at choosing partners. Perhaps in future – as our ability to test for specific genes increases – genomic compatibility will be as important as social compatibility!

The antenatal – or prenatal – period is important for health promotion. The arrival of a child, especially the first, is a time of change, upheaval and readjustment in the life of a couple. The aim of antenatal education, summarized in box 4.5, is to help the couple to take the necessary steps to ensure a successful pregnancy, to make the experience of childbirth a positive one, and to prepare for the demanding – and rewarding – task they will face in looking after their baby. Actions by the pregnant mother such as excessive alcohol intake and smoking can have adverse effects on the growth of their foetus, and support should be provided to help women address these issues. It is also a time when parent(s)-to-be are thinking about their present lifestyle and their future lives and are receptive to health promotion on many issues in addition to their future parenting role. Given the importance of this antenatal period, it is disappointing that a detailed systematic review carried by out by A. J. Gagnon (2000) reached the conclusion that '**the effects of general antenatal education for childbirth and/or parenthood remain unknown.**'

Health promotion in informal community settings is also offered by self-help groups such as the National Childbirth Trust, which supports parents after the birth of their child through a network of post-natal support groups. A great deal of information is available to parents from the mass media, although there are some major concerns. Often the people who need help the most – including the disadvantaged, persons from minority groups, single parents, young mothers – have limited access to services because of transport problems and language and cultural barriers. Most

Various studies have highlighted the significance of early childhood in shaping individuals' subsequent mental and physical health.

Box 4.5 What should antenatal health education cover

- *General*: building of confidence of future parents; the impact of a baby on a couple (especially first-time couples); twins and multiple births; maternity clothes; importance of social life; sex during pregnancy; sex and contraception after childbirth
- *Looking after oneself*: coping with changes in the body; tiredness; the importance of eating well and exercise; dealing with medicines and vaccinations; the risks from chicken pox; benefits of lifestyle changes, e.g. alcohol, tobacco smoking; travel
- *Father/partners*: feelings; understanding their partner; the role of antenatal classes; practical help before, during and after birth; sharing workload
- *Antenatal care*: what happens at antenatal clinics; purpose of tests and the ultrascan, what screening takes place, e.g. for Down's syndrome
- *Pregnancy*: early and later stages of pregnancy; effect on the body, weight gain; managing common symptoms, e.g. sickness, tiredness, dizziness, headaches, anaemia, thrush, heartburn; miscarriages

- *Childbirth*: the onset of childbirth, stages of labour; pain and its management; breathing and relaxation; the contribution and role of the birth partner; different kinds of birth; what happens after birth; colostrum and the initiation of breastfeeding
- *The baby at home*: feeding; breastfeeding; expressing and storage of breast milk; formula feeding, complementary feeding; care of the newborn baby; nappies and toilet training; sleeping position; common childhood illnesses; child health clinics; sources of help; health visitor and community midwife; support groups; sharing of load between partners and extended family
- *The future parenting role*: interactions with the developing child, including language; establishing routines, dealing with difficult situations including tantrums; discipline
- *Financial matters*: entitlement to maternity/paternity leave and other benefits; making a will

(Adapted from
http://www.nctpregnancyandbabycare.com)

education is directed at women, and there is a need for greater involvement of fathers. Families are overwhelmed with information from the mass media, the internet, families and health services on a vast range of topics, such as breastfeeding, the sleeping position of the baby, etc. This information can be both conflicting and confusing. It is especially important to balance the often rosy and sentimental image of child-rearing given in the media with a realistic understanding of the changes that will take place following the arrival of a baby and the disruption it will cause to routines, and the possible negative consequences, such as post-natal depression.

Activity 4.4

List the physical and relational changes that will take place in a couple on the arrival of their first baby. What should health promotion cover in order to prepare couples for this new challenge?

Preschool child, 0–4 years

The first years of life are a time of rapid physical growth of the body, including maturation of limbs and brain. This is accompanied by psychological changes such as the development of language, physical coordination and social interaction. An infant is completely dependent on the parents and other caretakers for physical and social needs. The key influences on the preschool child are the parents, brothers and sisters, significant others in the family, e.g. grandparents, and other caretakers, such as child minders and staff at day-care centres and nursery schools.

Parents can be under a great deal of stress and face social isolation, poverty and disadvantage. Impressed by evidence of the impact of out-of-home day care of children on improved educational and social achievement, the Acheson Report (1998) called for an expansion of affordable, high quality day care and preschool education, with extra resources for disadvantaged communities (see box 4.6).

Box 4.6 Early interventions and social inequalities

While remediable risk factors affecting health occur throughout the life course, childhood is a critical and vulnerable stage where poor socio-economic circumstances have lasting effects. Follow-up through life of successive samples of births has pointed to the crucial influence of early life on subsequent mental and physical health and development. The fact that adverse outcomes, for example, mental illness, short stature, obesity, delinquency and unemployment, cover a wide range, carries an important message. It suggests that policies which reduce such early adverse influences may result in multiple benefits, not only throughout the life course of that child but to the next generation.

(Acheson, 1998, p. 9)

As children get older they begin to take in more information from the world around them, through contact with others, from story books read to them by parents, and from television programmes targeted at the preschool child, such as *Tellytubbies* and *Sesame Street*. There is some controversy about the impact – positive or negative – of television on very young children. In 2004 a survey of 2,000 parents for *Mother and Baby* magazine found that nearly half (48 per cent) of all toddlers never eat with the rest of the family and instead eat on their own while watching television. In a survey by National Literacy Trust in 2001, three-quarters of 121 heads of nursery schools sampled in England expressed concern about declines in the language competence of three-year-olds on arrival at nursery school. Based on the assumption that the root cause of the problem was that adults are spending less time talking to babies, the National Literacy Trust launched its 'Talk to your Baby Campaign' in 2004 to encourage parents and caretakers of children under three to spend more time talking to their toddlers.

Pre-pubescent school-aged child, 5–9 years

Once children reach school age they become exposed to a wider circle of contacts and influences, including friends and teachers. They are likely to go out on their own and take more responsibility – a risky but essential part of the process of growing up. In school, children become aware of themselves in relation to their peers. Differences in size, weight, accent and clothing can become the subject of abuse and bullying, with resulting impact on mental health (see discussion of violence in schools in chapter 14).

With the acquisition of reading skills, children are exposed to health information through print media. As their cognitive skills develop, so does their capacity to understand health concepts and apply them to decision-making. Health promotion with the pre-adolescent child is carried out through both school and out-of-school activities, e.g. sports/other clubs and uniformed groups such as the Brownies and Cubs.

Pubescent and adolescent school child, 10–17 years

Adolescence has physical and social dimensions.

- **Physical dimensions**: Biological changes that take place during puberty include the development of sex organs, menstruation, secondary characteristics such as beard and pubic hair, the development of breasts, changes in the shape of the body, and the growth spurt. These changes can take place at different ages for different people, which can be a cause of anxiety.
- **Social dimension**: The transition from child to adult is marked in many cultures through special ceremonies and initiation rites.

> **Adolescence:** The period of psychological and social transition between childhood and adulthood.

> **Puberty:** The time when a person develops physical and reproductive maturity.

Young people are concerned about how their bodies develop compared with those of their friends – and in some case anxiety about body image can lead to eating disorders such as anorexia nervosa (see chapter 7 for a discussion of the influence of the mass media on body image).

Adolescence marks the achievement of adult levels of cognitive development, reasoning and thought processes. While the emergence of independent critical thought is something that education encourages, it sometimes leads to conflict with authority figures. Parent–adolescent conflict is typically based on 'the different ways in which parents and their children understand and define family rules, events, and regulations' (Steinberg, 1990).

At the time of adolescence, a young person looks beyond the home and is strongly influenced by their peers, youth culture, the media and the internet. Adolescence is a time of development of first relationships, experimentation and self-awareness. It is a time when sexuality may express itself in different ways, as heterosexual or gay. Young people may find it difficult to get practical help for contraception, so their first experiences of sex may be unprotected. Teenage pregnancy rates and rising levels of sexually transmitted infection provide compelling evidence of widespread unprotected sex. Alongside sex, other forms of risk-taking include the use of alcohol, smoking and drugs (see box 4.7). Health promotion to adolescents is carried out through personal social education and life skills in schools, peer education programmes out of school, the establishment of 'youth-friendly clinics', the mass media and the internet.

Box 4.7   Adolescent risk-taking behaviour

- One in every ten babies born in England is to a teenage mother. The United Kingdom has the highest levels of teenage pregnancy in Europe. Girls from the poorest backgrounds are ten times more likely to become teenage mothers than girls from professional backgrounds.
- As many as one in ten sexually active young women under the age of twenty-five may be infected with chlamydia.
- Prevalence of smoking increases with age: only 1 per cent of eleven-year-olds smoke, while 22 per cent of fifteen-year-olds do. More girls smoke than boys, with 11 per cent of teenage girls regularly smoking, in comparison to 8 per cent of boys.
- The prevalence of drinking alcohol has risen from 21 per cent of eleven- to fifteen-year-olds in 1998 and 1999 to 24 per cent in 2000 and 26 per cent in 2001, with levels of drinking greater among boys than girls.
- 20 per cent of eleven- to fifteen-year-olds in 2001 had used illegal drugs. The proportion of eleven- to fifteen-year-old boys taking drugs was higher (21 per cent) than that of girls (19 per cent). Cannabis was the most widley used illicit drug, taken by 13 per cent.

(Department of Health, 2004)

Young person, 18–24 years

The age of eighteen is when a young person becomes legally an adult – with the entitlement to vote, to buy alcohol and to be criminally responsible for any offences they commit. However, it is also a time of continued dependence on parents, which can result in tensions and conflicts. For some it is a time of leaving home and starting higher education at college or university – perhaps with a gap year for travelling and work. Leaving home is a period of exposure to new ideas, experimentation, making friends, and freedom from parental control. The many positive benefits can be offset by risks from sexually transmitted disease, alcohol and drugs, isolation, loneliness and mental illness. For those who leave school and start employment, the enhanced disposable income marks the beginnings of financial independence – although for those who still live at home some degree of dependence continues. This period of people's lives is for many a time of short-term and longer-term relationships, serial monogamy and multiple partners. Social life may revolve around cinemas, clubs, pubs and other night venues.

For young people, the main sources of health information are friends, the mass media, the internet and health services. Students have the opportunity to draw upon student counselling and health services and campus-based health promotion campaigns and other sources, including student newspapers and peer education programmes.

Middle adulthood, 25–49 years

Middle adulthood is a time for establishing regular patterns of work, changing jobs, moving home, forming and breaking relationships, starting a family and child-rearing. It is a time when many couples conceive, give birth and raise their children. For many people this is straightforward and rewarding. For some it happens with difficulty, and childbirth may only take place after extended consultations with fertility clinics and adoption services.

The birth of the first baby is an important event which changes the lives of parents as they adjust to the demands of the baby. It can be a time of stress and strain as well as, hopefully, of pleasure. The health promotion task is to assist the parents in their roles through providing support and advice on a range of health and parenting issues.

Parents are faced with an enormous amount of information about child-rearing from the mass media, their own parents and friends. One of the challenges of health

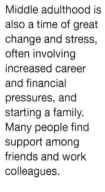

Middle adulthood is also a time of great change and stress, often involving increased career and financial pressures, and starting a family. Many people find support among friends and work colleagues.

promotion is to give the best advice possible according to current knowledge while not undermining the parents' confidence in their ability to cope. Unfortunately, as recent scares over MMR immunization have shown, parents can be confused by an overload of information in the media and distrust information from official sources.

Health promotion is carried out mainly through the mass media, the workplace and community development and through a range of health services, including family planning and antenatal services, maternity hospitals and child health services, e.g. immunization and home visits by health visitors (HDA, 2003).

Older adulthood, 50–69 years

Older adulthood is a time of many transitions and life events, such as the loss of parents and other relatives. For some, the departure of children for higher studies or taking jobs elsewhere can lead to a loss of role ('the empty nest syndrome'), while for others it is an opportunity to take on new challenges, such as foreign travel or learning new skills. It can be a time for thinking ahead about scaling down work and retirement. For those facing unemployment and age discrimination, it is a time of worry about the uncertain economic and social future.

As demands of child-rearing diminish, others emerge. Alongside looking after grandchildren, almost one-quarter of persons aged between fifty and sixty-five are caring for a sick, disabled or older person.

For women a major life event is the onset of menopause, which can have both a physical and a psychological impact. While it is debatable to what extent there is a male menopause, men also go through some kind of transition. Certainly for both men and women this is a time to review life's achievements and disappointments and experience a growing awareness of one's own mortality. For some this can be a period of considerable stress, especially if it coincides with multiple life events such as bereavement, divorce, unemployment, illness and retirement, the effects of which can be made worse by poverty and social exclusion. Ability to manage these life events depends heavily on the strength of one's networks, the presence of a supportive relationship and one's level of financial security.

This age is a time of onset of many chronic diseases, such as hypertension, diabetes and cancer, including breast and cervical cancer in women and prostate cancer in men. A reduction in physical activity that is not matched by a reduction in food intake leads to problems of overweight and obesity. Health promotion on exercise, diet and smoking cessation, combined with screening programmes and well-person clinics, are of particular importance for this age group. People aged fifty to seventy consider themselves a distinct group and do not necessarily identify with services for older persons. However, they are concerned about their future and making provisions for a healthy and fulfilling older age and are receptive to health improvement messages.

Most women will have had regular contact with antenatal, childbirth, child health and family planning services. This is not the case with men, who may have had very

Old age can be a particularly stressful time, involving multiple bereavements, ill health and financial insecurity. Simple tasks, such as paying bills and completing paperwork, can also become more difficult.

little contact with health services. A macho concept of masculinity reinforced through socialization and cultural values can lead to men denying symptoms of ill health, ignoring symptoms and other weaknesses, and only presenting themselves to health services when disease has advanced to a late stage. One of the challenges is to find ways of reaching men earlier with health promotion directed at lifestyle changes.

Health promotion is targeted to this age group through the mass media, the internet, primary care services (including well-person clinics), screening programmes and the workplace. It has been a policy for some workplaces to provide pre-retirement

Box 4.8 Benefits of promoting healthy active ageing among the fifty to seventy year group

Healthy active ageing results in
- fewer premature deaths in the highly productive stages of life
- fewer disabilities associated with chronic diseases
- lower costs related to medical treatment and care
- more people enjoying a positive quality of life as they grow older
- more people participating actively as they age in social, cultural, economic and political aspects of society – in paid and unpaid roles and in domestic, family and community life – with a resulting enhancement of the social capital of communities.

(Bowers et al., 2003)

education programmes to help persons plan for the future. While of considerable potential value, workplace-based programmes only reach those who are in work, and a challenge remains on the best ways to design community-based programmes to reach persons who are unemployed – either because of lack of work or incapacity.

Elderly person, 70+ years

It is useful to distinguish between the 'well old' and the 'frail old' – the latter requiring special support. Modern society places considerable value on youthfulness. One of the myths surrounding old age is that ill health is an inevitable consequence of aging and that it is not worth investing effort in the health of elderly people. It is important to counter ageism of this kind. It is certainly true that old age can be a time of decreasing physical function, e.g. vision, mobility, balance, sensitivity to temperature, and that older people are at particular risk of injury from falls, resulting in disability and death. Osteoporosis (brittle bones) affects more people, especially women, as they grow older (Department of Health, 2001c). However, the decline in health with old age is not inevitable and is aggravated by poverty, neglect, elder abuse and isolation, which in turn lead to poor nutrition, hypothermia and lowered resistance to illnesses such as flu.

> **Ageism:** Attitudes and actions that involve negative assumptions about and discriminate against older people.

Older people receive health promotion from the mass media, through community health services, social care services such as meals on wheels and home helps and day-care centres, and also through staff within institutional settings such as care homes and sheltered housing. While this group is less experienced in information technology than other age groups, there are growing numbers of 'silver surfers' who are going online and deriving benefit from the internet.

Health promotion to improve the quality of life of elderly people involves all three domains of the HESIAD approach:

- health education directed at countering negative stereotyping of elderly people and promoting beneficial activities such as diet and exercise
- service improvement such as improved health-care provision, community care and day centres
- advocacy to channel more resources to elderly people, address issues of poverty and discrimination, and protect against elder abuse.

The final stage in the human lifespan and the ultimate life event, death, remain shrouded in taboos, euphemisms and avoidance. Society is only just beginning to consider what might be meant by 'a good death'. A discipline of palliative care is emerging that, together with the hospice movement, is opening up discussions on the issues of geriatric care, pain, family care and the process of death itself. Key concerns for health promotion should be both the prevention of avoidable ill health in older persons and the strengthening of family and community capacity to care for sick and dying people and to cope with the grief and loss of bereavement.

Box 4.9 How to apply a lifespan approach

When planning health promotion in a community you need to decide which stages in the lifespan you should focus your attention on. This might be the age group which has a particular health need, e.g. those who are at risk of a particular illness or health problem. However, you might decide to intervene at an earlier stage to have an impact on future health. Questions you will need to ask are:

- What transitions, life events, and other changes are taking place at that stage and what influence would they have on the content and delivery of health promotion?
- What are the characteristics that make that cohort different from previous cohorts?
- How are health, education, employment, income and housing distributed between members of that age cohort and what are the factors that reinforce inequalities?
- What are the influences of social, cultural, economic and political factors on that cohort, including the family, social networks, cultural norms, employment, commercial pressures and government policies?
- What opportunities are there for health promotion, including the media, the internet, formal and informal educational systems, and specific settings such as the workplace and health facilities?
- What skills are needed to communicate with people at each stage in the lifespan?

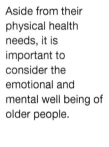

Aside from their physical health needs, it is important to consider the emotional and mental well being of older people.

A lifespan approach to health promotion

Applying a lifespan approach to health promotion allows you to address the changing needs, concerns, abilities and ways of accessing information during the life course. When faced with individuals and families, you need to tailor health promotion to their unique life course experiences. In planning health promotion in communities you need to decide which stage of the lifespan to target, using the methods and settings discussed in later chapters of this book.

Further reading

For a comprehensive review of influences on health and the evidence base of health promotion interventions in the life course, see:
Asthana, S., and Halliday, J. (2006). *What Works in Tackling Health Inequalities? Pathways, Policies and Practice through the Lifecourse.* Bristol: Policy Press.

A sociological perspective on the life course is provided by:
Hunt, S. (2005). *The Life Course: A Sociological Introduction.* Basingstoke: Palgrave Macmillian.

A general text on health promotion and the life course is provided by:
Leifer, G., and Hartston, H. J. (2004). *Growth and Development across the Lifespan: A Health Promotion Focus.* Oxford: W. B. Saunders.

PART II

Defining Health Promotion Strategy

Health Promotion Methods

CHAPTER
5 One-to-one
Communication

Contents

One-to-one Communication

Key issues within this chapter:

- One-to-one communication is widely used in many settings for health promotion and is a highly effective way of providing tailored advice.
- There are many barriers to effective one-to-one communication, including non-verbal communication, medical terminology, language, the context, and the relevance of the advice provided.
- Effective one-to-one communication is a skill that can be learnt and involves the application of a systematic approach to managing the encounter with the patient or client.

By the end of this chapter you should be able to:

- recognize different kinds of one-to-one communication used in health promotion
- identify the elements of effective one-to-one communication
- review your one-to-one communication and improve your own skills
- plan effective health promotion strategies that incorporate one-to-one communication approaches.

One-to-one communication can take place in health facilities and in workplace, home, community and other settings. It is used when talking with individuals ('clients') as part of general health promotion activities, in discussions with patients as part of treatment, in specific advice-giving or in more extended counselling. One-to-one usually involves direct face-to-face encounters, but we will also discuss its use in telephone advice lines. This chapter will look specifically at the basic communication process in one-to-one health promotion. While its main purpose is to introduce one-to-one communication, it will also introduce basic concepts of interpersonal communication which are part of group interactions discussed in the next chapter. Use of one-to-one in health facility settings will be further explored in chapter 12.

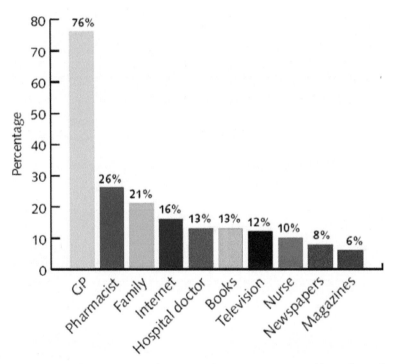

Figure 5.1 Sources of health information cited by respondents in a MORI poll (Department of Health, 2004)

The importance of one-to-one advice was shown in a MORI poll conducted with 2,023 persons aged over fifteen and presented in the report *Patient Choice* (MORI, 2003) and cited in *Choosing Health* (Department of Health, 2004). Respondents were asked which two or three persons they used most for health information. The GP and the pharmacist were the most frequently cited sources, with the family a close third.

Verbal and non-verbal communication

When people communicate they exchange information through words and non-verbal communication – also called body language. Non-verbal communication can involve:

- **body language:** hand gestures, head nodding, smiles, frowns
- **personal space:** proximity, touching
- **clothing and general appearance**
- **voice sounds:** loudness, pitch, 'ums' and 'ers'.

Box 5.1 How to listen actively

Listening to people involves more than just hearing what they say. It is a process of active listening:

- allowing time to explain, not interrupting
- giving encouragement – smiles, nods, encouraging remarks such as *'that's interesting'*, *'Really?'*, *'Please go on …'*, etc.
- asking questions for clarification: *'Can you explain what you meant by …?'*
- showing empathy: *'That must be a real problem'*, *'You must feel terrible'*, *'I am not surprised that you feel that way.'*
- looking interested – keeping eye contact, not looking at your watch or reading over notes
- keeping out interruptions – if someone calls you, say to them: *'I am seeing someone – I will call you back.'*
- summarizing: *'So what you mean is …?'*

Activity 5.1

Start a conversation with a friend and practise the active listening skills described in box 5.1.

Language and communication

Language is also one of the most important barriers to communication. A major reason for communication failure is the use of medical words – or jargon. We all have jargon words that we share with our colleagues that are perfectly understandable to us and even help communication by saving time. However, when the people with whom we are communicating do not share that jargon, there is communication failure. The problem of lack of understanding of medical terms was highlighted in a study by Davis et al. (2001), who found that patients with limited health literacy did not always understand such terms as blood in the stool, bowel, colon, growth, lesion, polyp, rectum, screening and tumour.

Misunderstandings can also extend to non-medical words. Whenever people come from different social and educational backgrounds, cultures and ethnic groups, there is a possibility of misunderstanding. Particular

Non-verbal leakage: When your body language gives an impression that you did not intend to convey, e.g. if, by yawning, looking at your watch or looking at your notes, you give the impression that you are not interested or are showing disapproval of what people are telling you.

problems are posed when English is not the mother tongue of the person with whom you are communicating. Even if their English appears good, they may not distinguish subtle nuances – e.g. the difference between you 'might', you 'can', you 'should', you 'may' and you 'ought'.

Box 5.2 Common barriers in interpersonal communication

- The *context* – unsuitable surroundings, e.g. formal situations, lack of privacy
- The *mismatch between the health promoter and the client* – e.g. in age, educational level, gender and ethnic background
- The *mental and emotional state of the person* – high levels of stress, anxiety, mental health or depression, or strong emotions such as anger and denial, which may prevent the person from paying attention and listening to what you are saying. This is especially important when the person is experiencing a crisis, e.g. bereavement, or discovering that he/she has a serious or even terminal illness.
- The *physical state of the person* – the symptoms experienced by the patient, e.g. pain or nausea, can act as barriers to communication. Disabilities such as deafness and problems with eyesight can affect communication.
- *Fear of being judged or confidentiality being compromised* – a person might withhold information, e.g. about their sexual orientation or potential risk behaviours, if they feel that they will be judged or treated in a negative way.
- *Failure to 'recognize' the uniqueness of the person* – this happens when the health promoter does not show respect and acknowledge the uniqueness of the person and their experiences, concerns and needs, and they are treated as just one of many patients or clients. Patients feel ignored, undervalued and not treated as a real person.
- The *language used* – using technical terms, e.g. units of alcohol rather than actual drinks; assuming that the person with whom you are talking is familiar with parts of the body and their basic function: the difficulty that people have in understanding 'probability' and 'risk'
- The *nature of the advice* – giving vague information, e.g. asking the client to take more exercise or cut down on salt rather than specifying exactly what kind of exercise to take or how much salt is enough
- The *subject matter* – embarrassment of both parties when dealing with sensitive subjects, such as sex, alcoholism and death; the reluctance to break bad news

---

Activity 5.2

What could you do to overcome each of the barriers in box 5.2?

Language is one of the most important barriers to communication. Think of a time when you found it difficult to communicate effectively in a one-to-one setting. What problems did you face and how did you deal with them?

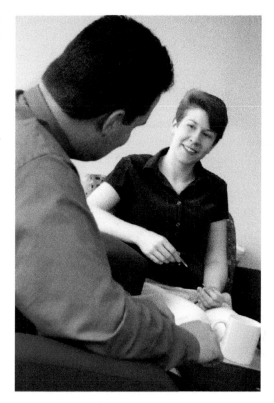

Health worker–patient communication

The interaction between health workers and patients has been the subject of extensive research. This has involved both observation of health worker–patient encounters and interviewing each about their perceptions of the interaction. A psychological perspective sees communication failure due to differences in understandings, language, perceptions and communication skills. A sociological perspective sees the encounter between health worker and patient as one of negotiation, power and control over access to information. Health worker–patient communication studies indicate that:

- patients want to know about the course of their illness, and what they can do, but are often dissatisfied with their experiences and the information received. Patients prefer advice that is tailored to their specific needs rather than generalized messages. In the age of the internet, patients can have considerable access to health information and can sometimes know as much as (or even more than) the health-care provider about the disease and treatment options.

- patients may not feel able to ask questions or pass on vital information about their problem because they feel pressurized by the short time available, they feel socially distant from the health worker, they are afraid of negative reactions, they may feel too proud to admit they are facing problems, or they mistakenly believe that nothing can be done to help them.

- health workers do not always communicate effectively. They may mistakenly believe they are being friendly when their actual body language suggests the opposite. Doctors may hold back information because they feel that the patient will not be able to understand the issues involved. They may hide behind euphemisms to avoid sensitive issues such as pain, sexual dysfunction, terminal illness and death. They may feel more familiar with the traditional medical model in which the health worker is the expert and the patient a passive recipient of advice and not feel comfortable with the alternative more modern partnership, or 'expert patient' approach, described in chapter 12, in which the health worker and patient together negotiate an appropriate solution to the patient's needs.
- some patients may feel more comfortable speaking to a nurse than a doctor. Other patients might be offended by being passed on to a nurse and (mistakenly) feel that they are being fobbed off.

Various options for improving the quality of health–worker patient communication include:

- providing training for health workers in communication skills, especially on ways of showing rapport, finding out patients' needs and concerns, active listening, managing their non-verbal communication, giving information, discussing treatment options and showing empathy and being supportive. The best way of providing this training is through approaches where they can practise skills through role-playing encounters with pretend patients, being videoed and receiving feedback and advice from the trainer.
- providing training to patients in assertiveness (see chapter 6) and encouraging them to bring someone with them to the doctor – either a friend, a patient advocate or a translator.
- using interpreters if you expect any language problems (see box 5.4).

Box 5. 3 How to assess provider–patient interaction

- Is the consultation long enough to deal with the issues involved?
- Are questions asked about home and family situations that might affect the illness?
- Is the language used appropriate?
- Is key information provided?
- Are opportunities provided for questions?
- Is the patient involved in the decision-making process?
- Is the advice provided tailored to the client's specific needs?

Box 5.4 How to work with interpreters

If you are working with people who do not speak English very well you may need to use an interpreter. The following is adapted from guidelines provided by the Queensland Health Authority in Australia.

Choosing the interpreter

- Make sure the interpreter speaks the correct dialect – e.g. spoken Arabic and Chinese can be very different according to the region.
- Make sure that the interpreter's background is acceptable. Some patients may not want to have interpreters from specific communities because of confidentiality fears or political reasons.
- It is usually best to use an interpreter of the same gender as the patient. If this is not possible, ask the patient if they are willing to accept the opposite gender.
- If volunteers are used, some training/orientation of interpreters should be provided, e.g. on the need for accurate translation, confidentiality and the translation of technical terms.
- It may be necessary to use professional interpreters when there are legal implications, e.g. for informed consent, domestic violence, sexual assault, child abuse or when information on treatment and medicines is being communicated.

During the session

- Face and speak directly to the client, not to the interpreter.
- Introduce the interpreter and explain his/her role in the meeting and the confidential nature of the process.
- Speak more slowly, keep the language simple, use short sentences and avoid jargon. Be careful of possible mistranslation. Interpreters may not understand medical terms – for example, 'rheumatic', as in rheumatic fever, may be translated as 'rheumatism'.
- Pause after two or three sentences to let the interpreter translate. Do not be surprised if the interpreter talks a lot after you have said something brief. It often takes more words to explain a concept in another language. If the issue is a sensitive one, the interpreter may feel the need to apologize for asking the question, and explain that they have to ask it.
- Check for understanding by asking questions.

(Adapted from *A Guide to Working with Interpreters*, www.health.qld.gov.au)

Counselling: A process for one-to-one communication that goes beyond just supplying information to clients and involves providing support, help in making difficult decisions and therapy to manage specific conditions.

Participatory one-to-one communication

In this book we advocate a participatory approach to one-to-one communication in order to promote health empowerment and informed decision-making. While the term 'counselling' is sometimes used to describe any form of participatory one-to-one communication, we prefer to reserve its use for more extended processes over a series of sessions that involve some form of therapeutic content. It is beyond the scope of this book to provide detailed coverage of counselling or the related approach coaching, and anyone interested is advised to carry out further reading and consider taking a training course.

Activity 5.3

Consider the following situations. In which of these would a shorter one-to-one participatory communication session be sufficient and which would require more extended counselling? What kind of issues would you need to consider with each of these situations?

- A family decision whether to have an abortion following results of a test on a foetus showing a genetic disorder
- A patient receiving treatment for a sexually transmitted infection
- A woman receiving news that she has tested positive for HIV
- A family making a decision whether to give their child the MMR immunization
- A mother with post-natal depression
- A person who is recovering from a heart attack
- A patient receiving a diagnosis that he has diabetes
- A person whose partner has died of cancer

Open-ended and closed questions: Closed questions are questions that require very specific answers of a 'yes' or 'no' kind. Open-ended questions use words such as 'why' and 'how' and encourage people to talk about their situation, e.g. *'Why do you think that happened?'*

Box 5.5 How to carry out participatory-one-to-one communication

Key elements are:
- establishing rapport, trust
- showing recognition that the person is unique and special
- maintaining confidentiality
- assessing needs
- asking open-ended questions
- active listening
- being aware of one's own feelings and values so that they do not influence the advice you give
- providing any necessary information
- helping the client to make decisions and set goals (using strategies such as listing the pros and cons of actions)
- building the client's confidence to put decisions into practice (self-efficacy).

Risks to avoid are:
- becoming overinvolved with the client and letting it affect your judgement
- letting your own feelings influence the process
- making negative judgements on the other person's actions
- going for the 'quick fix' and oversimplifying issues
- making someone feel overdependent on you to make decisions for them
- creating over confidence
- overlooking possible negative consequences of following your advice.

Self-management

Barlow et al. (2002) define self-management for chronic diseases as 'the individual's ability to manage the symptoms, treatment, physical and psychosocial consequences and life style changes inherent in living with a chronic condition. Efficacious self-management encompasses ability to monitor one's condition and to effect the cognitive, behavioural and emotional responses necessary to maintain a satisfactory quality of life. Thus a dynamic and continuous process of self-regulation is established with patient and health-care provider working in successful partnership.'

The concept of self-management is a key element of the expert patient approach described in chapter 12. Self-management programmes focus on two elements:

- improving people's ability to adhere to their treatment regime
- helping the individual to use their own skills, information and professional services to take effective control over their chronic condition.

Many self-management programmes use cognitive behavioural techniques which draw heavily on self-efficacy theory (see chapter 3).

Box 5.6 Case study: arthritis and self-management

More than eight million people in the UK have arthritis. Self-management programmes for people with arthritis focus on helping them mange their symptoms (especially pain), to live with the psychosocial consequences and lifestyle changes required (e.g. work), and to monitor their condition. The arthritis self-management programme is a community-based intervention for patients with mild to moderate arthritis and consists of six weekly sessions, each of two and a half hours' duration, delivered in community settings such as church halls by pairs of lay leaders, most of whom have arthritis themselves. Participants are encouraged to become active self-managers, able to select and carry out the strategies that best suit their needs. A randomized control trial by Professor Julie Barlow and her group at Coventry University showed that, four months after taking the self-management course, people were using exercise and relaxation techniques to improve their feelings of control. After twelve months, these improvements were maintained, with reports of less pain and fewer visits to the GP. The approach has also shown to be effective in other cultures, such as Bangladeshis in London.

(Barlow et al., 2000; Griffiths et al., 2005)

Burnout

Giving advice and trying to help people with problems such as HIV/AIDS and other chronic conditions can be very stressful and lead to a condition called 'burnout'. This can show itself in different ways, including tiredness, difficulty in sleep, depression and emotional numbness. Burnout can lead to staff and volunteers dropping out of health promotion programmes and can be prevented by:

- providing adequate training so that persons are fully prepared to deal with demanding situations such as giving advice, handling difficult situations and breaking bad news (box 5.7) and have realistic expectations of achievements
- providing a supportive work environment where problems of stress and burnout are recognized at an early stage and opportunities are provided to share difficulties with colleagues and managers
- encouraging the helper to have a balanced work–home relationship – especially a rich and varied personal life which provides opportunities to engage in a wide variety of activities and relationships.

Box 5.7 How to break bad news

One-to-one communication sometimes involves having to break bad news to someone. This is never easy, but here are some suggestions to follow.

DO:
1 Have the facts to hand.
2 Ensure enough time is available.
3 Control potential interruptions – switch off bleepers/mobile phones;
   – ask colleagues not to disturb you;
   – divert phone calls;
   – use a 'do not disturb' sign if in a general office.
4 Check if your patient wishes anyone else to be present.
5 Negotiate the approximate duration of the consultation and explain the need to take notes.
6 Clarify what your patient knows or suspects.
7 Be prepared to follow the patient's agenda.
8 Observe and acknowledge your patient's emotional reactions, such as nervousness or fear.
9 Stop if your patient indicates that they do not wish to continue.

DO NOT:
1 Make assumptions about
   – the impact of the news;
   – the patient's readiness to hear the news;
   – who else should be present;
   – the patient's priorities;
   – the patient's understanding.
2 Give too much information at one time.
3 Decide what is most important for the patient.
4 Give inappropriate reassurance.
5 Answer questions unless you have the facts to hand.
6 Hurry the consultation.
7 Use euphemisms, e.g. 'little ulcer' when you mean 'cancer'.
8 Block emotional expression from the patient.
9 Break bad news to relatives before telling the patient.
10 Agree to a relative's demands that you withhold information from the patient.

(http://www.breakingbadnews.co.uk)

Breaking bad news is a challenging situation. Think of a time when you have had to break bad news. What approach did you take, and why?

Telephone advice lines

Telephone advice lines provide confidential advice to people on a range of issues. Some systems have a menu of standard pre-recorded messages on frequently asked topics. Others use paid staff or volunteers to provide tailor-made advice.

> ### Box 5.8 NHS Direct telephone helpline
>
> NHS Direct was established in 2000 and provides general help and advice to some seven million people each year through a telephone helpline and through 6.5 million visits to the NHS Direct website. The most recent developments have been extending NHS Direct services through digital television channels, providing information on local services through www.nhs.uk, and including health information in Thomson Local directories (Department of Health, 2004).

You should find out about local advice lines and promote them in the communities in which you work. You might even consider setting up one yourself.

One-to-one communication and health promotion

Person-to-person communication is an important health promotion technique because it allows opportunities for the tailoring of information, feedback and developing health empowerment and participation. A major health promotion strategy is to provide the necessary training and support to expand both the quality and the quantity of person-to-person communication on health matters. This requires the learning of new skills as well as a reassessment and realignment of the relationship between the health promoter and the community. In this realignment the patient/client moves from the position of a passive recipient of information to that of an equal partner in the process of negotiation of health issues.

Box 5.9 How to assess the quality of one-to-one communication

Here is a simple checklist you can use to assess the quality of one-to-one communication.

- Has the person been put at ease?
- Is the environment conducive – in a private place, free from noise and distractions?
- Has the person been given a chance to explain exactly what their problem is and what they need?
- Has the educator/counsellor gained the trust of the person?
- Has the educator/counsellor used active listening skills?
- Is the body language helpful, e.g. smiles, looks of concern, gestures, posture?
- Was the person encouraged to ask questions?
- Has the educator/counsellor asked sufficient questions to understand the problem and give the appropriate advice?
- Was sufficient allowance made for cultural differences between the educator/counsellor and the person?
- Is the advice presented relevant/balanced and accurate? Is it grounded on evidence-based practice?
- Is the advice presented clearly using appropriate language? Was the person given alternative options and allowed to make a decision?
- Does the advice take into account what the person already knows about the health topic?
- Does the advice take into account the family situation of the person and the influence of partners or significant others?
- Have all the questions of the person been answered and their needs met?
- Was sufficient time available to meet the needs of the person?
- Has feedback been obtained at the end of the session to confirm that everything has been understood?

Further reading

For practical guidelines on communication skills, assertiveness, overcoming communication barriers and dealing with difficult situations, see:

- Sully, P., and Dallas, J. (2004). *Essential Communication Skills for Nursing*. St Louis: Mosby.

For detailed treatment of the theory underlying communication skills and specific areas such as non-verbal communication, questioning, listening, group dynamics and interviewing, see:

- Hargie, O. (ed.) (1996). *The Handbook of Communication Skills*. London: Routledge.

For a review of interpersonal skills and communication between health workers and patients, see:

- Silverman, J., Kurtz, S., and Draper, J. (1998). *Skills for Communicating with Patients*. Abingdon: Radcliffe Medical Press.

Health Promotion
with Groups

Contents

Health Promotion with Groups

Key issues within this chapter:

- Group work is widely used in many settings for the organization and management of health promotion activities, for facilitating self-help, and for promoting health empowerment and the development of skills such as assertiveness.

- Many factors affect the success or failure of groups, and it is important to have an understanding of group dynamics and participatory learning methods.

- Small-group teaching involves analysing the learning needs of a group and selecting suitable learning methods to meet those needs.

By the end of this chapter you should be able to:

- understand the contribution of working in groups to health promotion

- apply an understanding of group dynamics to the setting up and facilitation of groups

- be aware of specific group methods, including participatory learning, assertiveness training and the setting up of self-help groups

- plan small-group teaching sessions to promote specific learning needs.

Why are groups important in health promotion?

Important groups for health promotion include:

- **teaching/learning groups** – A small group is an ideal medium for learning because people are able to participate, ask questions and share their experiences with each other. Groups are often more effective in promoting changes in lifestyle than a one-to-one situation because their members have expressed their commitment publicly and feel pressure from the others to put their commitment into practice. Small-group teaching can be used to develop problem-solving skills, explore values and beliefs, and deal with sensitive issues such as sex.

  > **A group:** Any number of people who (i) interact with one another, (ii) are psychologically aware of one another and (iii) perceive themselves to be a group. (Schein, 1980)

- **self-help groups** – Belonging to a group benefits members directly through the help they give each other. Support and practical advice from someone else who has had a similar problem is often more useful than receiving advice from an outsider. Many people with problems feel very isolated and find it helpful to meet others with similar experiences.

- **problem-solving groups and teams** – Planning and implementing health promotion activities will usually involve setting up committees or working in planning teams with other people. You may need to set up groups in order to gather ideas and information or make suggestions, coordinate activities, and bring together people with different skills and backgrounds to find the best possible solution to a problem.

  > **Group dynamics:** The study of the functioning of groups.

- **community-based groups** – These often involve committees that enable people to participate in the management of activities, give their views and liaise with the health services. The success or failure of such activities depends heavily on how well groups function, and we discuss this further in chapter 11.

Box 6.1 Self-help groups

Self-help groups are groups of people with a similar need who support each other. They may spontaneously emerge or be deliberately set up by someone. In its early stages a self-help group is often inward-looking, dealing with the needs of its members. It can become more outgoing in its orientation and evolve into an action group, then link with other similar self-help groups to become part of a national movement. The Patient UK website (www.patient.co.uk) lists more than 2,000 patient support and self-help groups covering conditions as diverse as Alzheimer's, cancer, asthma, diabetes, alcohol, mental health, women's health and heart disease. They provide forums through which members support each other and act as pressure groups for improving service provision.

Group dynamics

The study of groups has been greatly influenced by the pioneering work of the psychologist Kurt Lewin (Lewin, 1948), who advanced the view that the concept of a group went beyond just a collection of people and was defined by the degree of inter-dependence of the members.

Activity 6.1

Spend five minutes observing groups of four, five or six people in some everyday settings. What kinds of interactions do you see? How does that group make decisions? How do the interactions change as the numbers of people increase? What lessons can you draw for health promotion?

Working in groups can be highly effective and get good results. It can also be frustrating and difficult and lead to failure for a range of reasons:

- lack of a common purpose; everyone wants something different
- some individuals dominate the discussion, others are silent and do not contribute
- disagreements, personality clashes and conflicts among the members
- members fail to perform assigned tasks
- poor and irregular attendance
- everyone talks but nobody is willing to make decisions.

Research on group dynamics suggests the following to be important in determining the effectiveness of group functioning: the characteristics of the group, including size and membership; the nature of the tasks undertaken; the decision-making processes; the roles of members; group processes; and pattern of leadership.

Size of group – The kinds of interactions among people, the opportunities for exchange of ideas and the success in achieving objectives are affected by the group size. With too few members, most people will have a chance to contribute, but there will be less experience to draw on. With too many people, it is difficult for everyone to contribute in discussion and harder to reach a shared decision. Many feel that eight to twelve persons is an ideal size, but it really depends on the aims and purpose of the group.

Background of the group members – Who the members are and their reasons for attending are of enormous importance to the function of a group. Persons may have a 'hidden agenda' and see its function as meeting their own personal needs rather than that of the group.

The purpose of the group and the tasks it sets out to accomplish – Another way of thinking about different kinds of groups is to classify them according to whether they are concerned mainly with producing results (task-oriented) or with promoting the wellbeing of their members (process-oriented).

No two groups are the same. When working with a group, it is important to take into consideration its size, the background of its members, its purpose and how it is to be led.

The presence or absence of effective leadership – An effective leader or facilitator can make all the difference. Among leadership tasks are those involved with *group maintenance* – dealing with the wellbeing of the group – and *task maintenance*, such as helping the group achieve its purpose. You will find more about the leadership styles and functions in chapter 16.

Group decision-making

How well a group makes decisions will depend on many factors, including the complexity of the decision required, the range of skills/expertise in the group, and the amount of relevant information available to the members. One way of reaching a decision in a group is through *consensus* – with everyone's agreement. This is often the best way – provided you are sure that everyone really does agree and they are not just keeping their disagreement silent because they feel inhibited to give their opinion. With a larger group it can be difficult to get everyone to agree. A vote can be taken and the majority view followed. But if you do make decisions by voting, you must take care that those with minority views do not feel left out and so drop out of future activities.

Some of the different reasons why groups find it difficult to make decisions are given in box 6.2. To overcome these problems, members must be honest with themselves and openly discuss them and try to find a solution. Good leadership is essential to resolve these difficulties and make effective decisions.

Box 6.2 Obstacles to group decision-making

- *Fear of consequences:* People may be afraid that employers or other influential people will criticize them for taking a particular decision.
- *Conflicting loyalties:* There can be divided loyalties among the different members, to employers, communities, churches, etc.
- *Disagreements and personalities:* Personal behaviour and disagreements between group members can interfere with decision-making (see section on individual behaviour below).
- *Hidden agenda:* Individual group members may try to influence the whole group to follow their particular interests.
- *Inadequate information:* The decision may be made based on the personal opinions of the group members rather than on the facts of the situation.
- *Inadequate leadership:* No one is given responsibility for coordination and leading the group so it drifts aimlessly.

Activity 6.2

Think about your own experiences with groups and make a list of the problems that you have experienced and compare them with those in box 6.2. What suggestions do you have for resolving those problems?

Small-group teaching

Teaching: Facilitation of learning.

Groups are an ideal way for people to learn because everyone can participate. The following principles of adult learning can be applied to group teaching to faciliate an interactive session.

- People learn better if the information you present is linked to their experiences and builds on what they already know. Always ask questions at the beginning to find out what people know, think and feel about the topic.
- Your audience will only pay attention to you if the content of your teaching is relevant to what they want to know about, is put across in an interesting way and uses a variety of teaching styles.
- Complicated information should be introduced step by step in a logical, organized way. Learning can be helped by well-chosen visual aids such as pictures and charts. Essential information can be on a handout and the time saved used for discussion.
- Take care not to overload your learners with too many new ideas in one session, as there is a limit to the amount of information that can be absorbed at one sitting. Use a range of teaching approaches, such as talks, discussion, exercises

and active learning methods. Build in frequent breaks between sessions where people can relax and stretch their legs. Twenty minutes at a time is probably the longest that people can concentrate.

- Information presented in a teaching session is quickly forgotten. Some further input, either by the student's own reading or reminders by the teacher, is needed for the information to be retained in long-term memory.
- Your audience may have enjoyed themselves and express appreciation but may not have learnt anything! The only way in which you can find out whether learning has taken place is by obtaining some feedback – either asking questions or observing their performance to see if they have improved.
- You should provide opportunities for your students to practise their newly acquired skills in a safe, friendly and tolerant environment where they can make mistakes and receive helpful criticism without feeling threatened.
- People learn better if they are allowed to discover principles for themselves and activities are built into the learning process. Use active methods as follows:
  - *more active methods:* practice in real situations with supervision, practice in class situation, e.g. role play, and discussion
  - *less active methods:* observing a drama or demonstration, looking at pictures, written examples, paper and pencil exercises, individual reading.

Active learning: Make students think and apply the knowledge through a task.
Be clear: Use visual aids, speak clearly, use simple language.
Make it meaningful: Explain in advance what you are going to teach; explain all new words and ideas; relate what you teach to students' lives and work; give examples; summarize main points at end.
Encourage participation: Stimulate discussion and involve the group in the learning.
Ensure mastery: Check understanding and competence reached.
Give feedback: Tell the learners what their progress is.

(Taken from Hubley, 2003)

After the session it is important to evaluate the quality of the the group learning experience in terms of content, delivery and the environment. The following typical questions could be asked.

- Was the information presented in a logical, sequenced way?
- Were complex points explained clearly?
- Was all the necessary content included?
- Were the learning objectives (facts, decision-making skills, communication skills and attitude change) met?
- Was unnecessary repetition and overload avoided?
- Were visual aids used, appropriately and clearly?
- Was there interaction with the audience?
- Did the session generate questions?

- Was the session interesting and fun?
- Was the room suitable (light, temperature, quiet, good acoustics)?
- Could everyone hear what was being said?
- Was the seating appropriate?

Activity 6.3

Sit in on some group teaching and apply the assessment checklist above. Suggest ways in which you think the group teaching could be improved.

Box 6.3 A good visual aid

A visual aid can be a photograph, extracts from a magazine or newspaper, a poster, information on a flip-chart, an overhead projector transparency, a PowerPoint presentation or a video. A good visual aid:

- explains complex ideas
- gains attention and holds interest
- triggers discussion
- creates a shared experience
- makes key points memorable
- is relevant to the session
- is clear and without distracting content.

Box 6.4 Examples of types of learning for HIV/AIDS (adapted from Hubley 1995)

Type of learning	Examples: AIDS and STDs	Teaching method
Facts: may be simple or complex, familiar or new, compatible or in conflict with existing knowledge.	The nature of AIDS and HIV; how HIV is and is not transmitted; how it affects the body; the effect of HIV on the body's immune system	Teaching fact involves the following steps: presenting the information logically in a step-by-step fashion; relating the information to previous knowledge; using visual aids to explain relationships; and avoiding presenting too much information in one session and causing overload.
Decision-making skills: involve application of knowledge to make decisions covering personal and family life or one's professional role.	Which mode of safer sex is most suited to one's lifestyle; how to select the best advice to meet a client's needs during counselling; how to set up an AIDS education programme in a workplace or community	Decision-making skills are taught first by providing the necessary basic information; then demonstrating the skills with worked-out examples presented as case studies; then allowing the students to practise making the decisions in realistic situations such as case studies, role plays and field exercises.

Type of learning	Examples:-AIDS and STDs	Teaching method
Communication skills: verbal and non-verbal skills involved in giving information, persuading and teaching	Negotiating with partner about safe sex and use of condoms; discussing sex with one's children; counselling a client on sensitive issues; giving a talk on AIDS; leading a group discussion	First demonstrate good communication to the learners and then let all trainees practise the skills with each other in role plays. For example, you can ask someone to give advice to another person on a sensitive subject (e.g. whether they should have unsafe sex); to pretend to be a parent talking to their adolescent daughter about sex or someone discussing with their sexual partner about using condoms; to give a talk to the others acting as the audience; or to give a counselling session. Afterwards, everyone can discuss how well the communication was carried out. It is helpful to video the session and let the person watch him/herself afterwards.
Practical/manual skills (psychomotor skills): manipulating and handling objects	Putting on a condom correctly; disposing of injection needles safely; operating a steam sterilizer; disposal of infected materials	Demonstrate the skill and provide opportunities to practise in pretend and real-life situations.
Attitudes and values (feelings)	Confronting prejudice about homosexuals, sex workers and drug users and people living with AIDS/HIV; sensitivity, compassion, tolerance and patience in counselling; willingness to understand and respect other persons' viewpoints and maintain confidentiality	Discuss the importance of particular attitudes; use role plays where participants act out particular situations and experience what it is like to be another person (e.g. a woman receiving inappropriate advice). Involve persons affected by the problem in the training (e.g. those who are HIV positive). The trainers themselves should show consideration, concern, tolerance and commitment and provide a role model.

Activity 6.4

Below are listed some outputs from group teaching sessions. Decide to which of the following kinds of learning each belongs: factual learning, decision-making (problem-solving) skills, communication skills, psychomotor skills, attitudes/feelings?

1 An environmental health officer knowing how to prepare a leaflet

2 A father being able to list the advantages of breastfeeding

3 The ability to demonstrate to mothers how to prepare fruit smoothies

4 A practice nurse wanting to spend time promoting blood-pressure awareness among patients

5 A man using a blood-pressure monitoring machine

6 A health trainer being able to list the sources of vitamin D

7 Parents choosing a balanced diet from available foods

8 A health trainer knowing the procedures for referral of TB patients

9 A GP referring a patient to an exercise-promotion programme

10 A councillor being able to write down the reasons why exercise promotion will benefit the community

11 A dietitian being able to plan how to set up a 'five a day' programme in their community

12 A community worker wanting to spend time in the community promoting injury prevention

13 A teacher being aware of the adolescent sexual health services provided by the primary-care group

14 A play-group worker being aware of the importance of doing health promotion work.

Answers: (1) decision-making (content of leaflet) as well as psychomotor (how to print and bind pages) skills;
(2) factual knowledge;
(3) factual knowledge about fruits, psychomotor skills in preparation of fruit and using a blender, communication skills on how to give a demonstration;
(4) attitude towards the benefits of blood-pressure monitoring;
(5) psychomotor skills of using a blood-pressure monitoring machine as well as decision-making skills in assessing the results;
(6) factual knowledge;
(7) factual knowledge of nutrients and sources of foods, decision-making skills as to choosing combinations;
(8) factual knowledge of procedures;
(9) decision-making skills of deciding in a given case whether to refer and knowledge of various options for referral;
(10) factual learning;
(11) decision-making skills on how to prepare community intervention strategy;
(12) attitude towards the value of injury prevention;
(13) factual knowledge of adolescent sexual health services;
(14) attitude towards the benefits of health promotion.

Small-group teaching in an informal environment allows members of the group to participate. It is a particularly useful method for raising consciousness of health issues common to a particular group – for example, women's health awareness.

Consciousness-raising, health empowerment and assertiveness groups

The women's health movement pioneered the use of consciousness-raising groups in which participants discussed their lives, reflected, and considered the implications for themselves and the people around them (Morgen, 2002). Similar consciousness-raising activities can be carried out with other groups of people and topics. This approach is similar to that developed by Freire (1972) and discussed in chapter 11. In Freire's approach, small groups called culture circles were shown a representation of their situation in pictures, given a chance to reflect on those images, and through discussion develop critical awareness or 'conscientization' and then action. The adult education and participatory learning movement absorbed this approach and has developed a wide variety of participatory tools using pictures, drama and games to support this process, e.g. Werner and Bower (1982), Hope and Timmel (1995) and INTRAH (1987).

As we explained in chapter 1, the concept of health empowerment can usefully be considered as a combination of health literacy and self-efficacy, with the former covering the understandings about health issues and the latter covering people's ability to control and change their lives. Thus people must have not only an understanding of health issues to make health decisions but also the confidence and skills to put those decisions into practice.

Assertiveness: Putting forward your own point of view in a positive, non-aggressive way.

> **Box 6.5 How to do assertiveness training**
>
> Assertiveness training involves working in small groups and using a variety of approaches, including self-examination, case studies and role plays, to develop self-awareness and skills in specific techniques for asserting one's viewpoint without resorting to aggressive responses. The aim is to control your verbal and non-verbal behaviour and avoid aggressive approaches which aggravate the situation further. The overall approach in assertiveness training can be summarized as:
>
> - ***listening to what the other person has to say***: showing that you understand the person's point of view, explaining how their actions make you feel, saying that you too have needs that should be respected and explaining what those needs are
> - ***saying no***: making it clear that you understand the other person's position but speaking in a positive way – 'I would prefer not to, I would rather not, I don't want to ...'
> - ***broken record***: continuing to repeat your point of view even if the other person tries to change the subject
> - ***fog***: defusing the situation by appearing to agree with the person – 'Yes, I can see how you must feel about this' – not allowing yourself to be provoked into a negative attacking response, keeping your cool.

One way of providing this confidence is through assertiveness training, described in box 6.5. Assertiveness training gained prominence through the women's health movement and has been used in health promotion. Assertiveness, unlike aggressive behaviour, is a positive attribute. It is promoted through a combination of activities which build up feelings of self-worth and self-esteem and also help people to acquire specific skills to handle pressure from others, such as bullying, abusive behaviour and influence from one's networks, including peers and family health-damaging behaviours.

Participatory learning methods

Participatory learning methods involve group discussion, puzzles, games, group exercises and role play to encourage members of a group to explore new ideas, share experiences, discover principles for themselves and have fun while learning. They are particularly useful when the group members have previous negative experience of learning when at school and feel uncomfortable in a formal learning environment. When used properly, participatory learning methods can build up individual and group confidence and lead to group decision-making and action. Some useful participatory learning methods as well as guidelines on running participatory group discussions are described in box 6.6.

Ice-breaker: An activity at the beginning of a course or group activity that helps people get to know each other and feel comfortable about working together.

Box 6.6 How to use participatory learning methods

Role play – Role play is the use of drama in which people act out situations for themselves in order to acquire communication and problem-solving skills and understand situations. Role plays can vary in length between an extended session lasting a whole day to a ten-minute activity within a training class.

Role play is a very direct way of learning; you are given a role and have to think and speak immediately without detailed planning. Learning takes place through active experience; it is not passive. Role play can be used to explore events that have already happened or which might happen. It uses situations in which the members of the group are likely to find themselves later in their lives and gives them the chance to consider different ways of responding within those situations. Some people find it easier to explain an experience through acting it out rather than reporting it or writing it down.

In role play group members can practise giving advice and making difficult decisions in a realistic situation. However, it is a 'safe' environment. You can make mistakes and try again, which is not possible in real life, where mistakes could have disastrous consequences. It is possible to try several versions and have the group discuss which role play it thinks best and why. Role plays can help a group:

- to get to know each other better
- to think about a particular topic, problem or issue
- to practise for a particular event such as a meeting or interview
- to be more sympathetic to points of view of other people
- to acquire social skills such as cooperation
- to acquire communication skills.

Games – Games are entertaining, encourage cooperation and discussion, and are good 'ice-breakers' at the beginning of a workshop to introduce participants and encourage an open approach to discussion. Games can also present information and ideas on health in exciting and challenging ways. Examples include card games involving the sorting of pictures or matching ideas, puzzles where you have to work out the solution to a problem from clues, and group games involving solving problems.

Discussion posters (picture codes) – Pictures are used to trigger a discussion. The picture is shown to a group and the facilitator encourages discussion by asking questions: *What do you see in this picture? What is the problem shown? How do you think it can be solved?*

Trigger videos – Show a short five-minute video which shows a situation or issue. Then invite the group to discuss the topic and reach a conclusion. Videos specifically designed to act as triggers are sometimes available – or you can select an excerpt from a longer video.

(Adapted from Hubley, 2003)

Box 6.7 How to facilitate group discussions

1 Seating people in a circle is best for discussions. In a circle there is no 'head' and everyone is equal. Sitting in a 'U' shape is the next best.
2 Tell your audience at the start that they will all be taking part in a discussion. Emphasize that you will *not* be doing all the talking.
3 Begin with easy questions. If you will be discussing more than one subject, begin with what you think people will be more free to talk about. This builds up people's confidence.
4 If you ask a question and no one answers, ask it again, using slightly different words.
5 Do not give up if answers are slow in coming. It will take people time to 'warm up' to this new way of learning.
6 Always respond with enthusiasm to any answer. Praise the people who answer, even if the answer is wrong: 'Thank you for your thoughts', 'That's interesting', or 'Good for you for speaking up'.
7 Be sure to look around at everyone in the group. It is easy to look at only the one or two people who are answering all the questions, and this discourages the others.
8 If someone asks you a question, a good way of keeping the discussion going is to direct the question back to the group: 'That's a very good question, Jane. What do you think, Rachael?'
9 The best discussions are short and leave people wishing for more. After an hour or so our minds begin to wander and not much more learning can take place.
10 Practice makes perfect! Before you lead the real discussion, it is very helpful to practise. Ask some of your family and friends to sit around and pretend that they are the people to whom you will be speaking. Ask them the same questions you will be asking your 'real audience', to find out what their response is.

(From Hubley, 2003)

Activity 6.5

Use the checklist provided on the next page to prepare a plan for a one-hour group session on one of the following: managing blood pressure, increasing fruit and vegetable consumption, dealing with problems of dog fouling on children's playgrounds or reducing the risk of falls among elderly people.

Box 6.8 How to plan a group learning session

You can use the following checklist to plan your group session.

1 What specific kinds of learning do I want to promote during the session (see box 6.4)?
   - *Factual knowledge* – specific facts about the health topic that they need to make informed decisions
   - *Decision-making or problem-solving skills* – how to make decisions, e.g. plan a diet, organize a budget, set objectives for life, choose the best form of exercise
   - *Communication skills* – e.g. assertiveness, discussing sensitive issues, getting their point across to health workers, communicating with their children, etc.
   - *Psychomotor (manual) skills* – e.g. preparing and cooking foods, using a blood-pressure monitor, massage techniques, measuring blood-sugar level, etc.
   - *Attitudes* – e.g. sensitivity to the needs of others, importance of taking regular exercise, diet, talking to your baby, etc.

2 How many people should I involve in the group? Who will be the participants?
3 How will I present the information? Will I use a visual aid (e.g. overhead projector or PowerPoint)?
4 How can I make the presentation interactive to avoid it seeming like a lecture?
5 How will I trigger discussion and participation? Will I use a group task or a trigger video?
6 How will I structure the time in the session? How long will the session last? What will be the balance of time between presentation of information and participatory activities? How much time should I leave for questions and summarizing main points?
7 How will I split up the group into smaller groups?
8 How will I manage the feedback from the group sessions?
9 What kind of follow-up would I want from the session and how can I encourage it?
10 How can I evaluate it? What questions or activities could I include that would tell me what people have learnt from the session?

Further reading

For further information on the theory and practice of working with groups, see:

- Benson, J. (2000). *Working More Creatively with Groups*. London: Routledge.
- Doel, M., and Sawdon, C. (1999). *The Essential Groupworker: Teaching and Learning Creative Groupwork*. London: Jessica Kingsley.
- Heron, J. (1999). *The Complete Facilitator's Handbook*. London: Kogan Page.

7 Mass Media

Contents

CHAPTER

7 Mass Media

Key issues within this chapter:

- Mass media can have positive and negative effects on health.
- Mass media operate at international, national and local/community level.
- Mass media can influence health through the advertising of commercial products, the coverage of news topics, the portrayal of role models, health promotion campaigns and social marketing.

By the end of this chapter you should be able to:

- understand the contribution of the mass media to health promotion at community, national and international level
- identify ways of maximizing the beneficial and minimizing the harmful impacts of mass media
- understand the steps involved in planning mass media
- mobilize mass media operating at the local/community level.

From early childhood we are surrounded by mass media, informing, entertaining and trying to sell us products. In this chapter we will look at the ways in which they can influence health for good – and for bad – and will explore some of the ways in which they have been used to promote health. In the past mass media operated mainly at the national and regional level. With increasing availability of local and community media, options are opening up to work with mass media at the community level.

The range of magazines available on any high street is likely to offer something of interest to anyone. However, each magazine is effectively targeted at a niche market, such as men interested in cars, sport or men's health issues.

Types of mass media

The mass media consist of television, radio, newspapers, magazines and direct mail. The internet can also be considered a form of mass media; however, with its many unique elements, we are considering it separately in chapter 9. A defining feature of the mass media is their capacity to reach large numbers of people quickly. While their approach is considered to be broad-based, the ability of magazines to target niche markets, the profiling of the readership of newspapers according social characteristics, the use of direct mail and the careful attention paid towards the positioning of billboards means that it is also possible to tailor mass media to specific audiences.

Early ideas concerning the mass media saw them operating like an aerosol – spraying information out to individuals who may or may not act on the information received. We now see the process of receiving and acting on mass media as a more complex process. People receive them as individuals, but they also watch and listen in families or groups, which becomes a social experience leading to discussion and possible action. The impact of the mass media is mediated through interpersonal communication, when people pass on the information received to others in their networks. While the mass media may influence people to act directly, they can also have indirect effects, raising awareness about issues, promoting debate/discussion, and increasing willingness to receive new ideas and to take part in community action. This chapter will focus mainly on the influence of mass media on individuals and communities, and chapter 10 will consider their role in advocacy and policy change.

The influence of mass media on health

A broad view of the impact of mass media on health needs to look at their totality at the different levels of society, the different ways in which they can be used and their effects at the level of the individual, the social network, and the public and policy agenda (see figure 7.1).

Figure 7.1
Influences of mass media on health

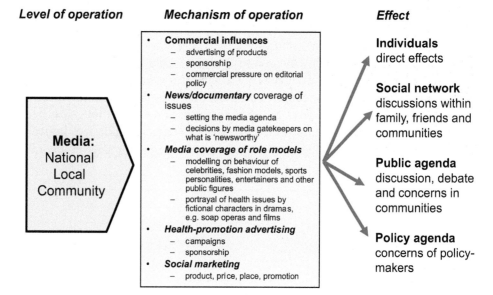

Advertising of health damaging products

Mass media can have a negative influence on health through the advertising of health-damaging products such as tobacco, alcohol, and foods high in fat and sugar. A particular concern in recent years has been the advertising targeted at children, adolescents and young people, e.g. the promotion of fast foods, 'alcopops' and 'designer drinks'. Companies can openly influence consumers through 'placement' of their products within films and television programmes, and through sponsorship of sports and televised events. They can also have a more sinister hidden influence via the large sums of money paid for advertising, which can influence editorial decisions on programme content.

Public health measures to control commercial interests range from the introduction of bans on the advertising of tobacco to regulations on the kinds of images that can be associated with the product, as in alcohol advertising in UK. There is ongoing debate as to whether controls on advertising should be extended to include foods high in fats and sugars, such as fast foods, soft drinks and snack foods. Another area of concern is the issue of the advertising of patent medicines and – a more recent trend in some countries – the advertising of prescription drugs direct to consumers.

An important issue is to get the right balance between the control of advertising and the education of the public to become more critical consumers of the sorts of information presented in advertisements.

Advertisements openly set out to influence people. In societies such as the United Kingdom people have grown up with mass media, and many have become savvy and discerning; they are not merely malleable consumers who accept everything (including health promotion campaigns!) at face value. More insidious, however, are the hidden influences and commercial pressures that are not part of advertisements, such as product placements, news reports of actions carried out by celebrities, and the exploits of fictional characters portrayed in the media.

In their defence, companies using advertising often claim that they are meeting existing needs rather than creating new ones. They also state that their aim is not to change people's behaviour, but rather to promote brand loyalty or influence people to switch to their brand of products rather than those of a competitor. Most health promoters do not agree with this and argue that advertising legitimizes unhealthy lifestyles and has a strong influence on the way people look at themselves, their lives and their needs.

> ### Activity 7.1
>
> Make a list of the foods and drinks you have consumed in the last week. Which of these are promoted by advertising? Has the advertising influence your decisions?

News coverage on media and the way prevention and cure are addressed

Mass media play an important role in influencing public perspectives on health issues – 'agenda-setting'. Most of our understanding of the world around us comes from news reports and the way they 'frame the issue' and influence our perceptions or the world about us (Wallack et al., 1993). On a positive note, the public are interested in health, and the media respond to this interest by providing a great deal of coverage on health issues. However, this coverage usually gives more attention to 'miracle cures', 'breakthroughs' and 'health scares' than to balanced reporting of less glamorous issues such as prevention. Decisions made by television, radio and newspaper editors on what is 'newsworthy' – and therefore on what deserves to be reported – can raise or lower the profile of health issues in the public mind. Many interest groups, pressure groups and commercial organizations compete to get their cause raised in the media, and the voices of health promotion agencies are often drowned. An example of this was the high profile given in the media to scares about side effects of the MMR immunization. The way the media report on health issues also influences or 'frames' the way people look at an issue. For example, in the United Kingdom HIV/AIDS was initially reported as a disease affecting gays and drug injectors, so the heterosexual population discounted it as a potentially serious issue. The challenge for health promotion is to find ways of increasing coverage of health promotion issues and encouraging responsible reporting. You will find more on media advocacy in chapter 10.

> **Activity 7.2**
>
> Look out for health topics in the news in newspapers, radio and television over the next week. How are health issues covered in these news reports? Why do you think those topics were covered in news reports? Do you think that coverage has been helpful for health promotion?

Modelling on 'celebrities' and fictional characters

Some of the public model their behaviour on the actions, behaviours and lifestyle of celebrities featured in news reports, used in advertisements or appearing in game shows and chat shows, as well as fictional characters in drama productions. The importance of role models has a theoretical underpinning in the social learning theory of Alfred Bandura, which we discussed in chapter 3. According to this theory, humans can learn by observing and modelling themselves on other characters. In the case of the mass media, the influence of a particular role model can be positive or negative and depends on the extent to which an individual identifies with, and feels emotional attachment towards, that person.

A positive influence was the intense media coverage of the admission of the basketball star Magic Johnson in 1991 that he was HIV positive. This had a considerable effect on a generation of young black people in the United States for whom he was an important role model. Negative influences of role models include celebrities who make heavy use of alcohol and tobacco, who have unprotected casual sex, or who are very thin. The former Wimbledon tennis champion Boris Becker achieved notoriety in 2000 when the media reported that he had had unprotected sex in the closet of a London restaurant with a Russian model who later gave birth to their daughter. By way of atonement, in April 2006 he announced that he was going to appear in a series of television advertisements in Germany to promote condoms as part of a government-sponsored AIDS awareness campaign (Leidig, 2006).

The influence extends to fictional characters in dramas. Furnham et al. (1997) carried out a content analysis of references to alcohol consumption in twenty-five episodes of six UK television soap operas, including such well-known programmes as *Eastenders, Emmerdale, Neighbours and Coronation Street*. The soap operas were found to be portraying alcohol consumption as the norm without necessarily raising some of the problems generated. There was a reference to alcohol in every 3.5 minutes of programming, and alcohol was consumed more than soft drinks in a ratio of 2.1:1.

Box 7.1 Body image, women and the media

More than 60,000 persons in Britain have eating disorders, and most of these are women. Women's magazines and the media in general have been criticized for the way in which they present images of women's bodies. Women's magazines and the lifestyle/bestseller shelves of bookshops give a great deal of coverage to food and new diets. The issue of body image and the media formed the central thesis of the book *Fat is a Feminist Issue*, an anti-dieting book written in 1978 by the feminist therapist Susie Orbach. A concern about putting on weight and a belief in the protective benefits of smoking in preventing weight gain might also be a reason for the recent increases in smoking among women.

A content analysis of magazines targeted at teenage girls carried out by Mitchell (1997) found that teenage magazines gave minimal coverage to physical exercise. When content did deal with exercise, prominence was given to attractiveness as a reason for physical activity, with few articles given to health and wellbeing as a reason.

Alarmed at trends in eating disorders, the British Medical Association published a report in 2000 expressing concern at the way images in the media shape young persons' attitudes to eating, body shape and self-esteem. In particular, they drew attention to the waif-like figures of 'supermodels' used to promote fashion and advertise products. They highlighted the way these images reinforce the mistaken belief that 'thin equals healthy' and the widespread emphasis on dieting rather than healthy eating (BMA, 2000). Their report reached the conclusion that 'the degree of thinness exhibited by models chosen to promote products is both unachievable and biologically inappropriate'. Alarmed by this report, the then women's minister, Tessa Jowell, held a summit meeting at Downing Street with the bosses of a top modelling agency and a teenage magazine to discuss what could be done.

More sensationally, Voracek and Fisher (2002) reported in the *British Journal of Medicine* the results of their analysis of pictures of women appearing in 577 consecutive centrefolds of *Playboy* magazine, from 1953 to 2001. Over that period there was a significant decrease in bust size, hip size and body mass index (a measure of weight for height) which was below that of the level in the general population.

At the end of their report the British Medical Association made the following recommendations on the role of media in addressing eating disorders (BMA, 2000).

1   Broadcasters (or programme-makers) and magazine publishers should adopt a more responsible editorial attitude towards the depiction of extremely thin women as role models, and should portray a more realistic range of body images.
2   Producers of TV and printed advertisements should consider more carefully their use of thin women to advertise products, in particular the Independent Television Commission should review its policy on the use of thin models to advertise products other than slimming aids.
3   Health professionals should work with the television industry to increase awareness of the possible impact of programming on young people, and encourage the inclusion of healthy eating patterns into their programming.

The way people view their own bodies can be powerfully influenced and distorted by the media.

Activity 7.3

Go to a magazine stand and look at the images of men and women in the magazines. What kind of body image is portrayed? Would you consider the body image promoted to be a healthy one?

Health promotion advertising and sponsorship

Campaign: A short, intensive programme by the mass media, often supported by other activities such as public events and endorsement by celebrities.

Health promotion media campaigns are deliberate attempts to promote health using paid advertisements. Campaigns are conducted at a national, a regional and – with the advent of local media – a community level. A recent innovation is the advertising at and sponsorship of sporting events by health promotion. For example, the Queensland Cancer Fund in Australia conducted a Sunsmart skin-cancer prevention advertising campaign using the scoreboard at the Brisbane cricket ground (Lynch and Dunn, 2003).

Social marketing

Social marketing is a term coined by Kotler and Zaltman (1971) for the use of commercial advertising approaches to promote social objectives. It has been employed in the developing world to promote contraceptives, safer sex, oral rehydration solution and mosquito nets (Hubley, 2005) and in the industrialized world to promote oral health/fluoridation (Hastings et al., 1994; Schou, 1987), cardiovascular health (Farquhar et al., 1985; Lefebvre et al., 1987), stopping smoking (HDA, 2000a), sensible drinking (Murray and Douglas, 1988) and many other healthy behaviours (Hastings and Haywood, 1994; Ling et al., 1992; Hastings et al., 2002). Social marketing places great emphasis on understanding the consumer's perspective and separating out ('segmenting') the population into component groups – by age, ethnicity and gender, with their separate and distinct needs. Another aspect of commercial marketing that social marketing draws upon is exchange theory, which involves considering what the consumer has to pay in exchange for the product (Houston and Gassenheimer, 1987). In the case of health actions, applying exchange theory involves examining the 'costs', such as effort, time and money, to the person of implementing the desired actions (e.g. stopping smoking, taking exercise, avoiding the sun, etc.). Social marketing activities would then seek to convince people that the costs are worth paying. Social marketing also applies the traditional four 'Ps' of marketing:

> **Social marketing:**
> The design, implementation and control of programmes calculated to influence the acceptability of social ideas and involving considerations of product planning, pricing, communication, distribution and marketing research.

- **product** – careful consideration on what is to be promoted – the packaging of the 'product', attractiveness, relevance to the aspirations of the audience/consumer
- **price** – in money, time, convenience or effort
- **promotion** – choice of tools of change media to suit the audience – i.e. the mix of methods, including mass media and face-to-face
- **place** – the location or setting where the product is to be promoted, and issues of accessibility and convenience to the target audience of items needed for behaviour change (e.g. specific foods, exercise facilities, safety equipment, etc.).

Recent experience in the United Kingdom (French, 2004) led to the Health Development Authority adding a further two 'P's:

- **politics** – informing and persuading political players who can influence the success or failure of the programme
- **public** – strategies developed which recognize and address different sections of the public who may have distinct and separate needs.

> **Activity 7.4**
>
> Look at advertisements in a selection of magazines and also on television. What kinds of approaches do advertisers use to sell their products? How effective do you think their advertising is? What lessons could be applied for promoting health?

Local and community media

In writing about mass media, most twentieth-century writers highlighted the main weakness of mass-media approaches as being their broad nature and inability to target local communities selectively with tailored messages. They also point out that the mass media do not allow for the immediate feedback that you get with face-to-face communication, when you can tell immediately if the message is not being effective and are then able to modify your approach. Recent developments in community media are leading to a revision of these criticisms. An increasing amount is being broadcast locally, which provides opportunities for health promotion targeted at specific communities and also for communities to participate and provide feedback to the programme-makers. These include local BBC and commercial radio stations and also 'community media', which broadcast on TV and radio, through cable and satellite and, with the advent of high-speed broadband connections, through the internet.

There are a growing number of exciting community media initiatives using a wide range of languages and being targeted at young people, local residents, members of ethnic minority groups and faith groups. These encourage direct participation of local people in the production of programmes about community issues.

Box 7.2 Community media for health promotion: *Kismet Road*

Community Channel is a company limited by guarantee owned by the Media Trust and funded by the Volunteering and Charitable Giving Unit of the Home Office. A special focus of the channel is to encourage volunteering and films made by local communities, and it also runs themed weeks on topics that include health. About one million people in the United Kingdom tune in regularly through digital, cable and freeview systems.

Kismet Road was a thirteen-part drama series based in Bradford which was in three languages – English, Punjabi and Urdu. The project was commissioned by the Bradford Health Authority, funded mainly by the Department of Health, and was broadcast on the Community Channel. Twelve focus-group studies were carried out to identify priority issues for the Asian community. Health issues addressed in the drama series included coronary heart disease, diabetes, asthma, and drug and alcohol dependency, and more controversial taboo issues covered were impotence, abortion, gay sex, forced marriages and racist behaviour by health workers. British Asian writers prepared the scripts (www.communitychannel.org).

Activity 7.5

Make a list of the local media in your community. Note down the different ways in which you might involve them in health promotion.

Media formats

You have already seen how health information can be presented in advertisements, news reports and drama. These are only a few of the many formats possible – see boxes 7.3 and 7.4.

Formats: The different ways in which material and information are presented in a given medium.

Box 7.3 Formats on radio and television

- News
- Spot announcements
- Slogans and jingles
- Discussions
- 'Phone-in' programmes
- Interview and chat shows
- Documentaries
- Drama and soap operas
- Music
- Quizzes and panel games
- Magazine programmes

Box 7.4 Formats in newspapers

- News
- Announcements of future events
- Advertisements
- Features
- Special interest sections
- Letters from readers
- Advice columns

Using theory for planning mass media: the six-stage model of communication

We use a framework (figure 7.2) which identifies six stages through which communications pass in order to achieve health improvements. Successful negotiation of each stage requires the application of different concepts and theories (Hubley, 2003).

Stage 1: reaching the intended audience – A communication must be seen or heard by its intended audience. This requires carrying out research on your intended audience to find out their watching, listening and reading habits.

Stage 2: attracting the audience's attention – Any communication must attract attention so that people will make the effort to listen/read it and not switch to other channels or skip to other parts of the newspaper or magazine. Media use a range of approaches to attract and hold their audience's attention, including unusual pictures, strong images, headlines, cartoons, music and choice of content.

Audience research: The process of carrying out research on the media habits of the community, such as watching, listening and reading habits, favourite programmes and information sources. Most newspapers, radio and television stations publish viewing/listening figures and profiles of their audiences.

Figure 7.2 The six-stage model of communication

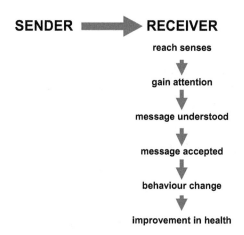

SENDER ➡ RECEIVER

reach senses
↓
gain attention
↓
message understood
↓
message accepted
↓
behaviour change
↓
improvement in health

Pre-testing: The process of trying out draft or 'prototype' materials on samples of the intended audience to test for understanding and the ability to attract attention, gain interest and generate impact.

Stage 3: understanding the message (perception) – Once a person pays attention to a message they then try to understand it – i.e. make sense of the words and pictures – a process that psychologists call perception. Perception is a highly *subjective* process. Two people may hear the same radio programme or see the same poster and interpret the message quite differently from each other and from the intended meaning.

Stage 4: promoting change (acceptance) – A communication should be believed and accepted. Successful negotiation of this stage involves drawing upon research into factors influencing changes in beliefs, attitudes and behaviour change (discussed in chapter 3). There is a rich literature on communications research into the influences of message design and sources on the credibility of messages.

Stage 5: producing a change in behaviour – A communication may result in a change in beliefs and attitude but still not influence behaviour. This is usually because of pressure/influence from others or the need for enabling factors such as money, time and services – see the discussions of behaviour change in chapter 3.

Stage six: improvement in health – Improvements in health only take place if the actions people are being asked to take are relevant to the health issue.

Appeals and mass media

Messages in posters and advertisements can be expressed in different ways. Among the options are:

Appeal: The way in which a message is presented, such as using logical arguments, humour or fear (scare tactics).

- **logical arguments** based on information, facts and health benefits. These can be one-sided arguments that just present the benefits of action or two-sided arguments that present the advantages and disadvantages of taking action.

- **emotional appeals** that use pictures, music, testimonials and shock/scare tactics to arouse strong feelings and emotions. These might build on positive images of love and belonging, the promotion of values such as a caring adult or responsible parent, on masculinity and femininity, or on success and status. Shock tactics use fear in an attempt to jolt the person into action.
- **humour**, which can help people identify with a situation, to see things from a different perspective, and to defuse potentially frightening or embarrassing subjects. For example, the Health Education Authority used the comedian John Cleese in a series of advertisements between 1992 and 1995 directed at getting adults to give up smoking.

Box 7.5 The debate about using fear and shock tactics

There is ongoing debate about the use of fear and shock approaches to health promotion (Hill et al., 1998; Hastings and MacFadyen, 2002; Green and Witte, 2006).

The idea of presenting strong negative information to make people change their behaviour is controversial. Originally theorists suggested that mild fear can arouse interest, create concern and lead to change, but that too much fear can lead to people denying and rejecting the message.

Early responses in the United Kingdom to AIDS involved strong fear messages with pictures of tombstones. A fear-arousing image of the Grim Reaper in a bowling alley knocking down people was used to promote AIDS awareness in Australia. There was a strong reaction to these negative messages by health promoters, who became reluctant to use fear appeals and preferred using humour and other types of appeal.

However, attitudes have shifted back towards the benefits of fear as a tactic. In recent years viewers have been shown harrowing emotional appeals exhibiting the negative consequences of smoking, taking drugs, and drinking and driving. Considerable impact was registered by Australian mass-media anti-smoking campaigns using fear-arousing images – most notably a TV advertisement that showed a person wringing out black tar from a sponge and another with pictures of arteries oozing white sticky material (Hill et al., 1998). Evaluations of these campaigns indicate that such approaches can be highly effective, especially if they are combined with real-life testimonials from persons – especially children – whose lives have been affected by the issue. The weight of evidence is shifting towards an acceptance of the idea that fear and emotional appeals have a role in health promotion, both in acting as a trigger to motivate people to change their behaviour and also in reinforcing the commitment of people to continue to practise healthy behaviours (Montazeri and McEwen, 1997; Grey et al., 2000).

But alongside issues of effectiveness there is a critical ethical question. Is the arousal of fear, guilt, anxiety and panic a price worth paying to get messages across? One approach is to use fear only when there are clearly indicated and feasible actions that people can carry out. Anti-smoking mass-media campaigns using shock messages now give details of stop-smoking clinics and telephone help lines, so there are clear options for people to follow.

In addition to these ethical concerns, there is also a question of where people stand in the debates on health promotion approaches discussed in chapter 1. Many persons in health promotion have been reluctant to use emotional and fear messages, which they see as taking a medical model/individualistic/persuasion approach and would rather use a health empowerment strategy, which keeps the decision-making in people's own hands.

> ### Activity 7.6
>
> Are there issues where you think the use of fear in health promotion can be justified? What do you see as the good and bad points of using fear/shock appeals in health promotion?

Entertainment education – drama and popular music

There is a long tradition of using broadcast drama as a vehicle for public education. Probably the best-known example in the United Kingdom was the launch in 1951 of the radio drama serial *The Archers* as a vehicle for introducing farming information (Fraser and Restrepo-Estrada, 1998). Health issues such as alcohol, unexpected pregnancy, suicide attempts, cancers, etc., are frequently used in the plot lines of television soap operas. For example, in the 25 April 2001 episode of the soap opera *Coronation Street* a well-known character, Alma, was required to have a repeat cervical smear (having previously missed many smear tests), and in the next episode was diagnosed with cervical cancer. Her cancer storyline featured in twenty-three of the following episodes, and within six weeks she was dead. A retrospective study of cervical smears in the Lancashire and Greater Manchester zones of the NHS found that uptake of cervical smear tests had increased 21 per cent – from 65,714 in 2000 to 79,712 in 2001 – with no other obvious explanation apart from the *Coronation Street* episodes (Howe et al., 2002). This provided a powerful demonstration of the enormous potential scope of soap operas for health promotion.

The inclusion of a cancer storyline in that episode of *Coronation Street* had been a decision of the scriptwriters and was not a planned health promotion activity. At present the intentional linkage of entertainment and health promotion is being carried out mainly in the developing world. The focal point for the international movement for 'entertainment education' is the Population Communication Institute of Johns Hopkins University, whose members from Africa, Asia and Latin America use television drama and popular songs for health promotion.

How effective are the mass media for health promotion?

There is ongoing debate about the effectiveness of the mass media for health promotion. The conventional wisdom of early writers such as the influential communications scholar Everett Rogers was that they are very effective at promoting awareness but less effective than interpersonal communication for promoting behaviour change, which requires person-to-person approaches (Rogers, 1983). This view is challenged by supporters of the use of mass media in health promotion, who point to the very low cost per person reached by the mass media compared with interpersonal channels and also the success of the commercial world in using the media to promote products.

The decline in smoking in the United Kingdom has been put forward as evidence of the impact of the vigorous anti-smoking media campaigns initiated in the 1970s, although it also reveals some of the shortcomings. As shown in figure 1.4 in chapter 1, over the last thirty years inequalities in smoking between social classes in Britain have increased. A possible explanation is that health promotion mass-media messages were selectively taken up by professional groups, with their higher educational, financial and social status. An implication of this is that, in order to address inequalities and promote social inclusion, the mass media need to be supplemented with face-to-face methods such as community development (for a discussion of the contribution of the mass media to inequalities in health and social exclusion, see Hastings et al., 1998).

In assessing the potential contribution of mass-media health promotion, the following also need to be considered.

- While advertising increases sales of products, it is misleading to draw the conclusion that health promotion advertising will also be effective. Outcomes such as stopping smoking, moderating alcohol consumption, changing diet, taking exercise and preventing obesity are more complex to achieve compared with purchasing a product because they involve changing long-term lifestyle habits and addressing economic barriers and social pressures/norms.
- It is difficult to use evaluation designs such as randomized control trials with comparison communities as controls (see chapters 2 and 17). It is therefore more challenging to attribute any changes observed unambiguously to the effect of the mass media.
- Most early theories of the impact of the mass media are based on evaluation of health promotion carried out before 1980. It is possible that newer programmes using more sophisticated planning models incorporating audience research, pre-testing and principles of social marketing have more impact than predicted in these early theories.
- Most discussion of the advantages and disadvantages of mass-media health promotion focus on advertising for health promotion. Little research has been carried out on the effectiveness of other approaches, using dramas, documentaries, coverage of news stories and endorsement by celebrities.
- Local and community media are recent phenomena in the United Kingdom and there has been little in the way of evaluation of their unique ability to combine locally tailored campaigns and community involvement.

In 2004, the Health Development Agency reviewed a range of evaluations of mass-media campaigns in the United Kingdom and came to the conclusion that such campaigns were particularly appropriate when the aim was to reach a large number of people very quickly to spread awareness, public discussion and debate (HDA, 2004b). They considered mass media to achieve behaviour change mainly when that behaviour was relatively simple – e.g. a one-time behaviour such as going for immunization or a cholesterol screening test – and concluded that they could achieve more ambitious objectives provided that:

- the public is broken down or 'segmented' into different groups by age, ethnicity, social class and readiness to change, and that the messages are tailored to meet the needs of each group
- there was a generous budget to cover advertising and direct mail
- the exercise is carried out over an extended time period with repeated bursts reinforcing key messages
- accompanying back-up and reinforcement can be provided from services providing face-to-face communication in the community, such as nurses, doctors, teachers, etc.
- media journalists are supportive of health promotion and will provide sympathetic coverage of the campaign.

The use of mass media also raises issues of health promotion values, approaches and other debates reviewed in chapter 1. Some health promoters are uncomfortable with the media because they associate them with an individualistic persuasive approach directed at behaviour change and prefer instead to use participatory work with groups and communities to promote health empowerment and informed decision-making.

The planning process for mass-media health promotion

We set out in figure 7.3 a process for systematically planning mass-media health promotion. Decisions on the content and delivery of health promotion activities

Figure 7.3
A systematic approach to planning mass-media health promotion

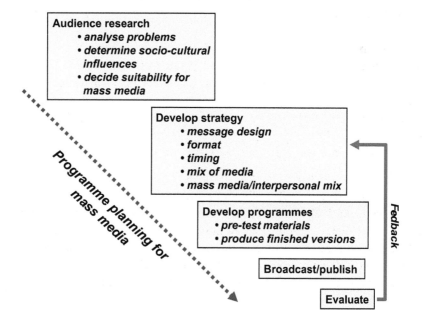

should draw on initial social research on what the target audience knows, believes and feels about the health issues. Health promotion should exploit the full potential of mass media, including both advertising and programme content, and be combined with other approaches, such as person-to-person methods/community development, service improvement and advocacy to promote healthy public policy.

> **Activity 7.7**
>
> Apply the approach used in figure 7.3 to one of the following issues or one of your own choice: smoking, obesity, injury prevention in the home, uptake of immunization, exercise promotion. Explain how you would carry out each of following steps: audience research, development of strategy, development of programme materials, and evaluation.

Further reading

For a review of the application of social marketing to health issues, see:
- Andreasen, A. R. (1995). *Marketing Social Change: Changing Behaviour to Promote Health, Social Development, and the Environment.* San Francisco: Jossey-Bass.

For a detailed discussion of the role of mass media in shaping the views of young people about sex, see:
- Buckingham, D., and Bragg, S. (2004). *Young People, Sex and the Media: The Facts of Life?* Basingstoke: Palgrave Macmillan.

A comprehensive collection of chapters on key aspects of the mass media, including theory, evaluation, and case studies, can be found in:
- Rice, R. E., and Atkin, C. K. (2001). *Public Communication Campaigns.* Thousand Oaks, CA: Sage.

8 Print Media

Contents

8 Print Media

Key issues within this chapter:

- Print media have a useful role in health promotion in providing information on health issues.
- The effectiveness of print media depends on achieving a match between the readability of the materials and the level of literacy and health literacy in the intended readership.
- Health promotion needs to adopt a systematic approach to the development of print materials, including initial research to develop appropriate messages, good quality design using clear and attractive layouts, careful attention to ensure the readiblity of the content, and pre-testing for the comprehension, attention-generating potential and relevance of the content.

By the end of this chapter you should be able to:

- identify when print material can play a role in health promotion
- understand concepts such as health literacy, readability, layout, design, pre-testing
- be able to adopt a systematic approach to the design and use of print materials in health promotion.

Walk into any newsagent and you will find print media targeting all ages, educational levels and interests. Print material on health is available at the GP surgery and distributed through the mail, in wage packets and with medicine prescriptions. In this chapter we will look at some of the different ways in which print media can be used in health promotion. We will provide some practical guidelines on producing your own print media.

Literacy and numeracy

Health promotion through printed media depends on people's ability to read. Understanding health promotion communications on risk, probability and the likely consequence of health actions also depends on a certain basic level of numeracy. The Department for Education and Skills (2003b) estimates that up to 7 million adults in England cannot read or write as well as the average eleven-year-old and that 15 million people have difficulties with fractions, decimals and simple percentages. In justifying the Skills for Life national strategy for England, the DfES makes the point that 'People with poor literacy, language or numeracy skills are less productive at work, earn less and are more likely to suffer from ill health and social exclusion.' Similar pictures are evident in other parts of the UK. For example, in the Generic Skills Survey 2003 (Future Skills Wales Steering Group, 2003) potential employers reported issues related to inadequate literacy, numeracy and understanding of customer needs when recruiting staff. A self-perpetuating and mutually reinforcing connection therefore exists between poor literacy and numeracy skills and social exclusion, especially among marginalized groups such as homeless people, refugees, asylum-seekers, drug abusers and travelling families.

> **Literacy:** The ability of people to make sense of the printed word.

Health literacy

In chapter 1 we showed how the concept of health literacy can be combined with that of self-efficacy to provide the basis for health empowerment. While health literacy now has a broader meaning encompassing general understandings of health information, it has its origins in practical concerns about the ability of people to understand information in printed materials, especially instructions on the use of medicines. Much of the early interest in health literacy came from the United States. The Ad Hoc Committee on Health Literacy for the Council on Scientific Affairs of the American Medical Association (1999) defined health literacy as 'a constellation of skills, including the ability to perform basic reading and numerical tasks required to function in the health-care environment. Patients with adequate health literacy can read, understand, and act on health-care information.' Various studies in the United States have demonstrated that patients with low health literacy – especially older people – lack essential information about their specific condition and are at risk of increased hospitalization. Typical of such studies is Schillinger et al. (2002), who found that diabetics with poor health literacy could not read or understand labels on pill bottles and had worse blood-sugar control and higher rates of preventable vision impairment.

One of the more difficult dimensions of health literacy is that of risk. Many people find it difficult to comprehend percentages and probabilities, which are vital to an understanding of risk associated with different health practices.

Measurement scales to evaluate a person's health literacy are described in a useful manual produced by the American Medical Association (Weiss, 2003). These involve tasks such as getting people to read aloud a range of health-related terms and to read and explain a set of health instructions (e.g. on a medicine label).

Box 8.1 How to write simple English

- Have the intended reader clearly in mind when you are writing.
- Use words that are likely to be familiar to the reader.
- Avoid jargon – if you really need to use a technical word it needs to be defined.
- Keep acronyms (e.g. HDA, HAZ, etc.) to a minimum.
- If there is a choice between a long word and a short word, use the short word!
- Use concrete language rather than general phrases – e.g. instead of saying 'engage with the community', say 'go and meet the community'. Instead of 'interact with your children', say 'talk with your children'.
- Try reading it aloud. If it is difficult to read aloud you need to rewrite it.
- Use short sentences and paragraphs. Commas and full stops are your friends!
- Use lists and bullet points.
- Pre-test what you have written by giving it to someone and asking if they understand it.

Readability

Approaches developed for measuring readability (see box 8.2) have included scoring text according to its use of difficult, uncommon and long words and long sentences. Alternatively, in the Cloze procedure, words are deleted according to various criteria and the text is then given to test subjects, who are asked to fill in the blanks to give the whole meaning. One of the simplest and most valid readability tests is the SMOG (simplified measure of gobbledygook) grading readability formula, developed by G. Harry McLaughlin in 1969, which is based on sentence length and the occurrence of words with three or more syllables.

Readability: The extent to which the meaning of a piece of writing can be understood. Readability depends on the choice of words, length of sentences and complexity of ideas.

As is typical of a number of studies, Beaver and Luker (1997) assessed the readability of fifty leaflets distributed through health-centre waiting areas, hospitals and charities in the UK to women with breast cancer. SMOG scores indicated an average readability level of fifteen years, and the authors concluded that the general population may not understand the information contained within the booklets. By way of comparison, the SMOG scores of leader articles in *The Sun* and *The Guardian* newspapers during that same period were twelve years and eighteen years respectively. A similar study of printed materials in environmental health departments is provided in box 8.3. The general conclusion drawn from these and other studies of readability is that health promotion printed materials are often pitched at too high a level.

Legibility: The ease with which letters and words in text can be recognized. It depends on the choice of font, the size of the type and how clearly it has been printed.

Beaver and Luker (1997) also compared the readability of their breast cancer leaflets with that of articles on health in women's magazines. A particularly interesting finding was that the women's magazines had the same high reading age of fifteen years as the leaflets – yet, despite this, the women's magazines were still widely read and popular. This shows that readability is only one of many factors that make text accessible. Other important design features that are not measured in readability formulae include an attractive style, the use of photographs and colour, the layout, and a content that is relevant and interesting to the reader.

Testing for readability is now becoming standard practice in health promotion. However, some have questioned what they see as an excessive reliance on readability formulas in designing printed texts. Later in this chapter you will see that readability is only one of many factors to be taken into account when designing print materials. It is also necessary to consider design, layout, clarity and perceived relevance to the reader.

Box 8.2 How to do readability tests

To test text for readability using the SMOG test:

1 Count off ten consecutive sentences near the beginning, in the middle and near the end of the text. Anything ending with a full stop, a question mark or an exclamation mark is considered a sentence.
2 Circle all the words containing three or more syllables and add up the number of words circled. Hyphenated words are considered a single word, Abbreviations should be read out in order to count how many syllables are involved (UN is two syllables, HDA and UNICEF are three syllables).
3 Estimate the square root of the total number of polysyllabic words counted. You can do this by finding the nearest perfect square to the number and taking its square root.
4 Add the number 8 to that square root. The resulting number is the SMOG readability grade or reading age level.

A leaflet targeted at an adult of low educational level, e.g. an early school leaver, should have a reading level of not more than ten years, and even this low level may not be understood by someone with a low literacy level.

For example, if there were thirty-nine polysyllabic words, the nearest perfect square would be 36 and the square root would be 6. The SMOG score would be 6 + 8, i.e. fourteen years.

For further information on the SMOG test, see the excellent guide 'Making health communication programmes work', at www.cancer.gov/pinkbook.

Leaflets are one of the most widely used methods of health promotion. For example, they are commonly found in GPs' waiting rooms.

Leaflets

Leaflets are the most basic print media in health promotion. Given out during face-to-face sessions, they can act as a take-home 'portable memory' that people can use to remind themselves of key points. They can be left in public places, health centres and doctors' surgeries, where people can pick them up discretely if they are too shy to ask. People can keep them in the house for reference and pass them on to others.

The basic leaflet is a single sheet of A4 paper folded two or three times that can be printed or produced just using a photocopier. Modern printing techniques have greatly expanded the range of possible designs. You can now create leaflets easily in a wide range of sizes and formats, with pull-out and pop-up sections and indexes, and in many different shapes, to look like envelopes, condoms, keys, etc. However, the basic components of a leaflet – as with all print media – are the same: words, pictures, typeface and layout.

Are leaflets effective in health promotion? A case study of leaflets on environmental health issues is presented in box 8.3. A study by Heaney et al. (2001) found that postal distribution of two self-care manuals by twenty GP practices in Lothian, Scotland, did not result in any change in the use of health services. Little et al. (1998) carried out a randomized control trial of the effect of GPs in Southampton sending out a 'What shall I do?' leaflet to patients' homes on self-management for forty-two common minor illnesses. A follow-up one year later showed that patients valued the leaflet. However, it had only a small effect in reducing attendance for minor illnesses and did not cut the overall number of consultations with GPs. The overall conclusion of the *British Medical Journal* was that 'Most patients find information about minor illnesses provided by post useful, and it helps their confidence in managing minor illness.' However, the pessimistic verdict of the authors was that 'information booklets on minor illness may have a limited role in the NHS'.

Leaflets are a passive form of communication and inevitably have limits compared with more active approaches. A study by Leiner et al. (2004) compared the use of leaflets with an animated cartoon film for educating parents about polio immunization and, not surprisingly, found that the video had a greater effect. The lessons are clear: leaflets should be used in a support role to other methods (e.g. the mass media) and in situations where they can be distributed directly (e.g. by post and through clinics and pharmacies). Even then, the internet might be a more cost-effective way of providing the same information (see chapter 9).

> **Visual literacy:** The ability of people to understand pictures and illustrations using different graphic formats.

Box 8.3 Case study: readability of environmental health promotion materials

Harvey and Fleming (2003) studied leaflets used by five environmental health departments in England, Scotland and Northern Ireland. The leaflets came from a variety of sources: 'in-house', central government, charities, trade unions and manufacturers of commercial products such as disinfectants. In their evaluation, the authors applied the SMOG test directly to the leaflets and carried out a survey in which they asked samples of the target audiences to complete a short checklist and rate each leaflet according to:

- the clarity of the layout
- the adequacy of the amount of text on each page – whether too much or too little
- the size of the lettering used and the ease of reading
- the ease of following the information in the leaflet
- the ease of understanding the words and phrases used

- whether they felt that simpler words could be used
- whether they felt the leaflet could be understood by other people
- how useful they felt the leaflet to be
- whether they felt that the leaflet could be improved and, if so, how.

They found that many of the leaflets were at a higher level of readability than their intended audience and were rated poorly by the respondents in the study. Leaflets produced in-house were often of poor quality. While materials produced by commercial companies were of good quality, readers were distracted by pictures of products and brand names and were misled into believing that the environmental health departments endorsed those products. The authors concluded that, when selecting leaflets for health promotion, more use should be made of readability scoring and checklists to screen out poorly designed materials.

> **Activity 8.1**
>
> Carry out a SMOG test on a health promotion leaflet. Is the reading age of the leaflet appropriate to what you think is the intended target audience? Assess what you feel are the intended audience and aims of the leaflet. Do you feel that the leaflet meets the purposes for which it is intended? How do you think it could be improved?

Visual communication and visual literacy

Well-chosen pictures or diagrams enhance the visual quality of print media, arouse interest, attract attention, and convey meanings and ideas, including the appearance of symptoms and comparisons in size and cycles of disease. However, visuals in health promotion communications can also be misunderstood, lead people to jump to the wrong conclusions about the purpose and relevance of a communication, provoke strong reactions and cause offence. These problems are especially common when people from one cultural background see print materials intended for those from another culture.

In our discussion of non-verbal communication and body language in chapter 5 you saw how people read meaning from a person's general appearance, hair style, clothing and jewellery to make judgements about that person's background, and perceived similarity to themselves. Not surprisingly, this also happens when people see pictures of people in print media. An inappropriate picture can lead to people rejecting messages as irrelevant to their own lives or drawing a different meaning from that originally intended. The following three kinds of pictures commonly cause problems:

- representation of objects (e.g. foods, clothing, utensils) that are inappropriate to the intended user
- statistical charts such as histograms and trend diagrams
- representations of parts of the body that cause offence within some cultures.

Guidelines on pre-testing of print media including pictures are given later in this chapter.

> **Activity 8.2**
>
> Collect some health promotion leaflets and posters and look at the pictures they use. Are the pictures clear to you? Are there any pictures that you think are inappropriate? Ask someone from another cultural background to look at those pictures and see if their views agree with your own. Can you reach any conclusions about what makes a good picture?

Posters

Many people in health promotion have reacted against posters completely, seeing them as a throwback to old-fashioned approaches to health promotion using persuasion and victim blaming. However, well-designed posters have their uses. They can present information in a simple, eye-catching and memorable way and stimulate discussion. Posters can be put up in public places such as health centres, GP surgeries, pharmacies, community centres, shop windows and notice boards in the workplace. It is also possible to rent spaces to display posters in streets, on signboards and inside and outside buses. If the poster is attractive and well designed, people – especially young children and teenagers – may even put them up in their homes. A variant on a poster is a calendar, in which the pages change each month to display a new image and message.

By themselves, posters have little value. They are useful mainly to bring a topic to the attention of the community, to reinforce a message that people are already receiving through other channels such as radio and individual communication, and to provide a talking point for discussion. Examples of the appropriate use of posters include reinforcing the main theme of a media campaign or a theme for a talk at a clinic; in a community hall to draw attention to a local issue; and displayed outside a shop to say that health products are available.

A good poster should have a very simple message and not try to say too much. It should be attractive, with eye-catching pictures, strong colours and interesting content to gain attention so people will want to display it. However, most importantly, it must be appropriate to the intended audience and communicate an unambiguous and clear message.

Box 8.4 Case study: Posters and the promotion of exercise

A poster was put up for four weeks in a Birmingham shopping mall to encourage shoppers to use the stairs rather than the escalators. 658 persons were interviewed to determine the impact of the poster. Use of stairs increased significantly during the intervention periods. Applying the stages of change model (see chapter 3), the interviewers found that the poster had more impact on people who were already thinking about increasing their exercise than on the 'pre-contemplators', who were found to be less likely to see the posters and take action. The study reached the conclusion that a poster was an effective method for motivating those who had already considered changing their behaviour but was less effective for those who had not considered making any change (Kerr et al., 2000).

> **Activity 8.3**
>
> What kind of poster would appeal to an older person, a teenager, a preschool child, a family with children, a patient visiting the doctor? Where could you display the poster to reach your intended audience?

Displaying printed materials

You need to give careful thought to how you will distribute your printed materials and where to display your posters. This involves finding out where your intended targets spend their time and so will be likely to see and pick up your materials. A common approach is to put up displays of printed materials in a public place, such as a health centre notice board. Unfortunately such displays are often just a selection of posters put up with little thought – the end result being a jumbled mess. Care and attention is needed to produce an eye-catching and coordinated display of relevant visual materials with take-home leaflets. It is a good idea to focus on one theme at a time and change the display regularly so that people do not get bored by seeing the same material all the time.

Using materials with different cultures and languages

Print materials designed for one culture usually have to be adapted before they can be used with another, to ensure that language, illustrations and advice given are appropriate and acceptable to the user (see, for example, the excellent discussion of the appropriateness of breast cancer printed materials for Hispanics in the United States by Massett, 1996). Even when the intended users speak English, difficulties can be experienced. If English is their second language, they may have a lower reading ability than the general population, assign different meanings to words and misunderstand nuances in language. The best approach is to involve members of the intended community in both developing and pre-testing the materials.

If you translate your materials into other languages you will have to take care to ensure that the finished product captures your intended meaning (Bhatt, 1997). Problems can arise when ideas and concepts are originally written in English and then translated into another language. Ideas easily expressed in English can be difficult to convey in other languages, which might not have equivalent words. This is especially the case for abstract concepts such as empowerment, beliefs and culture or specific medical terms. It is sometimes better to use the English word and then explain the meaning. Words can easily be mistranslated and acquire a very different meaning – for example, the words 'oily fish' might be translated as 'fried fish' or the concept 'sensible drinking' might be incorrectly translated to imply that 'drinking is sensible'. You will need to brief the translator on exactly what you want. Sometimes there are taboos about using certain words in writing that might cause offence. You need to make sure that the translation uses those dialects and normal everyday expressions spoken by the intended target audience.

A framework for producing a leaflet

A review in the United Kingdom by Mary Dixon-Woods (2000) showed that there were as many as 4,894 leaflets on the databases maintained by the Health Education Board for Scotland and the Help for Health Trust's Healthbox – a testimony to the widespread popularity of leaflets in health promotion. Her review highlighted the diversity of organizations involved and the 'ill-coordinated and ill-regulated' nature of the leaflet production process, which resulted in duplication of effort on some health topics, neglect of others and a lack of quality control. Her findings, alongside others such as the review of leaflets in environmental health services in box 8.3, emphasize the need to adopt a systematic process for design of printed materials such as the one provided in figure 8.1.

Needs assessment	*Is a suitable leaflet already available?* *Why has a need for a leaflet arisen?* *What research has been carried out on needs?* *At whom is it directed?*	**Figure 8.1** Key decisions in preparing a leaflet
Concept design	*What is the purpose of the leaflet?* *How is it planned to be used?* *What is it asking the reader to do?* *What support information needs to be presented?*	
Graphic design and pre-testing	*Who will set out the art work?* *What words will be used?* *What pictures will be used?* *Other decisions – picture style, fonts, use of colour, layout?* *How will you pre-test the draft version?*	
Production	*How will you produce the finished version?* *How many copies will you print and how much will it cost?*	
Distribution	*How will you distribute the leaflet?*	
Evaluation	*How will you evaluate the impact of the leaflet?*	

Needs assessment

A decision to produce an item of print material will have come about because of a need expressed by health workers or members of the community or through research findings. The information in box 8.5, from the National Cancer Institute in the United

States, shows how valuable initial research can be to understand what information is needed and how this should be communicated – including the language, reading level and channels for distribution. Before spending time producing your own leaflet it is worth finding out if something suitable already exists which could be used in its present form or be adapted to meet your needs.

Box 8.5 Cancer-risk message concept development

The National Cancer Institute in the United States provides cancer-risk information to the public. A series of focus groups was organized to learn what the public thought of different methods for communicating risks, and the feedback received emphasized the importance of careful choice of words in risk communication.

- Participants said that they wanted cancer-risk messages to give them hope for preventing cancer and that risk information is less threatening when written in optimistic terms.
- When faced with 'bad news' about cancer risks, they said that they look for reasons why it does not apply to them.
- They wanted risk messages to address key questions, such as 'How serious is the risk?' and 'What can be done to reduce or avoid the risk?', as well as to explain how and where to get additional information.
- Word choice also influences how information is perceived; 'risk' raises alarm, while 'chance' minimizes it.
- Use of vague or unfamiliar terms (including 'fourfold', 'relative risk', 'lifetime risk') gives people reason to discount the information.
- Combining brief text and visuals (such as charts and graphs) can increase attention and understanding.
- Statistical risk information was difficult for many participants to follow; percentages were more understandable than ratios, but in either case accompanying explanations of the seriousness of the risk were needed.
- Participants were interested in the complete picture – that is, what is known and what is not yet known about a risk, and what it means for ordinary people.
- The source of risk information affects credibility, with participants saying that they are less likely to trust the media or a source with a business interest and more likely to trust risk information supplied by a doctor or medical journal.

Adapted from National Cancer Institute (1998)

Concept design

You will need to define clearly the purpose of the leaflet. Is it intended to be used on its own, to support face-to-face advice, or to complement a mass-media programme? What advice will you be giving? You need to ensure that the advice/message is accurate, appropriate and acceptable to the age and culture of the target audience. How much supporting information will you present in the leaflet? A model, such as the health belief model (see chapter 3), provides a useful checklist of key points to put across in a leaflet to ensure people realize: 1) its relevance to them; 2) that the health issue is serious; 3) that there is a need for action; and 4) that the benefits of taking action outweigh the disadvantages. A leaflet also needs to address any issues that might have emerged from initial research with the intended audience.

Graphic design and pre-testing

This stage includes the various decisions involved in translating the concept into the finished product, such as the choice of words, pictures, fonts, headings, colour, etc. The leaflet should be attractive so that it stands out and people want to read it. The words and pictures should be clear and easily understood by the intended audience. You will need to control the language – especially technical words – and make sure that the readability matches the reading level of the intended reader. You will need to pre-test a draft version of the leaflet with some people from the intended audience to check that the content is attractive, understandable, acceptable, does not contain anything offensive and provides the information that is wanted. Further guidelines are provided in box 8.6.

Production

This stage involves the actual printing of the leaflet. You will need to get costings for the printing. The cost of material will depend on your choice of paper, whether you are using full colour or just one or two colours, the number of pages, how many folds are involved and the number of copies (size of the 'print run').

Distribution

You need to decide how you are going to distribute the materials to the target audience. If you send them out to other people to distribute, you need to give clear instructions. Some leaflets may be wasted if they are left at places where they are not taken up. It is usually a good idea to distribute only some of your materials at the beginning, monitor the use, and send the rest to where they are needed most.

Box 8.6 How to design the text

It is best to leave graphic design to specialists. However, it is helpful to have an understanding of some of the basic concepts so that you can design your own simple materials and work in effective partnership with designers.

- Make the structure clear with the use of headings, spacing, indenting, bullets.
- Use plenty of 'white space' in margins and between paragraphs. Do not make the text look too crammed. Keep paragraphs short.
- Present information in lists and bullet points.
- Modern computers give a wide choice of typefaces or 'fonts'. Choose one that can be easily read.
- Lower-case lettering is easier to read than UPPER case (capital letters).
- Lines that are too short or too long result in inefficient eye movements. Lengths of 6 to 9 cm or seven to eight words are the quickest to read.
- Right-hand margins that are not 'justified', i.e. 'ragged', are easiest to read.
- 10-, 11-, and 12-point type are easiest to read, but 12 point is preferable. Materials for persons with dyslexia and older persons should be at least 12 point.
- Text can be emphasized by using a **bold** typeface, by surrounding it with 'white space', by placing in a box or by having it in a different colour.
- Persons with dyslexia find it difficult to read text against a pure white or a patterned background. It is better to use an off-white or light coloured background.

Evaluation

In the short term you need to find out how many copies of the leaflet reached the intended audience. You then need to ascertain whether people have made use of the materials and taken action. It is a good idea to build some form of feedback into the leaflet, e.g. an address for someone to write to or a telephone number. You could also ask health workers to monitor their patients/clients to look for evidence that the leaflet has been used. Another approach is to carry out a survey of the target audience to establish whether they have seen, read or used the leaflet.

Pre-testing: Showing draft (prototype) materials to a sample of the intended target audience to check for attractiveness of content, understanding, acceptability and relevance.

Pre-testing

Pre-testing involves showing first drafts ('prototypes') to intended readers to identify any potential problems before the final version is printed (see box 8.7). It is also a good idea to show materials to gatekeepers (e.g. teachers, parents, health workers) to check that they are happy with the materials being distributed on their premises.

Box 8.7 How to pre-test printed materials

Give the materials to people who are typical of your intended user and ask them the following questions.

- Do the materials provide the information that you need? If not, what is missing?
- Is the advice acceptable? Is it culturally acceptable? Can you put it into practice?
- Is there anything that is controversial and causes offence – either words or pictures?
- Are the colours appropriate? (Colours can have different meanings within different cultures.)
- Is the typeface clear and easy to read? (Materials targeted at older persons will need a larger typeface.)
- Is it attractive to look at? Does it stand out? Would you pick it up and take it away?
- Is the length too short, too long or about right?
- Can you remember the main points? (Too much information, distracting details and technical terms can all reduce recall.)
- Is the size appropriate? Can it fit in a pocket and be easily carried about? If it is something confidential, can it easily be concealed?
- What is your overall opinion about this material?

Piloting leaflets helps to test their effectiveness and to learn more about the target audience's needs.

> **Activity 8.4**
>
> Use the checklist in box 8.7 to assess a health promotion leaflet and poster. Then show them to someone from the intended audience and ask them what they think of it. What conclusions can you draw about the suitability of that material?

Print media and debates in health promotion

Printed materials have an important role in health promotion, but their use has to be seen within the context of the debates in health promotion reviewed in chapter 1. In a thought-provoking and very comprehensive review of printed materials in health- care settings, Mary Dixon-Woods (2001) challenges what she sees as the very limited current view of the role and functions of printed materials. She considers that most leaflets are produced within a medical model, individualistic persuasion approach to health pro-motion – i.e. to address perceived deficits in a patient's knowledge in order to persuade them to comply with medical treatment, follow drug regimes and change their behav-iour. She argues that leaflets could be developed within a health empowerment approach – to provide information to enable patients to become partners with health-care work-ers in the process of recovery, to make informed decisions, to relieve anxieties and to promote patient satisfaction. If a health empowerment perspective is adopted, leaflets should not be evaluated on behaviour change but through outcomes such as increased satisfaction and patients' confidence in their ability to manage their illnesses.

In discussions of participatory learning in chapter 6 we described how printed materials have been used to trigger discussion and consciousness-raising. A common mistake in health promotion is to focus on materials rather than processes. The first priority should be to decide on the health promotion approach to use. Once that deci-sion has been made you can decide how the health promotion can be supported by printed materials.

Further reading

For discussion of concepts of graphic design and the layout of texts, see the two handbooks by Dabner:

- Dabner, D. (2003). *Design and Layout: Understanding and Using Graphics.* London: Batsford.
- Dabner, D. (2004). *Graphic Design School: The Principles and Practices of Graphic Design.* London: Thames & Hudson.

For a detailed guide on the production of printed materials on health topics aimed at health workers, see:

- Duman, M. (2005). *Producing Patient Information: How to Research, Develop and Produce Effective Information Resources.* London: King's Fund.

CHAPTER **9** Electronic Media and the Internet

Contents

CHAPTER 9 Electronic Media and the Internet

Key issues within this chapter:

- The internet and other electronic media, such as mobile phones and stand-alone computer technologies, are valuable resources for health promotion.
- The internet is a source of information for the public and a means of networking among health promotion workers.
- A strength of the internet is its interactive nature and its potential to provide advice that is tailored to the needs of individuals.
- Challenges posed by the internet are the lack of controls on the quality of information provided and the difficulty that some sections of the community find in accessing information.

By the end of this chapter you should be able to:

- critically assess the potential of the internet and new technologies for health promotion
- understand the features that make a website useful for health promotion
- make better use of the internet to meet your own information needs
- incorporate web-based strategies into your health promotion.

A revolution in information technology is changing the world around us. Not only has it resulted in a quantum leap in the amount of information available but it has shrunk the world. A UK Cabinet Office report (2005) estimated that 48 per cent of the 460 million people in the European Union have access to the internet. This revolution is bringing enormous benefits to health promotion, enabling us to seek out information, network with colleagues, form global movements and make information available on demand to people in their homes. However, it has also created new problems and challenges. In this chapter we will review the use of electronic media for health promotion.

Stand-alone computer-based technologies

CD-ROMs/DVDs/multi-media

Music, games and other information can be delivered to specific target groups through CD-ROMs and DVDs. This is especially useful for large amounts of information that might take a long time to download from the internet. It is also a practical way of targeting information to a specific group.

Computer games

These include games that can be played on a normal computer, a games console or a mobile phone. Health promotion programmes have developed computer games on health themes that are distributed through CD-ROMs or can be downloaded from internet sites and played on a computer. For example, DCODE was a computer CD-ROM that was developed by the Health Education Authority to teach young people about drugs, and consisted of a series of games that provided information in a fun and entertaining way. The prize for completing the various sections was a computer programme that could be used to create and mix music.

> **Stand-alone computer-based technologies:** Technologies that can be used on their own without being connected to the internet. Most stand-alone computer-based technologies can also be delivered via the internet.

> **Web-based technologies:** Technologies that have to be connected to the internet.

Health-risk appraisal

One of the attractions of computers is that they are non-judgemental, so people can provide personal information without feeling threatened. Health-risk assessment is the term used for the process of collecting epidemiological risk factor information from a person, calculating mortality risks, and providing both feedback on health risks and tailored advice. Typically a person fills out a questionnaire – either on paper or directly onto a computer – and receives specific feedback on screen or as a printout with a personalized message. Such tailored communication is often based on theoretical models of health behaviour, such as the health belief model, the stages of change model and social cognitive theory described in chapter 3, and provides many advantages over 'one size fits all' standardized health promotion approaches. Evaluations have demonstrated the effectiveness of computer-based tailored communications for a wide range of health topics, including nutrition (Brug et al., 1998; Oenema et al., 2001), smoking cessation (Strecher et al., 2005), patient education (Kreuter and Strecher, 1996) and the wearing of hearing protection by factory workers (Lusk et al., 2003).

> **Activity 9.1**
>
> Use a search engine such as www.google.com to find a health-risk appraisal and complete the on-line questionnaire. How useful a process do you think this is?

Computer-generated printed advice

Computers can be used to generate tailored advice based on a patient's clinical records. A randomized trial by Jones et al. (1999) compared tailored advice for cancer patients generated by computer from patient records with leaflets providing standardized information. They found that patients offered the personalized advice were more likely to say that the information was relevant and they had learnt something new.

Touch screens

Touch-screen technology provides an interactive source of information for people who may not have access to the internet. A good example of the use of this for health promotion was the Three Cities Touch Screen Project that was set up in Sheffield, Nottingham and Leicester to reach black and ethnic minority groups. Information on ten health topics (diabetes, heart disease, hypertension, diet, smoking, alcohol, etc.) was developed in five Asian languages, and the machines were installed in libraries, GP surgeries and temples. A screensaver encouraged the user to pick up a telephone handset, and on selecting their choice of language they received instructions on how to use the touch screen to find the information they wanted (Jackson and Peters, 2003). Another example of touch-screen technology was a multimedia health promotion package to be placed in pharmacies, developed by the Department of Pharmacy at King's College, London. This package assessed the user's lifestyle and offered tailored advice on lifestyle change (Hariri et al., 2000).

Web-based health promotion

Information-rich websites

For most people the useful aspect of the internet are websites, which may be:

- websites of organizations involved in health promotion, which contain information about that organization, copies of publications and links to other websites, e.g. the website for the World Health Organization, at www.who.int.org
- websites dedicated to specific health topics – often set up by foundations but sometimes by private companies with advertising, e.g. the Ask Franks website on drugs, at www.talktofrank.com
- databases of bibliographic materials and research tools – the best-known example of which is the site for the National Library of Medicine, at www.ncbi.nlm.nih.gov, which gives access to their vast Medline database of journal articles on medical topics
- portals – websites which serve as gateways to a range of literature, e.g. the Department of Health website at www.dh.gov.uk.

Box 9.1 What do people use the internet for?

The Pew Internet & American Life Project carried out in 2001 a survey of 500 internet users who go online for health-care information (Fox and Rainie, 2001) and found the following:

- 93% of health seekers had gone online to look for information about a particular illness or condition.
- 65% had looked for information about nutrition, exercise, or weight control.
- 64% had looked for information about prescription drugs.
- 55% had gathered information before visiting a doctor.
- 48% had looked for information about alternative or experimental treatments or medicines.
- 39% had looked for information about a mental health issue such as depression or anxiety (up from 26% in August 2000).
- 33% had looked for information about a sensitive health topic that is difficult to talk about (up from 16% in August 2000).
- 32% had looked for information about a particular doctor or hospital.

The widespread availability of websites covering virtually all health topics has revolutionized access to health information and provides the public with a vast amount of specialist information. As early as 2002, a Euro-barometer survey of sources of information on health in the EU found that 23 per cent of people reported use of the internet to get information on health (European Opinion Research Group, 2003). The country with the longest experience of the internet is the United States and, in a national telephone survey in 2002, the Pew Internet Project (Bass et al., 2006) found that almost half of Americans over the age of eighteen (about 93 million) had carried out an internet search on a health topic (See box 9.1 for details of topics of online health searches from their survey carried out the previous year). The impact of the internet in the United States was further demonstrated in a survey of newly diagnosed cancer patients using the National Cancer Institute website. Users of the site were more likely to have prepared questions in advance for the doctor, to ask questions, to express a feeling of being in partnership with their doctor, to comply with treatment regimes and to have a feeling of self-efficacy – i.e. the characteristics that we defined in chapter 1 as being those of a health empowered person.

> **e-health:** the integration of health-care delivery and information delivery through the web and related technologies.

However, the positive benefits from use of the internet for health information need to be set against the possible negative consequences arising from the spread of misinformation due to the unregulated information on websites – especially from those sites with hidden agendas (e.g. those produced by pressure groups, commercial companies or other interest groups). Breast cancer is one of the most widely sought health topics on the internet and a search by Meric et al. (2002) found 600,000 'hits' when the term breast cancer was entered into search engines. However, when

Box 9.2 How to identify a good health promotion website

It should have:
- an easy-to-remember address
- relevance to the users
- frequently asked questions which give the information people are likely to want
- lots of free downloads of video, music and pictures
- images relevant to the topic and the user
- contact information – email, phone number and address.

It should be:
- interactive and not just full of pages that need to be read
- well signposted with links to other websites
- non-judgemental – giving information without passing judgement
- listed on search engines such as Google.

It should:
- not be too cluttered or busy
- not take a long time to download a page
- provide accurate and unbiased information (see box 17.7 for a checklist on how to tell if a website can be trusted).

Understanding how people use the internet helps to target health campaigns more effectively. Young people tend to spend more time than other groups surfing the web.

Activity 9.2

Consider your own experience of using internet websites. Do you agree with the criteria in box 9.2? Are there any criteria that you would like to add or remove from the list?

they reviewed the 200 most popular sites they found that these were not necessarily the ones that provided the highest quality of information. We return to this important issue of quality of information on internet websites in chapter 17, and in box 17.7 suggest quality criteria for assessing sites.

Web-based support groups

Increasingly, people are looking to web-based services for support. Drentea and Moren-Cross (2005) present a case study of an internet-based parents' support network and raise the intriguing question of whether such 'virtual communities'

Box 9.3 How to design websites that appeal to young people

Young people make heavy use of the internet for information, music and communication. Various qualitative research studies (e.g. Gray et al., 2002, 2005a, 2005b) highlight the increasing sophistication of adolescents in using the internet for learning about health. These studies also show that some young people have insufficient heath literacy to discriminate between material that can and that which cannot be trusted, and that there is a need for schools to provide guidance both on medical terms and in developing critical appraisal skills.

The Health Education Board for Scotland (2002) commissioned a research study including both quantitative and qualitative data on the use of the internet by young people in Scotland aged twelve to twenty. The respondents reported being heavily influenced by the style of presentation of websites and preferred sites that had easily digestible amounts of information and were

- more visual than textual
- simple, with language that was easy to understand
- colourful and visually appealing (especially for younger teenagers)
- highly interactive.

The interest of younger respondents was limited mainly to body image, sports/fitness and diet. Older respondents had a broader range of health interests, among them drugs, alcohol and smoking, body shape, sex and personal relationships. They suggested a range of approaches to presenting this information on the internet, which included:

- the provision of tailored programmes of advice
- a confidential email advice service from doctors/health specialists
- an agony aunt/uncle and a problem page with question and answer sections
- chatrooms on a range of topics where young people could swap advice anonymously
- health games and quizzes
- links to other relevant websites.

provide an alternative to person-to-person networks and enhance social capital in society. Mothers joined specific bulletin boards at that website using anonymous aliases in cohorts based on the expected month of their child's birth. There were as many as 500 persons in a cohort. During the course of their pregnancy, birth and post-natal period, mothers posted requests for information, anxieties about their child's development, advice to others and supportive messages to each other. When the births took place, they posted details and sent messages of congratulation to each other. Drentea and Moren-Cross demonstrated that this website was an important source of emotional support – especially for women who were socially isolated and did not get out of their homes very often. The anonymous nature of the bulletin encouraged free expression of feelings and openness.

Consistent with the above study of mothers and parenting, a study of online cancer support groups by Seale et al. (2006) found a similar valuable support role for cancer patients. However, they also showed gender differences in the way men used the support groups for prostate cancer and women used theirs for breast cancer. Men's concerns focused on treatment information, medical personnel and procedures, while women's forum postings centred more on the emotional support and concern with the impact of the disease on other people.

> ### Activity 9.3
>
> What communities and health issues do you think would be suitable for an online support group? What do you consider to be the strengths and weaknesses of online support groups compared with face-to-face support from families and community?

Website access for disabled persons

The internet has opened up many exciting possibilities for health promotion targeted at persons with disabilities. A UK Cabinet Office (2005) report on e-accessibility in the European Union noted that 39 per cent of the population have some sort of disability. However, that same study provided the disturbing findings that 70 per cent of internet sites in the EU were unsuitable for disabled persons and only 3 per cent fully met their criteria for web accessibility to disabled persons. When designing websites it is important to take into account their special needs to ensure the information provided is accessible. One of the best ways of ensuring access is to involve persons with disabilities in the development and testing of websites. The Web Accessibility Initiative (www.w3.org) works with organizations around the world to develop strategies, guidelines, and resources to help make the web accessible to people with disabilities. The advice presented below draws on their valuable and informative internet website.

Visual impairment – This category covers persons who are blind or partially sighted and those with colour blindness. Persons who are blind rely on screen readers and may also use text-based browsers – software that reads text on the internet and connects with a speech synthesizer or a Braille reader. Even partially sighted persons find it difficult to use websites and may need extra-large monitors, screen-enhancement software or particular combinations of text and background colour, such as a bright yellow font on a black background. One in twelve men and one in 200 women are colour blind, and this will affect the way they perceive colour combinations of text and background. A comprehensive set of guidelines on designing accessible websites for visually impaired persons has been produced by the Royal National Institute of the Blind.

Hearing impairment – Persons with hearing impairment make heavy use of the internet, especially for reading newspapers and for communicating with other persons through instant messaging and chatrooms. In designing websites to be accessible to the hearing impaired it is important to provide text transcripts of any audio files.

Box 9.4 How to design web pages to ensure access by disabled persons

- Keep the layout of pages consistent with clear navigation between pages, use headings and links that are easily identifiable, and include a site map that clearly – and in a text format - explains the organization of the site.
- Provide alternatives to frames.
- Avoid flickering, blinking and pop-ups.
- Take care when presenting information in tables to ensure that they make sense when translated by a screen reader.
- Design pages so the fonts can be enlarged easily by the user.
- Keep use of illustrations to a minimum, do not embed text in visuals, and make sure that any information in pictures is also described in words that can be read by a screen reader or provide a sound file that explains it.
- Avoid use of colour as a way to emphasize text on page. Take into account the needs of colour-blind persons when choosing colours or ensure that the user can adjust the font and background colours to suit their personal preferences.
- When essential information is provided in PDF form, also provide an HTML version.

Box 9.5 See it Right

The Royal National Institute of the Blind has established a 'See it Right' logo that it awards to websites that meet its criteria for access for the visually impaired.

Motor impairment – Motor impairment can include physical disability (e.g. from spinal injuries, cerebral palsy or arthritis) and pain that affects the hands and other parts of the body. Depending on their disability, persons with motor impairment might use a range of aids, including pointing devices attached to the head or mouth, voice-recognition software and eye-gaze recognition systems. In designing websites for use by motor-impaired persons it is important to include keyboard alternatives to the mouse and to ensure that sufficient time is allowed for the user to respond to requests for input.

Seizure disorders – Persons with seizure disorders such as epilepsy often turn off animations and blinking text. It is important to avoid flickering between 2 and 55 hz, which can trigger a seizure.

> **Activity 9.4**
>
> Spend some time with a person who has a disability. Ask them if they have any problems using the internet and how they have overcome those problems.

Publicizing a website

It is not enough posting a website – you have to take steps to promote it. One way is to send details to search engines so that it will get listed when people use that search engine to look for specific information. Commercial companies will pay large sums of

DIPEX home page

Members of Arsenal football club using the subject of testicular cancer to promote the Dipex website.

money to advertise their sites. An alternative is to try to get free publicity through writing to local media and newspapers. A useful approach is to launch the site with a publicity event. An example of this was the Dipex health website, which used footballers from Arsenal and the issue of testicular cancer at its launch during Men's Health Week in 2003 (Mayor, 2003).

Activity 9.5

Design an internet website on a health issue and for a target group of your own choice. Decide on the content, any special features and how you would launch it.

Mobile phones

It is possible to set up computer systems that can send a text message to large numbers of users. SMS or text messaging has been used to remind patients to take their medicines and to inform young people on sexual health topics. Receiving unsolicited text messages can be very irritating, so it is important to get permission before including someone's name on a list. Screening programmes for chlamydia for young people are offering the option of receiving test results by text message (See box 2.6 in chapter 2).

Automated dialling

Many of us find it an annoying and frustrating experience to receive telephone sales calls and will probably be critical of their use in health promotion. However, a randomized trial by Corkrey et al. (2005) in Australia found that an interactive automated telephone system increased cervical screening rates by 0.43 per cent at a very low cost per person reached. Unlike the case with commercial cold calling, those running the programme had sent out a letter on official headed paper one week before the call to explain that an automated telephone call would be made. During the call, through a series of interactive key pad prompts, the automated system explained the nature of the call, asked to speak to an eligible woman aged eighteen to sixty-nine, determined her screening status, delivered a message appropriate to that status, offered additional messages to counter common barriers, provided additional information on cervical screening and cancer, gave contact telephone numbers, and offered to arrange for someone to call back if required.

E-learning

The internet provides an ideal medium for distance learning. This could involve online courses which provide a structured learning programme on a topic. Such a course might be a short unit that takes only a few minutes, with immediate feedback through short questions, or a distance learning course spread over a few months which combines interactive sessions on the internet and a task that the learner can complete to receive a form of accreditation towards an academic qualification. A particularly valuable internet e-learning resource is the 'Supercourse', on which thousands of PowerPoint presentations on a wide range of topics in epidemiology, health promotion, behavioural science and other topics are available for the user.

The digital divide

It is easy to get carried away by technology just because it is new. Decisions about choice of technology depend on who you want to reach and what you want to communicate. It is important to make sure that your intended target group has access to the relevant technology. Sections of society being left behind in the information technology revolution – the 'digital divide' - include older persons, persons with little formal education, people for whom English is a second language, the socially disadvantaged and 'technophobes' (Christmann, 2005). The major challenges facing health promotion are the issue of equity and how to address inequalities in health. While information technology has an important place, it needs to be supplemented by other methods if we are to reach the communities who have the most need.

Electronic communication and the future

Will these new technologies replace other channels – especially face-to-face communication? The research study by Drentea and Moren-Cross (2005) described above suggests that the internet can be an important source of social support for isolated mothers, and so enrich social capital in society. However, the internet on its own is unlikely to replaced personalized advice. Hardyman et al. (2005) report on a survey of users of the website and telephone advice line run by the cancer society BACUP. Almost a quarter (23 per cent) of the help-line enquirers in their sample had already sought information from the website before telephoning. The researchers concluded that the website could not completely replace the telephone helpline and that a planned mix of the two is needed.

The unregulated nature of the internet and the lack of quality control of information make it essential to develop the health literacy of all sections of the community so that they become critical consumers of health information from the internet.

With a generation now reaching their teens who have grown up surrounded by information technology and are comfortable with accessing online information on health matters, the scope for using the internet for health promotion is vast. The fast pace of development of new technologies means that by the time this book is printed there may be new developments that did not even exist at the time it was written. By having our own dedicated website for this book we will also make use of this new technology in keeping you updated.

Further reading

The following journal article provides an authoritative overview of the research literature on the use of new technologies in health promotion:

- Suggs, L. S. (2006). A 10-year retrospective of research in new technologies for health communication. *Journal of Health Communication*, 11, 61–74.

This special edition of the journal *Health Education Research* is entirely devoted to research papers on the use of the internet in health education:

- Bernhardt, J. M., and Hubley, J. H. (eds) (2001). Health education and the internet. *Health Education Research – Theory and Practice*, 16, 643–763.

A comprehensive guide on how to take into account the special needs of disabled persons when designing websites is provided in:

- Paciello, M. (2000). *Web Accessibility for People with Disabilities*. Lawrence, KS: CMP Books.

CHAPTER
10 Advocacy

Contents

10 Advocacy

Key issues within this chapter:

- Advocacy to promote healthy public policies is a key health promotion activity.
- A wide range of organizations, including political parties, government departments, local services, voluntary bodies and pressure groups, influence policies on health issues.
- An important objective for advocacy activities is to get health issues on the agenda of policy-makers, the media and the public.
- Effective advocacy involves defining strategic objectives, forming partnerships and carrying out activities such as lobbying, speaking at public events, working with the media and direct action.

By the end of this chapter you should be able to:

- identify, for a given health issue, the different organizations that shape that issue
- understand the processes by which health issues get on the agenda of policy-makers, the media and the public
- develop an advocacy strategy to influence a health issue
- apply specific advocacy methods, including working with the media, public speaking and lobbying.

One of the goals of health promotion is to create supportive environments that help people to make healthy choices. This can involve relatively simple undertakings, such as making healthy foods available at a factory canteen, or complex measures at the national and international level, such as introducing laws to regulate the actions of tobacco companies or the labelling of food products. Advocacy can include actions by individuals, but more often it presupposes individuals and organizations coming together, building alliances and taking collective action. An essential part of advocacy is applying communication strategies to reach policy-makers and gatekeepers at all levels of decision-making, from the community, through the district, regional and national, to the international level.

> **Advocacy for health:**
> A combination of individual and social actions designed to gain political commitment, policy support, social acceptance and systems support for a particular health goal or programme.
> (WHO, 1995)

Policy and health

Among the kinds of policy changes that health promotion may seek to influence are:

- the introduction of new national laws or local by-laws, e.g. to ban a dangerous product
- the enforcement of existing regulations and laws, e.g. for food hygiene in kitchens, or the relaxation of such laws, e.g. so that needle-exchange systems for injecting drug users could be introduced in pharmacies and prisons as part of a harm reduction programme to reduce transmission of HIV
- the actions of health, social welfare and other public services, e.g. to allocate more money and resources to particular issues or to take specific action, such as introducing a crossing at a busy road near a school
- the promotion of intersectoral collaboration, e.g. between health and social services, to address health issues such as child safety
- the promotion of change in private companies, e.g. the environmental policies of multinational companies, the introduction of workplace policies for alcohol and HIV.

> **Health issue:** A health problem that has received mass-media coverage

> **Health agenda:** Health issues in the media, public or policy domain ranked according to the amount of time, attention and importance that they are given in discussion, debate and action.

Influences on health policy in the UK

While government sets the policy, many different groups and organizations (see figure 10.1) compete to influence that policy.

Figure 10.1 Some influences on UK health policy

Government is responsible for legislation and policy on health. Key figures are ministers as well as civil servants responsible for implementing policy. MPs mainly follow the directions of their political party through the system of 'whips', but they also play a role through their participation in advisory bodies and select committees.

Professional bodies, especially the British Medical Association and the Royal Colleges, have considerable influence through contacts with various policy-makers, through participation as invited members of committees and advisory bodies, and through their publications and media advocacy. Trade unions in general, and more specifically those representing health workers, also play a role.

Commercial companies wield considerable influence either directly (e.g. companies such as British American Tobacco) or through associations such as the Confederation of British Industry and the Association of the British Pharmaceutical Industry. They aim to affect policy through their donations to political parties, contacts with politicians, the involvement on their boards of policy-makers, sponsorship of public events, giving of grants to professional associations, and using the media for purposes of advertising and public relations. They may also seek to control policy directly or indirectly through professional lobbying companies. In return for a fee, these lobbying companies use their specialist expertise and understanding to promote their clients' cause, arrange introductions between their clients and policy-makers, and advise on strategies for advancing their clients' interests.

Alongside these organizations are a large range of health groups and alliances of varying influence – some operating within the framework of government on the 'inside', others operating 'outside' on the fringe (Allsop et al., 2004).

Globalization and health

In an increasingly globalized economy, a country's health policy is subject to international influences, both positive and negative.

The European Community, through the Commission, the Council of Ministers, the European Parliament and the European Court of Justice, is increasingly involved in health matters, taking a stance on issues such as control of tobacco and implementing regulations for food products and the work environment. These bodies also have an interest in regeneration programmes and social exclusion.

The United Nations provides the focus for the international community. It influences health through the work of agencies such as the World Health Organization (WHO) and also through conferences such as the Earth Summit at Rio in 1992. The WHO operates at both the international and the regional level. Its headquarters in Geneva provides technical support on health issues, including global responses to emergencies such as avian flu and severe acute respiratory syndrome (SARS), and forms the secretariat for the World Health Summit held in May each year, at which health ministers from all the UN member countries come together to discuss health issues and agree common strategies.

At the fifty-sixth World Health Assembly on 26 May 2003, the 192 members of the WHO unanimously adopted the Framework Convention on Tobacco Control (FCTC), which requires countries to impose restrictions on tobacco advertising, sponsorship and promotion, establish new labelling and clean indoor air controls, and strengthen legislation to clamp down on tobacco smuggling. By January 2006, 116 countries, including the United Kingdom, had ratified the framework convention as part of their national health policy. The framework convention has become one of the most rapidly embraced treaties in the United Nations system. It is the first international treaty negotiated by the WHO representing its commitment to adopting a more active role in health promotion.

The European regional office of the WHO is based in Copenhagen, Denmark, and has been an active force in the development of health promotion in Europe through movements such as the Healthy Cities and Healthy Schools programmes.

A major force in the globalization of health has been the emergence of multinational companies covering areas such as pharmaceuticals, energy, food and tobacco. These companies have considerable influence and their multinational nature and power allows them to escape accountability to governments for their actions.

Many different groups seek to influence government health policy, including voluntary sector organizations representing the interests of patients.

Health movements

An increased awareness of the limits of modern medicine, the blurring of the lay–professional boundaries in health care, government policies promoting the expert patient concept, and partnership working, together with an increased access to health information through the internet, have all contributed to a rise in the number of organizations involved in health activities. Among these are groups campaigning on women's health, AIDS, the rights of mental patients and disabled people, self-care and alternative health, environmental waste and many other issues. Their diverse goals include:

- seeking to change the health-care and public health systems
- seeking to shape priorities in the public funding of research in medical science, in some cases by directly funding research
- promoting the involvement of patients and consumers in the institutions involved in making health policy.

Various overlapping terms have been developed in an attempt to classify and understand the functioning of different groups. Brown et al. (2004) suggest the following three categories:

- **Health access movements** seek equitable access to health care and improved provision of health-care services. These include movements such as those seeking national health-care reform and freedom to choose the kind of health care available.

- **Embodied health movements** involve people who have been directly affected by specific illnesses and build on the insights that they have gained from their personal experiences. These groups challenge the findings of medical science on the cause, diagnosis, treatment and prevention of specific diseases. They also seek to draw attention to, achieve medical recognition of, and channel research funding towards illnesses that are contested by the medical establishment, e.g. Gulf War Syndrome and ME. (ME/CFS/PVFS – myalgic encephalopathy/chronic fatigue syndrome/post-viral fatigue syndrome).
- **Constituency-based health movements** address health inequality and health inequity based on race, ethnicity, gender, class and/or sexuality differences. These groups address both overemphasis on particular health issues/communities and neglect of others. Examples include the women's health movement and the gay and lesbian health movement.

Baggott et al. (2005), in their study of health consumer groups in the UK, suggest a useful three-way classification:

- **condition-based groups** – that focus on specific conditions, e.g. the British Heart Foundation
- **population-based groups** – concerned with patients, carers or a specific population sub-group, such as older people, children or ethnic minorities, across a range of conditions
- **formal alliance organizations** – umbrella groups of autonomous groups linked by a shared interest such as genetics or long-term illness.

Another useful approach, by Whiteley and Winyard (1987), organizes the groups according to the kinds of activities they carry out and, in particular, whether:

- they pursue an 'open strategy', such as lobbying a range of agencies, or a 'focused strategy', which concentrates mainly on specific government institutions
- they are promotional – i.e. they speak on behalf of a group of people, or 'representational', and are actually comprised of persons affected by the health issue
- they are 'accepted' or 'not accepted' by government
- their role is mainly lobbying or as a service provider.

While many health consumer groups carry out some advocacy, the main focus of pressure groups is on this activity. ASH – Action for Smoking and Health – provides a good example of a pressure group. It was set up by the Royal College of Physicians to campaign against smoking and is recognized and accepted by government, which provides funds for much of its work. Other pressure groups, e.g. Greenpeace, work outside the framework of government and have to raise their own funds. Pressure groups approach politicians directly but also seek to raise media and public support for issues through advertising, meetings, public relations, holding media events and direct action.

Pressure group: An organization that seeks to represent interests or preferences in society, has a certain degree of independence from government, and is not a recognized political party. (Baggott, 1995)

Box 10.1 Case study – Health consumer groups in the UK

Researchers in the study interviewed members from thity-nine health consumer groups in the UK across the following five conditions: heart and circulatory diseases; cancer; mental heath; maternity and childbirth; and arthritis and related conditions (Baggott et al., 2005).

When asked what importance they attached to different kinds of activities, the following areas of action scored the highest ratings (in each case percentage refers to the number of organizations citing that particular area of action): providing information (98%), publicity/raising awareness for the condition (97%), providing advice support (96%), influencing policy (84%), building networks (84%), fundraising (84%).

Policy activities they carried out included:

- national awareness weeks
- professional conferences
- networking with civil servants
- lobbying parliament
- responding to enquiries from the media
- actively seeking publicity
- fringe meetings at party conferences
- producing reports
- research.

There are many ways in which members of the public and independent pressure groups can attempt to influence health policy, such as signing petitions to lobby important decision-makers.

Health movements form a sub-group of social movements. A common element is that people come together and create a collective identity based on shared experiences of illnesses and a perception of having been neglected and exposed to discrimination by health services. While many are advocacy-oriented and work within the existing system, others have a more proactive approach and use direct action, including civil disobedience, to express their views.

> **Social movements:**
> Informal networks based on shared beliefs and solidarity which mobilize around conflictual issues and deploy frequent and varying forms of protest. (Della Porta and Diani, 1999)

Health movements have drawn attention to many examples of inadequate and sub-standard care and have been a catalyst for improvement in health services. However, their existence also raises important questions:

- How representative, by ethnicity, gender and socio-economic status, are the memberships of health consumer groups?
- To what extent does the increase in the number of health groups lead to fragmentation and competition? (See discussion on alliances below.)
- To what extent is policy distorted in favour of the health consumer groups who are the strongest and best organized?
- Given that the viability of groups depends on funding, to what extent are the strongest health groups those that follow government policy and therefore receive government funding?

Health movements represent an important new force in modern society, showing commitment, energy and skill in their operation. Health promotion programmes need to identify the movements relevant to their areas of interest, assess their community support and impact, and form strategic alliances to achieve common goals.

> **Activity 10.1**
>
> Make a list of the health movements with which you are familiar. What are their strengths and weaknesses? How do you think you would set about involving them in your health promotion work?

Health agenda-setting

If we can understand the processes by which issues get on the 'health agenda' we can use this information to promote health issues that we feel are neglected but important. One of the major tasks in health promotion is to understand how health concerns become health issues, and why some health issues get discussed and acted upon while others, equally or more important, are ignored.

In their review of agenda-setting, Dearing and Rogers (1996) identify three inter-related domains:

- **media agenda** – the priority and coverage given by the mass media to different issues, reflecting the decisions made by media 'gatekeepers' such as editors of newspapers and television news services on what they consider to be 'newsworthy'

- **public agenda** – the opinions of the public on the important issues of the day and the priorities for action, e.g. as expressed in responses in opinion polls
- **policy agenda** – the issues that policy-makers and legislators feel are the priorities – those that are debated in political and policy arenas and are expressed and acted upon in new legislation, policies, service developments and budgetary allocations.

Health issues often get onto the agenda following an event of some kind that triggers widespread media interest. For example, the death of the film star Rock Hudson of AIDS in 1987, the diagnosis of former US president Ronald Reagan of Alzheimer's disease, the mauling by a lion of the schizophrenia sufferer Ben Silcock, who strayed into the lion enclosure at in London Zoo in 1992, and the death from bowel cancer of a former captain of the England football team, Bobby Moore, in 1993 all led to increased public interest in the particular illnesses. In figure 10.2 we summarize some of the different factors that influence the health agenda.

> ### Activity 10.2
>
> Choose a health issue that has been in the news recently. Make a list of the possible reasons why that topic has received coverage. Choose a health topic that is important but has not received the coverage that you feel it should have done. Why do you think that topic has been neglected?

Figure 10.2 Setting the health agenda

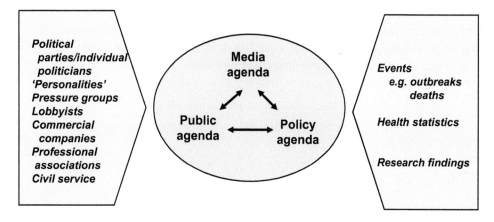

Planning advocacy programmes

You need to start by identifying precisely the cause or issue for which you are acting as advocate. You then need to ask and answer the following questions:

- What is the ultimate objective you wish to achieve?

- What are the intermediate objectives you need to achieve on the way to the ultimate objective?
- Who are the people you need to reach – the decision-makers and gatekeepers?
- At what level do they operate – community, organizational, district, regional, national or international?

Define policy changes needed

Identify key decision-makers/gatekeepers

Form alliances/networks

Prepare advocacy strategy
    Policy-makers
    Public support
    Media

Implement strategy

Review and refine strategy

Figure 10.3
Planning process
for advocacy

Defining policy changes

In deciding the objectives, you need to find a balance between what is desirable, what is absolutely essential and what is achievable given the time constraints and the resources available. Major changes in policy, including the passing of laws, can be complex, time-consuming and involve the parliamentary process. You might be able to achieve your goals through modification of existing policies or changes in the way they are implemented or enforced. For example, the introduction in pharmacies of needle-exchange programmes for injecting drug users was made possible by the police agreeing not to prosecute drug users who came to pharmacies to make use of this facility.

Box 10.2 How to identify key decision-makers, gatekeepers and stakeholders

You will need to identify all the key players for your issue and assess them according to the following questions:

- What organizations influence the health issue with which you are concerned?
- At what level do those influences operate – local, regional, national, international?
- Who are the people who control the decision-making?
- Who is sympathetic to your cause?
- Who is opposing you?
- Whose support is most important to influence the policy change?
- What could be done to increase support and minimize opposition?

Identifying and dealing with influential gatekeepers is often essential to implementing health campaigns. Think of a time when you have needed to negotiate with a gatekeeper. What problems did you face and how did you tackle them?

Identifying key decision-makers/gatekeepers

Gatekeepers: Persons with power and control over specific policies, with access to the policy-making process, or with resources that you may need for influencing policy.

You need to establish who are the key decision-makers or 'gatekeepers' for the policies with which you are concerned. These might be national, local or community politicians, people who sit on key decision-making bodies, civil servants who prepare draft policies, or people who control the agenda of committees that agree on policy. They might also be editors of national and local media who decide on the priorities for coverage of health issues.

Preparation, implementation and evaluation of advocacy strategy

An advocacy strategy is a plan that sets out the policies you are seeking to change, the methods you plan to use to influence that policy, and the timescale involved. For strategic planning methods, see chapter 16.

Forming coalitions, alliances and partnerships

Coalition: A group of like-minded people or organizations that work together to achieve common goals.

The more people you have on your side the greater your influence. Successful advocacy involves collaborative efforts by alliances that bring together the resources, time, energy and talents of many different people and organizations. The study described earlier (Baggott et al., 2005) found that the health consumer groups formed three kinds of alliances:

- **collaborative networks** involving ad hoc meetings held on an occasional and intermittent basis
- **informal alliances** involving regular meetings, sometimes over years, with the sharing of costs but no formal structure
- **formal alliances**, often involving the setting up of national organizations and employing staff to support their work.

Among the benefits of working in alliances identified by the health consumer groups in that study were the sharing of resources; drawing on each other's expertise; gaining access to other networks; and political advantage (i.e. 'strength in numbers').

Despite the many advantages of forming alliances, some barriers need to be overcome, especially differences among the group members according to:

- concepts of health promotion
- agendas, values, visions and aims
- concerns by smaller organizations that they might get swamped by larger ones
- concerns over loss of identity
- competition for funds
- concerns that the alliance might be slower to respond to political events.

Box 10.3 How to form partnerships and alliances

Prepare a list of possible partners – What are their interests? What is their mission statement/vision statement?

Prioritize your possible partners – Who could help you the most? Who is most likely to support your cause given their previous involvement in other issues? What positive features would they see in collaborating with you? With whom do you have contacts? How well are they regarded by other agencies? Do they have a track record of successfully implementing programmes?

Have an initial meeting – At this early stage the first priority is to get to know one another, explore mutual interests, and learn about how activities are planned (e.g. the time of year they develop their annual work plans and how far ahead they plan their activities).

Agree on possible partnership – Prepare a written agreement. Consider adopting a new name for the partnership that is relevant to its aims.

Establish a mechanism for partnership – Set up collaborative structures and communication channels (e.g. regular meetings, planning group, working group, action group, mailing lists).

Plan and implement joint activities – Design activities that use the strengths of each participating agency.

Review impact and plan further activities.

> ### Activity 10.3
>
> Take one of the following health issues: childhood accidents, breast cancer, obesity, the health of elderly people (or a health issue of your choice). Make a list of the organizations you might involve in an alliance. How would you set about forming an alliance?

Lobbying

Lobbying is a general term that covers activities aimed at influencing government and parliament. The term 'government' is used here to refer to the work of the ministers and other members of the government with responsibilities for the different departments in Whitehall and the civil servants that work there. Parliament consists of the wider political institutions, including both the office-holders and the backbenchers within the party in power, the opposition MPs and peers.

Lobbying typically involves actions such as:

- building up a contacts list and regularly sending out information, briefings and resource packs on key issues
- holding briefing meetings for politicians on health issues
- inviting MPs and peers to join the management board of your organization and to become patrons
- holding fringe meetings at party conferences
- forming a parliamentary officers' group around a health theme – e.g. the Mental Health Parliamentary Officers' Group, which meets on a regular basis
- participating in, and giving evidence to, the various advisory committees (e.g. the Advisory Committee on the Microbiological Safety of Foods), reference groups, royal commissions and public inquiries that the government sets up in Whitehall
- responding to requests by government to comment on consultation papers, including Green Papers (*Our Healthier Nation* was a Green Paper sent out in 1988 for consultation; it was followed in 1999 by the White Paper *Saving Lives*, which set out the policy that was drafted taking into account that earlier consultation).

Working with the press

As we discussed earlier in this chapter, and also in chapter 7, the media play an important role both in setting the agenda for health issues and defining and shaping the way the public and policy-makers view them. Working with the press is an important advocacy activity and you need to understand the way the media work and how you can get them to support your issues. In the 'how-tos' over the next few pages we present some basic tips on working with the media. If you want to develop this further in the course of your work you should make links with journalists and public relations experts who can help you to develop a media strategy.

Box 10.4 How to use local and community media

Read local papers and listen to local radio. Make a note of the names and email addresses of the journalists ('bylines') and broadcasters that cover health issues. For each type of media ask the following questions:

- What is their coverage in the community? Who reads/listens to them? What ages/ethnic groups?
- When are they listened to?
- What topics do they like to cover?
- On what days do they cover health topics?
- Who are the writers/presenters for health topics?

- Write to congratulate them on articles you approve of.
- Write in to tell them about what you are doing.
- Ask if you can meet up.
- Feed them stories that they might find interesting.
- Offer to give reactions to news stories.
- Don't pretend to be an expert on something you are not.
- Give them a local community angle to their health stories.

Box 10.5 How to plan a media event

Your aim is to get the press to give your activities priority and send a photographer to take that all-important picture that will make people read the story. Research your media. What things make it to their front page? What topics receive more column inches? What secures the big headlines?

Timing – Find out their deadlines and choose times accordingly. If you are targeting evening papers, plan your activities to be in the morning. Avoid clashes with competing events.

Be newsworthy – The media will only cover topics that they perceive are interesting, timely (a 'hot issue'), follow on from a previous story, contain human interest and deal with people, consist of tragedies, scandals, political intrigue or cover-up, concern famous people or people of local interest (a soap opera star will get more coverage than a politician!), or involve 'David and Goliath' conflicts between authorities and individuals.

Impact – Try for something unusual or unexpected, such as interesting pictures or catchy phrases or 'sound bites', and use slogans on a banner or placard which summarize the main points in a few words.

Give interviews – Find suitable spokespersons from the local community. Provide their contact details to the press and make sure that they are available (see the 'how-to' on giving interviews below).

The best way to let the media know what you are doing is by preparing a 'press release'. This is a written document of not more than one page in length, neatly typed with an attention-getting headline. It should provide information on what you are doing by answering the following questions:

- *What will be happening?* Describe the event. Give the names of important people participating and any details of activities that might make a good photograph.
- *Why will it take place?* Give background details; explain why the activity is taking place. Supply some facts and figures that can be quoted in a story (e.g. how many children died in road traffic accidents last year in that community).
- *Where will it take place?* Give precise details of how to get there.
- *When will it take place?* Give the date and time of day.

Box 10.6 How to speak in public

You may need to speak in public to convince a group of people why they should support your issue or to motivate your colleagues to continue to give support. With practice everyone can acquire skills in public speaking.

Plan the content carefully in advance. It takes a lot of expertise to write a speech that flows naturally. Rather than writing your complete speech it is better to jot down on cards or a sheet of paper the main points you want to get across and improvise the dialogue.

Watch experienced public speakers in action and learn from their example. A speech usually has three parts:

- the *beginning:* you tell them what you are going to say
- the *main part:* you say what you want to say
- the *ending:* you summarize the main points.

Speak loudly and clearly. Use body language – look in the faces of your audience and gesture (but not too much!). Make it interesting. Smile. Don't speak with the same tone of voice all the time: lowering your voice or using pauses is a good way to attract attention. Time your delivery with pauses so you can breathe. Use a microphone if available, but take care not to hold it either too far away so that it does not pick up, or too close so that there is distortion.

Here are some tips that professional speechwriters use.

- suspense: '*I have one more thing to say …*'
- rhetorical questions: '*How many of you have tried to …*'
- analogies: '*Safe sex is like …*'
- repetition: '*Education, education, education …*'

- triads – groups of three points: '*The three things we need to remember are …*'
- anecdotes: '*Last week I met someone with a …*'
- humour: '*I am reminded of the story about …*'

When dealing with difficult questions:

- answer as honestly as possible – if you don't know, don't be afraid of saying so (but avoid sounding weak and apologetic)
- get the audience on your side ('*That's a really tough question*')
- throw the question back ('*What do* you *think we should do?*')
- change the subject (but not too obviously!)
- do not get sidetracked by questions or allow them to interrupt the flow ('*Would you mind if I deal with that later?*')
- flatter the questioner ('*That's a really good question*')
- take questions in groups of three or four. In that way you can deal with the easy ones first and hopefully run out of time before you get to the more difficult ones!

Box 10.7 How to use the internet for advocacy

Set up a website:

- Provide information on your issue, such as a calendar of events, details of meetings, critical dates when policy decisions are being made by authorities, suggestions for letter-writing to decision-makers.
- Set up an online petition to which people can add their name.
- Invite visitors to your website to send an email describing their own advocacy activities and views about the topic.
- Compile a page of frequently asked questions (FAQs) on your issue.
- Include a web forum on which people can post and exchange messages.

Set up a list serve:

This is a system by which people subscribe online to receive regular email updates on issues and post responses and comments.

- You can use the list serve to build up a list of sympathetic people.
- You can encourage members to use the list serve for networking and sharing information on new developments in research, legislation and forthcoming media coverage.
- You can send alerts to encourage action, e.g. when a policy decision is being made, when a letter to a policy-maker or contact with the media would be appropriate, or when there are forthcoming activities, such as meetings being held.
- You can 'cross-post' emails to several discussion list serves to reach an even wider range of people. But make sure that the message you are sending is relevant to the objectives of each list serve so that you do not irritate the members with unwanted emails.

See also discussion of the internet in chapter 9.

Direct action

Direct action involves working outside the framework of conventional politics and in extreme cases deliberately breaking the law in order to highlight one's cause. Examples of direct action are the occupation in 1995 by the environmental group Greenpeace of the Shell Oil 4,000 tonnes storage and loading buoy Brent Spar to prevent it and its load of toxic and radioactive sludge being dumped into the North Sea; and the 'surfers against sewage' protest in 1990 involving activists in wetsuits and gas masks surfing in polluted coastal waters.

One person famous for his use of non-violent protests was Mahatma Gandhi. The methods he used to fight injustice and advance the cause of freedom for India are well worth studying as models of action. His approach, which he called *satyagraha*, meaning 'truth force', involved a range of methods, including hunger strikes, boycotts, sit-ins, strikes, mass 'stay at homes' and *civil disobedience* – which is the deliberate breaking of laws and being willing to go to prison for causes that one's conscience feels to be just. The aim is to capture the public's imagination by striking, symbolic acts and the honesty, conviction and sacrifice of those taking action. Direct action is most successful when it is staged as a media event and attracts press coverage.

Box 10.8 Case study – The BUGA UP direct action campaign

An example of direct action in health promotion was the Billboard Utilizing Graffitists Against Unhealthy Promotions (BUGA UP) campaign against tobacco advertising in Australia. This campaign started in 1978 and in the years up to the introduction of Australia's national ban on cigarette advertising in 1994 drew attention to the marketing of tobacco products using humour, parody and direct action, including:

- defacing tens of thousands of tobacco advertising billboards. This involved changing slogans, e.g. from 'Marlborough' to 'It's a bore'; from 'Enjoy your freedom' to Enjoy your cancer'; from 'John Player Special' to 'Lung Slayer Special'. Copies of some of the best changed billboards were put on T-shirts and posters and were widely circulated, especially among young people.
- setting up parody organizations, e.g. an 'Advertising Double Standards Council'.
- in 1982, when the Philip Morris tobacco company set up a search for an Australian Malborough Man, entering into the competition an elderly man in a wheelchair who still smoked through his tracheostomy
- busking as the 'Royal Carcinogenic Orchestra' outside a tobacco-sponsored series by the Royal Philharmonic Orchestra
- using a small plane to sky write 'Cancer country' at the men's singles final of the 1984 Malborough Open Tennis Championship.

BUGA UP captured the imagination of the country and had a Robin Hood effect, which helped to create a climate of opinion that led to Australia becoming a world leader in tobacco control measures. Inspired by this example, various copycat movements with highly inventive acronyms started in other countries. Among those in the UK were COUGHIN – Citizens' Organization, Using Grafitti for Health in Neighbourhoods – in Bristol and TREES – Those Resisting an Early End from Smoking – in London.

(Chapman, 1996)

Activity 10.4

Which health issues do you think might be serious enough to justify taking direct action? For one of these issues, suggest some direct actions that you could take as one part of health promotion advocacy.

Advocacy and debates in health promotion

While some form of advocacy is necessary for most health promotion activities, it is particularly important when adopting health empowerment approaches addressing social and structural factors operating at the national and international level. Advocacy is also the most difficult area of health promotion action, as it involves controversy, risk, exposure to criticisms, reprisals and – in the case of direct action – even imprisonment. Some of the lessons are that:

- there may be little you can do on your own to address a particular health issue. Find people with more influence and power who will support your case.
- it's always easier to ignore, discipline and attack individuals. If you are dealing with something controversial it is better to have your views coming from a *group* of people rather than named individuals, who can be exposed and publicly attacked
- it's much easier for officials to ignore criticism if no evidence is presented. So always support your case with accurate information. Include specific examples, with testimonies and photographs, of the harm that is being done by a particular policy.
- issues often have international dimensions and involve multinational companies. In that case you should form links with groups in other countries and international agencies. You should harness the power of email and the internet to link up with others who feel the same way you do and will support you.
- if your cause is a just one, you will have the support of a network of well-wishers within your country and abroad. Don't give up!

Activity 10.5

Choose a health issue and apply the systematic approach to advocacy planning shown in figure 10.3, working through each step. What difficulties do you think you might face in implementing this strategy and how could you overcome them?

Further reading

For a review of the mass media's role in determining which topics are at the centre of public attention and action, see the following:

- McCombs, M. (2004). *Setting the Agenda: the Mass Media and Public Opinion.* Cambridge: Polity.

The following two books by one of the pioneers of studies of media advocacy provide detailed analysis of the way in which the mass media can be used to influence the health agenda and frame public opinion:

- Wallack, L., Woodruff, K., Dorfman, L., and Diaz, I. (1999). *News for a Change: An Advocate's Guide to Working with the Media.* Thousand Oaks, CA: Sage.
- Wallack, L., Dorfman, L., Jernigan, D., and Themba-Nixon, M. (1993). *Media Advocacy and Public Health: Power for Prevention.* Newbury Park, CA: Sage.

PART III

Defining Health Promotion Strategy

Settings in Health Promotion

11 Community Settings

Contents

CHAPTER 11 Community Settings

Key issues within this chapter:

- The community is an important setting for health promotion.
- Communities can be defined in many ways, including by geographical boundary area, as an administrative area covered by a service, as a social network or as a group of people with shared characteristics.
- Many influences on health operate at the community level, among them norms, social networks, patterns of leadership, culture, religion, housing and environment.
- Working at the community level opens up opportunities for health empowerment and building up the capacity of communities to participate in meeting their health needs.
- The process of working at the community level involves the following stages: dialogue, making a community profile/needs assessment, and entry, initial and follow-up actions.

By the end of this chapter you should be able to:

- critically assess the potential of the community as a setting for health promotion
- understand the influences at the community level and be able to make a community profile
- describe the process of systematically working with communities to develop community participation and health empowerment.

'Working with – and for – communities to improve health and wellbeing' was one of ten areas of operation that the UK Faculty of Public Health considered core areas for public health practitioners in the UK. Many of the influences on health as well as opportunities for change operate at the community level. We need to take health promotion to where people live and spend their leisure time.

What is a community?

The term 'community' has many overlapping meanings, including:

- a neighbourhood – a group of houses within a defined geographical boundary. This might be a housing estate, a single block of flats, an inner-city area or a rural village.
- an administrative unit – for example, community services as distinct from hospital services, or the smallest unit in which the responsibilities and workload of a particular service might be organized (social work, school, domiciliary midwife, environmental health officer, etc.)
- a political unit – i.e. the basic unit that is used for political purposes, such as the constituency for an MP or a council ward.
- a social network of people that interact with each other (see chapter 3 for an introduction to social networks)
- a group of people with shared characteristics and similar needs, such as persons of a particular age (e.g. teenagers), an ethnic group (e.g. persons of Bangladeshi or Caribbean origins or Romanies), persons with a particular illness (e.g. diabetes) or persons sharing a particular sexual orientation (e.g. gay and lesbian). These may or may not live in the same neighbourhood – more typically they live across a city. This aspect of community overlaps with the concept of culture and subculture.

> **Community:** A specific group of people, often living in a defined geographical area, who share a common culture and who are arranged in a social structure according to relationships which have developed over a period of time. Members of a community gain their personal and social identity by sharing common beliefs, values and norms that have been developed in the past and may be modified in the future. They exhibit some awareness of their identity as a group, and share common needs and a commitment to meeting them. (WHO, 1998)

In this chapter we will take 'community' to mean neighbourhood, social network or group of people, while recognizing that this sometimes, but not always, overlaps with a community defined by administrative or political boundaries.

Outreach

Outreach is the most basic kind of work at the community level. The outreach worker might be a specially employed person, such as a health visitor, a social worker, a salaried community worker, a health trainer or a volunteer/peer educator recruited from the target community. This individual can target support and care directly to those with the most need and also serve as a bridge between community members and services. Probably the best-known outreach worker is the health visitor – now called a specialist community public health nurse (SCPHN).

> **Outreach:** Programmes where people go out into homes and other community settings to carry out health promotion activities.

Home visiting in the first two years of a child's life has been shown to have beneficial effects. A Cochrane systematic review by Bull et al. (2004) found that home visits by professionals or trained lay care-givers resulted in decreased rates of childhood injury and may possibly reduce rates of child abuse, incomplete immunization, hospital admission and childhood sickness.

Figure 11.1
Concepts and disciplines that provide the theoretical basis for community work

Community action for health: Collective efforts by communities which are directed towards increasing community control over the determinants of health, and thereby improving health.
(WHO, 1998)

Community development

Adult education theory and Paulo Freire

Primary health care and community participation

Self-help movement

Inequalities in health and social exclusion

Social networks and social capital

Partnership

Health promotion in community settings

The theoretical basis for community work

Work at the community level draws on the various traditions/disciplines summarized in figure 11.1.

Community development

Box 11.1 Community work

Community work is essentially concerned with affecting the course of social change through the two processes of analysing social situations and forming relationships with different groups to bring about some desirable change. It has three main aims: The first is the democratic process of involving people in thinking, deciding, planning and playing an active part in the development and operation of services that affect their daily lives; the second relates to the value for personal fulfilment of belonging to a community; the third is concerned with the need in community planning to think of actual people in relation to other people and the satisfaction of their needs as persons rather than to focus attention upon a series of separate needs and problems.

(Younghusband, 1968)

Community development in the United Kingdom derives from a range of community-based initiatives, most notably the community development projects initiated by the Home Office in the 1970s. Useful books setting out very clearly the methodology of working with communities were published, for example, Henderson and Thomas (2002) and Batten and Batten (1967). Most of these programmes involved action on housing, child care and the environment, but an increasing number in the health sector began to adopt principles of community development.

Adult education theory, community empowerment and community capacity

Health promotion at the community level draws heavily from adult and non-formal education theory – most notably from the work of the Brazilian adult educator Paulo Freire. Freire's approach to education evolved from his experience of adult literacy education with poor peasant communities in north-east Brazil. An important part of his approach was to make people aware that they created their own culture and therefore had the power to transform their surroundings.

> **Community health empowerment:** Individuals acting collectively to gain greater influence and control over the determinants of health and the quality of life in their community. It is an important goal in community action for health. (Adapted from WHO, 1998)

Freire was deeply critical of traditional top-down approaches of education and instead advocated a problem-posing approach involving dialogue between the community and educator: 'In problem-posing education, people develop their power to perceive critically the way they exist in the world with which and in which they find themselves; they come to see the world not as a static reality but as a reality in process, in transformation' (Freire, 1972). He advocated an approach to education which he called '*conscientization*', in which members of the community are encouraged to critically reflect on their situation and how they might transform it through action. This process he called 'praxis'. The term 'health empowerment', which we introduced in chapter 1, is broadly similar to that of conscientization. A related term, 'community capacity', has recently entered the discourse and provides another useful way of defining the aims of working at the community level to improve health (Norton et al., 2002).

> **Community capacity:** The sum total of understanding, skills and organizational structure that enable a community to identify, mobilize and address social and public health problems. (Adapted from Norton et al., 2002)

> **Activity 11.1**
>
> Make a list of the kinds of actions you would expect from a community that was empowered to improve its own health. How many of these might arise of their own accord and how many might require some kind of external support to initiate?

The self-help movement

Another influence on health promotion at the community level comes from the growing awareness of the value of self-help groups. One of the best examples of this has been the women's health movement, but self-help groups exist for virtually every health issue (See chapter 6 for more on setting up and supporting self-help groups). The initial focus of most self-help groups is on meeting the needs of its members. Once these are met, many groups move on to take up a campaigning approach to advocate for policy change and improved services (see chapter 10 on advocacy).

Among the wide variety of community groups are playgroups, often set up by parents themselves to provide child care and opportunities to try out new activities and make new friends.

> **Box 11.2 How to classify community groups**
>
> *Self-help groups*: groups run by people for their own benefit, such as cooperatives, stop-smoking groups, mother and toddler groups, playgroups
>
> *Representative groups*: groups elected by and answerable to the community, e.g. community associations, tenants' groups
>
> *Pressure groups*: groups of self-appointed citizens taking action on what they see to be the interests of the whole community – such as exerting pressure to improve the school, get rubbish collected or do something about a dangerous road
>
> *Traditional organizations*: well-established groups, usually meeting the needs of a particular section of the community, such as Rotary Club, Mothers' Union, Parent Teachers Association
>
> *Faith-based groups*: churches, temples, mosques or other religious organizations
>
> *Social groups*: groups that exist mainly to put on social events, e.g. sports clubs, music groups, carnivals, *melas*
>
> *Welfare groups*: groups that exist to improve welfare for others, e.g. supplying meals on wheels, night shelters for the homeless
>
> *Cultural groups*: groups held together by their cultural or ethnic background

Primary health care and community participation

The importance of community participation was a central focus of the concept of primary health care adopted at the World Health Assembly at Alma Ata in 1976. There is growing awareness of the potential value of these approaches for the industrialized developed nations (HDA, 2000a).

Inequalities in health and social exclusion

Concern about inequalities in health since the Black Report in 1980 (see chapter 1) has led to greater interest in community-based approaches. Early explanations of inequalities in health were based on victim-blaming notions such as people indulging in health-damaging behaviours. These have given way to more sophisticated understandings in which individual behaviours are seen in the context of social exclusion and structural forces in society.

Social networks and social capital

Social networks were introduced in chapter 3 as sources of information, social pressure and support/home care and provide one of the most useful ways of defining and describing communities. Depending on the community, social networks can involve a couple, parents and children, grandparents, other relatives or the whole community.

The importance of economic capital – income and wealth – in tackling poverty and inequalities in health has long been recognized. However, in recent years a greater awareness of the beneficial role of social networks has led to the introduction of the concept of social capital by agencies such as the World Bank (Campbell et al., 1999), which defines it as 'the institutions, relationships, and norms that shape the quality and quantity of a society's social interactions ... social capital is not just the sum of the institutions which underpin a society – it is the glue that holds them together.' Indicators used to measure social capital have included the amount of volunteering that takes place, community support structures, community trust in civil organizations, and the absence of violence and crime. Putnam (1995) goes on to say that 'by "social capital" I mean features of social life – networks, norms and trust – that enable participants to act together more effectively to pursue shared objectives.' Recent developments have broadened the concept of social capital to involve three dimensions – *binding* within a community, *bridging* between communities, and *linking* to the wider world.

The implications here are that health promotion should seek to build on and strengthen social capital in communities, which in turn will increase community capacity to provide mutual support and care (Kawachi, 1997).

Social exclusion: A term to describe the structures and dynamic processes of inequality among groups in society. Social exclusion refers to the inability of certain groups or individuals to participate fully in life due to structural inequalities in access to social, economic, political and cultural resources. These inequalities arise out of oppression related to race, class, gender, disability, sexual orientation, immigrant status and religion. (Adapted from Galabuzi, 2002)

Social inclusion: Activities designed to address social exclusion.

Activity 11.2

Take a community with which you are familiar. What are the current social networks and social capital in that community and what effect do they have on the health of the members? Suggest some ways in which the capacity of social networks and social capital could be strengthened.

Coalitions, partnerships and intersectoral collaboration

Partnership: Local collaboration by statutory, voluntary, community and private-sector organizations in planning and implementing economic, social and health programmes. (Henderson et al., 2004)

The term community coalition has been used for structures through which organizations or groups collaborate and work together for a common purpose. Another term used for this is partnerships. National health policy in the United Kingdom promotes partnership to foster 'intersectoral collaboration', i.e. communities, health services, local authorities, the private sector and voluntary organizations working together for a more effective deployment of effort (see figure 11.2). Such 'joined-up thinking' involves addressing the many barriers to collaboration, notably administrative and organizational, and those deriving from different professional values (Miller, 1998).

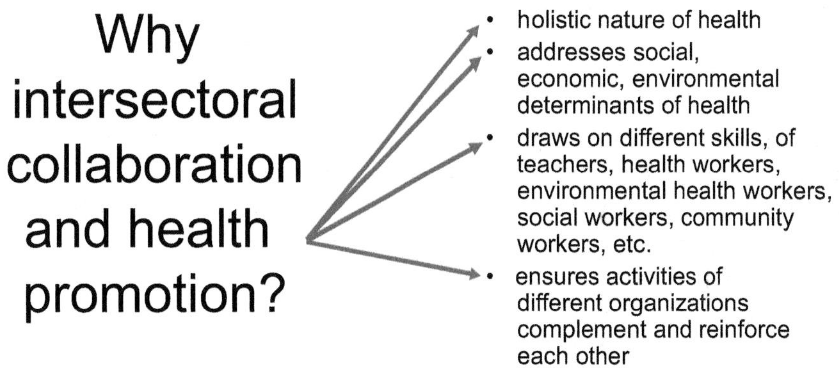

Figure 11.2
Benefits of intersectoral collaboration

Why intersectoral collaboration and health promotion?

- holistic nature of health
- addresses social, economic, environmental determinants of health
- draws on different skills, of teachers, health workers, environmental health workers, social workers, community workers, etc.
- ensures activities of different organizations complement and reinforce each other

Despite its obvious benefits, intersectoral collaboration can be difficult to achieve for a number of reasons:

Intersectoral: Activities that bring together in joint action different sectors, e.g. education, health, environment, industry.

- separate agendas and priorities of different departments
- different geographical boundary areas between departments
- lack of a forum for joint meetings, pressure of work making it difficult to find mutually convenient times for meetings and lack of encouragement from senior management for field staff to allocate time for meetings
- lack of trust between different departments because of previous experiences, specific personalities of staff and competition for the same funds

- lack of a shared value/vision of needs and different perspectives and core values
- issues of confidentiality that prevent sharing of information
- confusion over respective roles in health promotion.

Building blocks for community-level health promotion

Health promotion practice at the community level draws together a number of ideas or 'building blocks' which are represented in figure 11.3, taken from the HDA manual on Developing Healthier Communities (Henderson et al., 2004), which in turn draws on the work of Barr and Hashagen (2000).

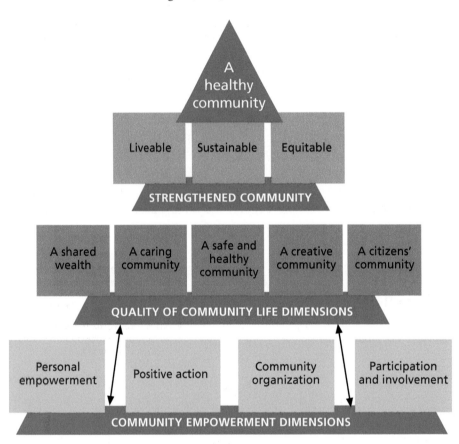

Figure 11.3
Building blocks for community development

Assessing the level of community participation

The terms 'participation' and 'involvement' are used very loosely to cover a wide range of activities. The American planner Sheryl Arnstein developed a measuring scale that gives at one end complete participation and at the other manipulation, where the community is given the illusion it is making decisions but in reality is being manipulated. Somewhere in the middle is consultation – asking the community's opinions but making the decisions yourself (Arnstein, 1969). You can use the simple checklist in box 11.3 – adapted from the work of Rifkin et al. (1988) – to estimate how much participation is taking place in a particular programme.

> ### Box 11.3 How to estimate how much participation is going on in a community programme
> - *What* activities and decisions does the community participate in? Is it involved in evaluating any of the activities?
> - *How* are priorities decided? Who makes the decisions?
> - *Who* controls the budget? Are community members involved in the management body/committee? If so, how are they chosen? Are they accountable to the rest of the community?
> - *Who* participates? Are all sections of the community represented – men, women, young people, ethnic groups?

Working with communities

Many community programmes go through a process of evolution which follows the stages in figure 11.4. This involves a cycle of initial actions, further actions, then evaluation, reflection and further actions.

Figure 11.4 The community development process

Further actions

Community capacity-building, setting up community organizations, the selection and training of community volunteers, resource mobilization and fundraising

Entry

Get to know the community: make contacts, find out about the local community. Use a range of data collection methods, including rapid appraisal. Work with existing groups, and where no groups exist bring people together.

Initial actions

On a topic which is achievable and a felt need shared by many people (used to build up the confidence of the community and trust in the field staff)

Evaluation, reflection and further actions

Community participation in evaluation, learning from experiences, community action planning

Entry

The entry stage involves finding out about the community so that you can plan appropriate activities. Details of the information that is helpful in making a community profile are given in box 11.4. Some of this may already be available in the form of records, published surveys or newspaper reports, but it may need to be supplemented by data gathered directly from the community through surveys, interviews with key informants, and community groups. It is helpful to use a mix of data-collection methods and compare ('triangulate') the results.

Box 11.4 How to decide what information you need for a community profile

The information required to plan a health promotion intervention depends on the health issues you are concerned about, but will usually involve the following:

Structure of the community
- numbers of houses, families, people
- age, cultural and ethnic mix
- employment/unemployment
- housing
- social networks

Organizations/resources/stakeholders: details of their previous history, present level and potential for future involvement in health promotion; felt and expressed needs; willingness to support health promotion
- pharmacies, health centres, GPs, health visitors, environmental health officers
- social services and other community services
- voluntary organizations working in the community
- leisure facilities, play schemes/playworkers
- leisure centres/sports facilities
- complementary medicine practitioners
- shops, cafes and other focal points
- community media, local newspapers
- clubs, associations, churches, mosques
- organizations such as scouts/guides/brigades
- youth groups
- community arts groups
- community groups, residents' associations

Sources of information (triangulation of data from the following)
- records of agencies
- previous local surveys
- newspaper reports
- minutes of local councils and community groups
- participatory rapid appraisal – mapping, seasonal calendars, problem ranking
- key informants, e.g. councillors, health workers, local leaders, long-established residents
- meeting with community groups

Activity 11.3

Using the list in box 11.4 as a guide, build up a profile of a community with which you are familiar. What does the information in your profile tell you about the health promotion needs and the kinds of actions you might be able to undertake?

Building up a profile of the local community is essential for planning community-based campaigns. For example, a busy market or shopping centre could prove to be a useful setting for health promotion activities.

Stakeholder: Anyone in a community with a vested interest in a particular issue.

Stakeholder analysis: The process of identifying local stakeholders, determining how they think about what is needed, what they feel about the activities you would like to carry out and whether they will give you support.

PRA (participatory rural appraisal): A method for collecting data on community needs that uses both qualitative and participatory approaches. Increasingly the alternative term PLA (participatory learning and appraisal) is used.

As part of this initial phase it is helpful to carry out a stakeholder analysis. Primary stakeholders are community members or beneficiaries of the proposed community health action, e.g. the elderly, youth, members of a minority group. Secondary stakeholders are other organizations and groups with a vested interest and who might affect the success or failure of your activity. Another name for these persons is gatekeepers. These will also depend on your activity and might include teachers, police, local GPs, community groups, churches, mosques, etc. Key stakeholders are those who will make a big difference to the success of the programme – or who could oppose it and prevent things from happening!

You can use many different methods to collect community data. Qualitative methods such as focus-group discussion are particularly useful for finding out community perceptions about the causes of problems and the scope for action. Quantitative information will give information on the size of a problem (see discussion of qualitative and quantitative information in box 3.6).

A useful approach is to encourage communities to describe their health needs using visual formats, community drama and games/exercises. There is growing interest in the use of participatory research and rapid appraisal collection methods, which were pioneered in developing countries (Rifkin and Pridmore, 2001). PRA is a process of working with a community over a few days or longer. Members of the community are encouraged to undertake a series of activities, which includes describing their community using both written and visual formats; mapping local resources, reflecting on their present status; and considering priorities for change (Ong et al., 1991; Murray et al., 1994; Jones, 1997).

Initial actions

You need to take care when choosing initial topics for community action. The aim is to encourage actions on issues that most people agree are problems, are held widely as felt needs, and can unite people in a common purpose. It is also important to choose goals that can be achieved in the short term, that will provide an immediate sense of achievement, and that will strengthen confidence to take on more ambitious aims. You may need to discourage communities from tackling issues that are difficult and for which there is divided opinion and so less chance for success.

Further actions

Building on the momentum and self-confidence of initial successes, other activities can be planned which might include more difficult and longer-term actions. As a consequence of those initial actions, individuals from the community may emerge as leaders and take on more extended roles in community activities. At this stage you might provide some training to introduce new skills and build community capacity. It might also be appropriate to build up community structures such as committees, form associations and recruit more community members. Alongside planning new activities, this stage often involves mobilizing local resources, fundraising and applying for grants.

Evaluation, reflection and further actions

Conventional evaluation methods such as randomized trials are difficult in community settings – especially when the community is involved in planning activities and setting targets. Health promotion at the community level emphasizes the concept of evaluation as an ongoing 'iterative' process of determining impact, learning lessons and using insights gained to redefine activities. Data are collected by community members, the various field workers involved in the actions, or external evaluators who are sensitive to the process-oriented goals of working at the community level. This kind of research has been called participatory evaluation or action research. The rationale for it comes from the ideas of Paulo Freire discussed above – especially praxis – which emphasize the importance of the community reflecting and learning from action. It also has roots in qualitative research and the participant observation methodology employed by sociologists and anthropologists to research communities.

An important aim of heath promotion in community settings is the development of processes such as participation, enhanced community capacity and health empowerment. It is important to choose indicators for evaluation that include measures of community participation such as those described in box 11.3.

Healthy cities programme

Under the auspices of the World Health Organization, a network of cities has formed where each has agreed to work towards the implementation within its own community of the vision of a healthy city (Davies and Kelly 1993; Farrington and Tsouros, 2006).

Box 11.5 What is a healthy city?

A healthy city is one which addresses the following issues:

- *Social environment* – the fostering of social networks and social capital through its layout, housing patterns, opportunities for interaction
- *Physical environment* – good air quality, waste collection, sewerage, water supply
- *Leisure/recreation* – green spaces, leisure facilities, playgrounds, sports facilities
- *Housing* – quality housing at affordable prices, freedom from overcrowding
- *Safety* – safe roads, crossing points, enforcement of road-safety measures
- *Security* – protection of the public, policing, freedom from crime
- *Health services* – accident and emergency services, preventive services, primary-care services
- *Food* – availability, pricing, quality control, food hygiene.

Activity 11.4

Consider a city that you know well. Make a list of the features that you think contribute to the health of the community in that city and another list of those which detract from health. What actions would you take to make it a healthy city?

Area-based regeneration

Among the common features of recent government initiatives to address inequalities and social exclusion in local communities are the use of small-area statistics to determine needs (see chapter 2); partnership between health, local authority and other agencies; improvement of services; and a commitment to working with community groups. Two recent examples of area-based approaches are the Neighbourhood Renewal Programme (Social Exclusion Unit, 2001; Neighbourhood Renewal Unit, 2002) and Health Action Zones (HDA, 2004a).

Peer education is particularly useful when working with certain tightly knit networks and communities, such as student or friendship groups.

Working with volunteers and peer education

One of the main resources in community-based programmes is the community members themselves. Community projects aim to involve local people and tap their interest, expertise and enthusiasm. This involvement could emerge spontaneously or it can come about through a deliberate programme of recruitment of volunteers. When volunteers come from within the target community, the term *peer education* is used to describe the approach. Peer education is particularly useful when working with tightly knit networks where it is difficult for outsiders to be accepted, such as drug injectors, prisoners and sex workers. Peer education has also been used to reach young people in community settings.

> **Peer education:** Community programmes in which members of a community or group of people are recruited, trained and supported to carry out health promotion among their peers.

Community arts and health

Community-based activities have often involved the arts – drama, music, the visual arts and murals. Activities based around the arts have the potential of involving everyone – regardless of age, background or ability – uniting a community and developing pride and self-confidence together with a greater self- and community awareness. Arts activities range from those with groups in a local community to the organization of larger-scale events such as festivals, carnivals and *melas* (HDA, 2000b).

Through their impact on social inclusion, empowerment and self-esteem, arts activities have clear relevance for health even if they do not explicitly address specific health topics. However, in recent years there has been growing interest in using community arts activities as an entry point for health promotion. This might involve the painting of murals, performing dance and drama, writing stories or producing an art exhibition – all with health themes. Community arts promote health in different ways. Firstly there is the impact on the persons involved – the process of researching the health issue and developing an arts activity provides many valuable learning opportunities. Secondly there is the impact on other members of the community who view performances and paintings, read stories, etc. Community arts approaches used in health promotion can include the following:

- **master class** approach – an arts instructor or artist in residence works with members of the community to develop a performance, an art exhibition, a book of stories – either through a one-off production or through the creation of an ongoing performance group
- **cooperative community approach** – community members cooperate to produce one single piece of art, e.g. a community mural
- **studio approach** – a studio is set up, with guidance available, open to all to come and produce their own work of art
- **health promotion agency as commissioner** – a health promotion agency hires a performing arts group to prepare a production on a health issue that is then shown in various community settings, e.g. community halls, schools, etc.

Theatre is a particularly powerful medium because of its impact on both performers and audience. Performers can be encouraged to research the topic and improvise the content and the audience can be invited during the course of the drama to comment on what is happening and suggest different actions that the characters might follow. Using the approach of Paulo Freire described above, theatre can be used to portray real situations and the audience can be stimulated afterwards to identify with the characters portrayed, reflect on the situations raised, and consider what action they could take to deal with the issues.

Box 11.6 Some examples of community-based initiatives

Breastfeeding welcome here – Northern Ireland

Businesses which are open to the general public, such as coffee shops, restaurants, shops, supermarkets and hairdressers, were invited to join the scheme and display a prominent sign with the logo and words 'Breastfeeding welcome here'. In order to join, they must fulfil the following criteria:

- breastfeeding should be acceptable in all areas open to the general public
- a mother who is breastfeeding would not be asked to stop breastfeeding or to move to another area to feed
- all staff members should made aware that the business is a member of the scheme.

'It's a goal!' Mental health promotion in a local football stadium in Macclesfield

A psychiatric nursing service was set up in Macclesfield town football stadium to carry out mental-health promotion with young men. The programme consisted of a six-week series of group sessions which used imagery from football to raise mental-health issues. An evaluation based on interviews with the participants in the group sessions found a high degree of acceptability for the approach (Pringle and Sayers, 2004).

Community cafe on a housing estate in South-East England

A local tenants'/residents' association received a grant from the council to set up a community cafe in a shopping centre on a housing estate. The purpose of the cafe was to provide food on a not-for-profit basis and also to act as a meeting place for community members, including elderly and young people. An evaluation was carried out with support from the Health Education Authority, using interviews and focus-group discussions with customers and volunteer workers. It found that the cafe fulfilled its aim of providing a meeting place, but the uptake/impact of the provision of food was less clear-cut (Kaduskar et al., 1999).

Doorstep walks to promote physical exercise in Salisbury

An alliance, called the Salisbury Walking Forum, consisting of various local organizations, including the Rambler's Association, the Wiltshire Wildlife Trust, the city council and the Salisbury Health Promotion Unit, was formed to promote brisk walking. It produced 2,000 information packs with details of ten local walks and information on the benefits of regular exercise which were distributed through leisure centres, libraries, social service departments, GP surgeries and health centres. An evaluation surveyed all local persons who had requested a copy of the pack. Of 229 returned questionnaires (71% response rate), 61% indicated that they had used the packs to plan walking activities; almost half of those had done six or more walks. Three-quarters of those who had used the pack said that participation in the initiative had improved their enjoyment of exercise (Vernon and Brewin, 1998).

The Edinburgh women's health shop

The women's health shop in Edinburgh opened for sixteen months with the aim of providing information in a high-street location. It was staffed by two health visitors, two clerical assistants and a community worker who all worked on a part-time basis. The shop was open for three and a half days each week. Materials – including fact sheets and books – were on display together with an exhibition and video. Any woman with a medical or personal enquiry (17% of women visiting) was seen in a private room by the nurse. During the lifetime of the project the shop was visited by 5,664 women and 400 men, an average of twenty-four people each working day. The most popular topics for discussion were women's health problems (Robinson and Roberts, 1985).

The community setting and debates in health promotion

Community development emphasizes health empowerment approaches, so it is perhaps not surprising that its use has been controversial and has posed many challenges. A difficulty often faced is how to ensure a genuine partnership between the various organizations involved and the community. This is especially so when stakeholders have different values and approaches, especially along the coercion–persuasion–health empowerment continuum that we highlighted in chapter 1. The potential conflict between the medical model and social model of health is particularly apparent when a programme is set up around a particular health issue which, while being based on government policy, may not necessarily reflect community priorities. This tension – and the mismatch between community development ideals and reality – was highlighted in a qualitative research study of the 'Breathing Space' scheme that was initiated within an urban regeneration programme. In response to a request by local community groups, this sought to target community norms on smoking in a low-income area in Edinburgh through working across four settings: community, primary care, workplace and youth. The study found that not all partners had an equivalent level of involvement and that the community did not necessarily see smoking as a priority issue within the context of their other needs. Health services did not fully understand the social dimensions of the community-development and health empowerment approach and tended to focus on activities that targeted individual behaviour change (Ritchie et al., 2004).

It would be wrong to claim that community participation can overcome all the problems facing communities. Some health educators have been criticized for emphasizing community development and health empowerment while ignoring action to deal with structural influences on health that operate at regional, national and international levels. Government policies and the forces of globalization can only be tackled at national and international level.

Community participation is not always a feasible strategy. You may not have the time yourself or have access to other fieldworkers for the demanding task of working with local communities, holding dialogue or supporting community organizations. Then you may have no other choice but to make use of the mass media, schools and health facilities. In urban areas, your target group may be scattered throughout the city, so it is not viable to bring them together for common action, and an outreach approach may be best. However, in many situations a genuine community-based approach is both desirable and possible – *but can only be achieved if you plan for it.* This involves considering the processes and strategies presented in this chapter and the guidelines in box 11.7.

Box 11.7 How to implement health promotion in community settings

- Base the programme on an understanding of the local community and their felt needs.
- Identify and involve all the relevant stakeholders.
- Set up a partnership structure with the involvement of the community.
- Brief all partners on concepts of community participation and health empowerment.
- Use well-trained fieldworkers who understand participatory approaches.
- Have flexible, open-ended objectives and a realistic timescale.
- Build in dialogue and participatory learning experiences.
- Provide support and training for volunteer lay workers.
- Involve the community in evaluation.

Further reading

A collection of essays by leading figures in the field of community devopment that provides a comprehensive overview of the theory and the application of the principles and practice of community development and its role in the health empowerment of communities is:

- Minkler, M. (ed.) (1997). *Community Organizing and Community Building for Health.* New Brunswick, NJ: Rutgers University Press.

For a comprehensive introduction of community-development approaches in health promotion with clear guidelines on action, see the following:

- Henderson, P., Summer, S., You, C., and Raj, T. (2004). *Developing Healthier Communities: An Introductory Course for People using Community Development Approaches to Improve Health and Tackle Health Inequalities.* London: Health Development Agency.

For a discussion of community organization and its contribution to building social capital, see:

- Gittell, R., and Vidal, A. (2002). *Community Organizing: Building Social Capital as a Development Strategy.* Thousand Oaks, CA: Sage.

CHAPTER **12** Health-Facility Settings

Contents

12 Health-Facility Settings

Key issues within this chapter:

- Health facilities are important settings for health promotion.
- There is a need to improve the quantity and quality of health promotion provided within health facilities.
- Health promotion activities include patient education and outreach from health services into communities.
- Well-planned programmes of tailored patient education are necessary to promote adherence to medication, adoption of lifestyle changes, utilization of health services and informed decision-making on self-care.

By the end of this chapter you should be able to:

- critically assess the potential of health facilities as a setting for health promotion
- describe the role of health promotion in key health settings – hospitals, pharmacies and primary care
- be able to plan a programme of patient education for a health setting.

The settings approach and health facilities

Health promotion should be an integral part of all health activities – public or private, curative or preventive, community or hospital, inpatient and outpatient. Depending on the kind of facility it is and the community that it serves, its specific contribution will include a mix of the following:

- health promotion activities with members of the community that come for treatment, preventive services, counselling, etc.
- communication between health staff and inpatients and outpatients on treatment, use of medicines, self-care
- rehabilitation and self-care of patients and families after major illnesses and surgical procedures
- outreach health promotion by staff to the surrounding community.

Activity 12.1

Take one of the following settings and make a list of the different ways in which it can be used for health promotion.

- Pharmacy in high street
- GP surgery with nurse, health visitor, community midwife, district nurse, health trainers
- Health centre
- Cardiac rehabilitation unit
- Outpatient physiotherapy unit
- Children's ward
- Maternity hospital

Box 12.1 A health promoting setting

A health promoting facility will:

- consider the needs of the community in which it is located, including specific health problems, ages and ethnic mix, and have health promotion activities that meet those needs
- treat the patients and staff with respect and a high degree of professional service.
- maximize the potential of the entire setting for health promotion, including waiting areas, cafeterias, toilets and encounters of staff with patients/families
- have clearly defined health promotion and patient-education responsibilities for everyone working in the setting
- have a staff-development programme in health promotion with opportunities for training, sharing of experiences and support.

Primary-care settings

GPs, either in their own practices or in health centres, practice nurses, health visitors, pharmacists and health trainers all operate in primary-care settings. Health promotion within primary-care settings involves a combination of all or some of the following:

- educational work carried out with patients in order to assist in their treatment and recovery as well as with healthy persons accessing preventive services, such as family planning, antenatal care, child immunization/child health clinics
- well-person clinics that invite healthy persons to come for health promotion activities
- outreach activities in the community through home visits
- community-based activities working with schools, environmental health services, social services, care institutions
- community development working directly with neighbourhood and community groups.

The patient journey:
The pattern of use/uptake and movements between formal and informal health-care workers and services by a patient during the management of their illness.

Box 12.2 How to recognize a health promoting waiting area

A waiting area should:

- be comfortable, relaxing and not too noisy
- be clean with sufficient accessible seating
- have activities for children (and magazines for adults!)
- keep appointment times and minimize delays
- keep people informed how long they will have to wait
- make information available (e.g. have leaflets to pick up, relevant posters on walls)
- treat patients as people, not objects
- recognize patients with anxieties and provide information and help.

Patient education

Structured patient education: A planned course that covers all relevant aspects of the health issue, i.e. is flexible in content, is relevant to a person's clinical and psychological needs, and is adaptable to a person's educational and cultural background. (Adapted from Department of Health, 2001b)

As shown in box 12.3, there are many points of contact between the public and staff in health facilities. Patient education, the term used for health education carried out with patients in health-care settings, can involve one-to-one or group sessions with patients and also – where appropriate – with partners/relatives of patients. It should form part of all contacts between persons in health-care settings and be tailored to the specific needs of the patient. While it is carried out by health workers (e.g. doctor, dentist, practice nurse, attached health visitor, district nurse and pharmacist), even non-medical persons (e.g. receptionists, cleaners, catering staff) have a potential role in providing information. Patient education can be integrated into the normal patient–health worker consultation process but can also be carried out as a separate individual or group session or indirectly through media, displays, take-home materials and leaflets in waiting areas.

Box 12.3 Number of daily contacts between the public and the NHS

Point of contact with public	contacts per day
Consult GP or practice nurse	890,000
Total community contacts	315,000
Outpatient attendances	122,000
A & E attendances	44,000
In bed as emergency admission to hospital	996,000
Courses of NHS dental treatment for adults	74,000
In bed as elective admission to hospital	38,000
NHS sight tests	26,000
NHS direct calls	18,000
Walk-in centres	4,000
Ward attendances	3,000

Source: Department of Health, 2004.

Depending on the health topic and the needs of the individual, patient education can be used to achieve all or some of the following outcomes:

- providing specific information about a health topic
- imparting specific skills, e.g. injections, preparing foods, etc.
- ensuring correct use of medicines and recognition of possible side effects
- managing symptoms, e.g. pain
- inducing specific lifestyle changes required for rehabilitation, e.g. smoking, alcohol, weight reduction
- allaying anxieties/teaching stress management
- building confidence (self-efficacy).

Activity 12.2

Use the list above to suggest objectives for patient education for one of the following topics:

- asthma patient
- child with diabetes
- person with HIV/AIDS receiving anti-retroviral drugs
- middle-aged woman with high blood pressure
- spouse worried about the mental health of their partner

Patient education serves a number of different purposes. It can be particularly important for ensuring patients' compliance with the use of prescribed medication.

We discussed the theory and practice for one-to-one and group communication and the use of tailored communication approaches in chapters 5 and 6. The use of printed materials, such as leaflets in patient education, was considered in chapter 8 and electronic media in chapter 9.

Box 12.4 How to help people to use medicines properly

One of the important priorities of patient education is to ensure that patients adhere to prescribed doses. Medicines are only effective if people take the correct dose, at the right time and under the right conditions (e.g. with or without food) for the total time necessary to achieve complete treatment. Following medication regimes may be particularly complicated for patients with chronic conditions, who may have to take a wide range of medicines, each with its own specific conditions. Studies of patient compliance suggest that people may not take their medicines properly/complete the dose for the following reasons:

- they do not understand the treatment regime (inadequate or non-existent instructions)
- they forget
- they experience side effects
- they lack commitment to the specific medicines prescribed

- they cannot open the packaging
- they find the tablets too difficult to swallow
- they are feeling better and do not see the need for completion
- they have travelled away from home and did not take the medicines with them.

Some helpful strategies
Review the medical prescription:

- Are more appropriate drug regimes available, e.g. shorter times for completion of treatment, or longer-acting drugs to reduce the number of times someone needs to take medicine?
- Is a more acceptable presentation possible, e.g. sugar coated or liquid form?
- Is modified packaging necessary, such as blister packs which set out pills in correct order/combinations, rather than screw-topped containers?

Explain carefully:

- Spend time explaining the importance of adherence and help people to choose strategies that can help them.
- Provide clear instructions in written or pictorial form about how and when to take the medicine.
- Involve partners or other family members so they can remind the patient if appropriate.
- Discuss the use of reminders, e.g. text messaging, calendars to put on the wall, pill boxes compartmentalized for the various medicines, to assist the patient.

Who should implement patient education?

Health promotion should be integrated into all patient–health worker encounters, whether with doctors, nurses, health trainers or other persons. However, it is sometimes appropriate to carry out patient education sessions in other contexts, e.g. as group health promotion sessions. An important question is who should run these sessions? The evaluation of the impact of smoking cessation advice offered by doctors provides evidence of the high credibility given to doctors. However, the heavy load of GPs considerably restricts the amount of time they can spend with their patients. Nurses have more time and, provided they have the direct support of the GPs, can also have high credibility. A randomized control trial of 1,173 patients with heart disease from nineteen general practices in Scotland investigated the impact of nurses running secondary prevention clinics, which involved the monitoring of blood pressure and lipid cholesterol levels, promoting aspirin use, undertaking lifestyle assessment, and providing advice on heath behaviours. At the end of one year patients attending the clinics showed significant gains (Campbell et al., 1998).

Opportunistic health promotion

People without symptoms may also use primary-care services for a range of reasons, including family planning, antenatal care, immunizing children, flu injections, and to get sick notes. While they come for a specific reason, this provides a good opportunity to discuss other relevant matters, e.g. weight, smoking, diabetes, etc.

Health promotion debates and health settings

In chapter 1 we considered debates in health promotion, in particular medical and social models of health, individualistic and structuralistic approaches, and the role of coercion, persuasion and health empowerment. Much of what takes place under the name of patient education is carried out within the medical model or the individualistic, persuasive or 'patient compliance' strategy. However, increasing attention is given to health empowerment approaches in which the communication between health provider and patient shifts from information *transfer* to information *exchange* (Lee and Garvin, 2003) – see box 12.5.

Box 12.5 Approaches to patient education

	Patient-compliance approach	Health empowerment approach
Alternative names used in the field to describe the approach	Persuasive Individualist	Patient empowerment Expert patient
Conceptual model	Medical model	Health empowerment model
Perception of the patient	Patient is irrational, passive, forgetful and incompetent. Patient's role is to follow advice given by health-care worker.	Patient is expert in their own needs and active participant in process of recovery.
Approach	Paternalistic Patients are not interested in controversies but want the doctor to make decisions on their behalf.	Empowering Patient is seen as responsible and interested in their health and wants to be a partner in the decision-making process. Patients have a right to information.

Box 12.5 *continued*

	Patient-compliance approach	**Health empowerment approach**
View of needs of patients	Patients need simple information that is clearly presented to match their educational level and reading skills. Health workers need to decide what information should be given to patients. Information presented should be evidence-based.	Patients need information that will help them to decide what is best for themselves to do. Patients are the best persons to decide what information they need.
Objectives for patient education	To remedy deficits in information of patients, to promote compliance with medicines, to promote appropriate use of health services, including reduction in demand.	To promote patient satisfaction, appropriate self-care and informed decision-making and to reduce anxiety.

Activity 12.3

Consider the two approaches to patient education outlined in box 12.5. List what you consider the strengths and weaknesses of each. What approach do you consider appropriate?

The expert patient

With improvements in overall health status and greater longevity, there are increasing numbers of people living with a long-term chronic illness, such as cancer, heart disease, stroke, arthritis, mental illness, diabetes and asthma. The *expert patient approach* is a core element of national policy for supporting people with chronic illness (Department of Health, 2001b). Using techniques such as self-management, discussed in chapter 5, the expert patient approach (see box 12.6) represents a shift towards patient-centred care which assigns a key role to health promotion and health empowerment.

The expert patient: An approach that sees the patient in a partnership role with the health provider in taking decisions about the management of his or her condition.

Box 12.6 Vision for a successful expert patient programme

The Department of Health (2001b) set out the following vision for a successful expert patient programme:

- Many more patients with chronic diseases improve, remain stable or deteriorate more slowly.
- Many more patients can manage effectively specific aspects of their condition (such as pain, complications, use of medication).
- Patients with chronic diseases who become expert are likely to be less severely incapacitated by fatigue, sleep disturbance and low levels of energy.
- Most patients with chronic diseases have skills to cope with the emotional consequences of their disease.
- Many people with chronic diseases gain and retain employment.
- Many more patients with chronic diseases successfully use health promoting strategies (for example, improving diet, exercise, weight control).
- Most patients with chronic diseases are effective in accessing appropriate health and social care services.
- People with chronic diseases make greater use of adult education and employment training programmes.
- Many more patients with chronic diseases are well informed about their condition and medication, feel empowered in their relationship with health-care professionals, and have higher self-esteem.
- People with chronic diseases spend fewer days a year as hospital inpatients or attending outpatient clinics.
- People with chronic diseases contribute their skills and insights for the further improvement of services.
- People with chronic diseases work as counsellors, information workers and advocates for others.

Activity 12.4

Consider the vision for a successful expert patient programme set out in box 12.6.
Make a list of the different ways in which a health programme might support the realization of this vision.

The well-person clinic

Well-person clinics deliberately invite people to attend for health promotion activities such as screening and health education. They have been targeted mainly at adult men and women – especially those in late middle age, at the time of the onset of chronic illnesses, but have also been successfully used with adolescents (Walker et al., 2002). Many GPs have age–sex registers of their patients which make it easy to identify and contact those persons of a particular age and risk category. A typical well-person clinic will start with some kind of health risk appraisal to screen for conditions appropriate for that age group. For the older adult this might be blood pressure, blood serum cholesterol or diabetes, and to explore existing patterns of health and risk factors in their family history and lifestyle, e.g. weight, diet, alcohol consumption and smoking. This is followed up with a tailored mix of activities that combines treatment for specific conditions with support for lifestyle change.

Box 12.7 How to run a well-person clinic

Well-person clinics are run for different sections of the community – men, women, the over fifties, adolescents – and involve the following decisions:

Who should be invited?
All persons in the community who fit the chosen category of provision.

Who should run it?
It depends on the focus, but either a nurse or doctor – preferably of the same gender/age/ethnic background as that of the users.

Activities to carry out
- Check for general health, e.g. hypertension, diabetes, cholesterol, eye health, sexual dysfunction.
- Find out and respond to any special concerns, e.g. about personal life, sexual health, parenting and work.
- Provide advice where appropriate on exercise, smoking, diet and alcohol and other concerns. Advice should be non-judgemental and practical.
- Provide help on how to put advice into practice, e.g. how to give up smoking, what kinds of exercise are appropriate, how to modify food intake.
- Refer people to other agencies in the community, e.g. fitness centres, leisure centres, walking groups, food cooperatives, smoking clinics, self-help groups, social services, citizens' advice bureaus.
- Involve the partner where necessary (and with the client's permission), e.g. on lifestyle changes.

The pharmacist

Pharmacies are an under-utilized but valuable resource for health promotion in the community. They are open all day and see both sick and healthy people, and their location in high streets makes them highly accessible. Many people use them as a first point of enquiry if they have a health problem and find them more accessible than their GP. Pharmacists can advise individuals when self-medication with over-the-counter medicines is appropriate and when they should see a doctor. Pharmacists can also explain the use of medicines and any possible side effects.

A survey which found that community pharmacists had a high level of knowledge about folic acid and often saw women planning pregnancy earlier than both GPs and midwives was the trigger for the 1996 national folic acid campaign by the Health Education Authority in England. Increasingly, health promotion programmes have explored different approaches for involving pharmacists. Touch-screen information systems and leaflets provide useful sources of information for topics on which people might be shy to ask the pharmacist directly. In a useful review of the role of pharmacies in health promotion, Anderson (2000) describes a range of initiatives involving community pharmacies, including setting up health-information centres, lending

Community pharmacists have a high level of knowledge about medicines and their side effects and are a valuable, if under-used, resource for health promotion.

libraries with books and videos, providing advice about stopping smoking, providing counselling on health issues, holding a women's health afternoon, and lunchtime talks.

While pharmacists have a high level of understanding of health issues, they may need training in health promotion and communication skills. Sinclair et al. (1997, 1998) trained community pharmacists in Grampian, Scotland, in smoking counselling based on the stages of change model (see chapter 3). An evaluation found that customers who were counselled by trained pharmacists were significantly more likely to have stopped smoking after nine months than customers of pharmacists who had not received the training.

Box 12.8 Using pharmacy shop windows to promote emergency contraception

Hammersmith and Hounslow Health Authority and the local pharmaceutical committee approached local pharmacists to include a display on emergency contraception in their front window and make leaflets available inside. During the four-week campaign, enquiries about emergency contraception increased threefold and those about pregnancy doubled. The number of emergency contraceptives distributed during the campaign increased. Most persons making enquiries were teenage females. (Sharma and Anderson, 1998).

Activity 12.5

Visit your local pharmacist. Make a list of the various ways in which it is involved in health promotion. Suggest ways in which the quantity and quality of health promotion could be improved.

The hospital as a setting

Although they are seen mainly as places for treatment and curative care, hospitals have the potential to act as a major resource for health promotion in their communities – with inpatients in hospital wards and their visitors, outpatients, persons attending at special clinics (e.g. genital urinary) and those using accident and emergency services. Health promotion can prepare the patient for surgery and for discharge home, brief partners/relatives on home support, and reduce the likelihood of recurrence and the need for future treatment. Admission to hospital is a traumatic experience involving considerable upheaval; it can be a major event in a person's life course and provides a point for taking stock of one's lifestyle and making changes. Health promotion can alleviate this stress and maximize the health benefits of the experience. Links can be promoted between hospitals, primary health care and community services. For example, accident and emergency services deal with the acute impact of alcohol-related violence, injuries in the home, poisonings, and road traffic accidents, but preventive measures and rehabilitation services are located in the community. It is important that effective links are made so that people attending accident and emergency departments are given information about where they can receive further health promoting advice and support.

Activity 12.6

Think of a hospital that you have visited or in which you have been a patient. Make a list of the various ways in which health promotion could be carried out in that hospital. Compare your list with the actions in the Budapest Declaration in box 12.9.

The health promoting hospital

The health promoting hospital movement applies the settings approach to hospitals. The movement started in Europe and its aims were set out in the Budapest Declaration in 1991.

Box 12.9 Budapest Declaration on Health Promoting Hospitals 1991

Beyond the assurance of good quality medical services and health care, a health promoting hospital should:

1 provide opportunities throughout the hospital to develop health-oriented perspectives, objectives and structures
2 develop a common corporate identity which embraces the aims of the health promoting hospital
3 raise awareness of the impact of its environment on the health of patients, staff and community. The physical environment of the buildings should support, maintain and improve the healing process.
4 encourage an active and participatory role for patients according to their specific health potentials
5 encourage participatory, health-gain-oriented procedures
6 create healthy working conditions for all staff
7 strive to make the health promoting hospital a model for health services and workplaces
8 maintain and promote collaboration between community-based heath-promotion initiatives and local governments
9 improve communication and collaboration between existing social and health services in the community
10 improve the range of support given to patients and their relatives through community-based social and health services and/or volunteer groups and organizations

11 identify and acknowledge specific target groups (e.g. age, duration of illness, etc.) within the hospital and their specific health needs

12 acknowledge differences in value sets, needs and cultural conditions for individuals and different population groups

13 create supportive, humane and stimulating living environments, especially for long-term and chronic patients

14 improve the health promoting quality and the variety of food services for patients and personnel

15 enhance the provision and quality of information, communication and educational programmes and skill training for patients and relatives

16 enhance the provision and quality of educational programmes and skill training for staff

17 develop an epidemiological database specially related to the prevention of illness and injury and communicate this information to public policy-makers and to other institutions in the community.

The principles in the Budapest Declaration were later expanded into the Vienna Recommendations on Health Promoting Hospitals, adopted at the third Workshop of National/Regional Health Promoting Hospitals Network Coordinators, held in Vienna on 16 April 1997.

In 2004 the European region of the World Health Organization published a set of standards for health promotion in hospitals which they had piloted in **thirty-six hospitals in nine European countries (WHO, 2004a). The standards are related to the patient's pathway and define the responsibilities.**

- **Standard 1** demands that a hospital has a written policy for health promotion. This policy, which is aimed at patients, relatives and staff, must be implemented as part of the overall organization quality system and is aiming to improve health outcomes.
- **Standard 2** describes the organization's obligation to ensure the assessment of the patients' needs for health promotion, disease prevention and rehabilitation.
- **Standard 3** states that the organization must provide the patient with information on significant factors concerning their disease or health condition, and that health promotion interventions should be established in all patients' pathways.
- **Standard 4** gives the management the responsibility to establish conditions for the development of the hospital as a healthy workplace.
- **Standard 5** deals with continuity and cooperation, demanding a planned approach to collaboration with other health service sectors and institutions.

Effective communication between health workers, patients and their families is a core element of health promotion in hospitals. In box 12.10 we list in full the objectives and criteria used for Standard 3.

Box 12.10 Standard 3: Communication with patients on hospital wards

Objective:

To ensure that the patient is informed about planned activities, to empower the patient in an active partnership in planned activities, and to facilitate integration of health promotion activities in all patient pathways.

3.1 Based on the health promotion needs assessment, the patient is informed of factors impacting on their health and, in partnership with the patient, a plan for relevant activities for health promotion is agreed.

3.2 Patients are given clear, understandable and appropriate information about their actual condition, treatment and care and factors influencing their health.

3.3 The organization ensures that health promotion is systematically offered to all patients based on assessed needs.

3.4 The organization ensures that both information given to the patient and health promoting activities are documented and evaluated, including whether expected and planned results have been achieved.

3.5 The organization ensures that all patients, staff and visitors have access to general information on factors influencing health.

Facilitating the treatment and recovery of patients in hospitals

Hospitals are under pressure to discharge patients as early as possible into the community to free up beds for other patients. Health promotion can play an important role in preparing people for hospital, speeding up recovery and enabling the patient to function to his or her potential, minimizing recurrence of the condition and future demands on hospital services (see box 12.11).

Box 12.11 Case study: Smoking cessation programme in surgical pre-admission clinics

A pilot study by Haddock and Burrows (1997) evaluated the impact of a nurse running a smoking cessation programme in surgical pre-admission clinics at the Chesterfield and North Derbyshire Royal Hospital NHS Trust in Chesterfield. The intervention consisted of a single face-to-face individual counselling session lasting 20 to 40 minutes given by a nurse to thirty patients. As control, thirty other patients received the routine information normally provided at such clinics. Patients in the intervention group were also given a leaflet and provided with advice about smoking cessation aids such as nicotine replacement therapy, referred to their GPs and practice nurses for advice about smoking cessation clinics, and given a diary to record their smoking behaviour. The evaluation found that the intervention had a significant impact, with 80 per cent of the persons in the intervention group stopping or reducing smoking compared with 50 per cent of the control group.

Communication with patients on hospital wards

In box 12.12 we provide some practical guidelines on working with people in hospital and speeding the recovery process.

> **An empowered patient:**
> A patient who has the necessary information, skills and confidence to play an active role in their recovery.

Box 12.12 How to help your patient get better

- Provide any information they need, both verbally and through leaflets, to speed up their recovery.
- Give them a chance to practise any skills they will need to help their recovery and reassure them that they can do what is necessary.
- Give them encouragement. Boost their confidence but keep expectations realistic.
- Find out if they have any concerns or anxieties and try to deal with them.
- Get them to think ahead and find out if there are any obstacles that might prevent them putting your advice into practice. Discuss possible strategies to overcome those obstacles.
- Explain about any medicines they need to take. Discuss practical strategies for remembering medicine procedures such as timings and dosages.
- Tell them where they can get help (e.g. from telephone advice lines).
- Suggest that they join a self-help group – give them details.
- Ask them to invite a partner, relative or friend to come in and participate in your advice session.

Maternity hospitals

The maternity hospital is unusual among hospitals because the users are healthy persons. Health promotion at this point can have a beneficial impact on the health of the mother, the process and outcome of childbirth, and the future health of the baby. As discussed in chapter 4, childbirth is a major event in the lives of families when parents are highly receptive to suggestions for actions on health matters. Health promotion in maternity hospitals takes place during antenatal clinics, as part of 'parent-craft' sessions (see box 4.5 on the content of antenatal education) and during the period the mother is with the newborn baby in the hospital. The Baby Friendly Hospital initiative is an international movement to reorient maternity hospitals so that they provide maximum support for breastfeeding. Broadfoot et al. (2005) carried out a survey of thirty-three maternity units in Scotland and 464,246 infants who were born in them between 1995 and 2002. Babies born in a hospital that had received the UK Baby Friendly Hospital award were 28 per cent more likely to be exclusively breastfed at seven days of post-natal age than those born in other maternity units. Breastfeeding rates had increased significantly faster in hospitals which had achieved Baby Friendly status.

Critical issues for health promotion in health-care settings

While health-facility settings have a considerable potential for health promotion, the reality often falls short of this ideal.

Uptake of health services

One of the major challenges is to ensure that the people who have the greatest need make full use of health services and their health promotion activities. Alongside the cultural and psychological barriers reviewed in chapter 3 are the effects of social exclusion. A contributing factor to social inequalities in health is the under-utilization of health services – especially preventive services such as immunization, antenatal care and screening. The radical GP Julian Tudor Hart (Tudor Hart, 1971) coined the term 'inverse care law', which states that the people who need services most are least able to use them. Any activity to increase health promotion in health-care settings needs to be accompanied by measures to ensure that the services are used to their full potential by those sections of society with the greatest need.

> ## Box 12.13 Case study: Barriers to the uptake of services for coronary heart disease (Tod et al., 2001)
>
> In a research study in Yorkshire, qualitative research was carried out with patients with stable angina, primary-care staff and community groups and identified six barriers that prevented or delayed people taking up health services.
>
> 1 *Structural* – difficulties in transport and access to health services, inconvenience of location of surgery and opening times, appointment systems with difficulty in contacting the surgery by phone, the need to wait a few days before seeing a doctor, the absence of a nurse-led clinic and perception of the general practitioner as always busy.
> 2 *Personal* – fear of the consequences of diagnosis of illness, denial of illness and resort to self-management.
> 3 *Social and cultural* – local social mores that overvalued self-reliance, coping with pain, stoicism and tolerating extreme discomfort.
> 4 *Past experience and expectations* – previous bad experiences of person or family members resulting in low expectations of health services.
> 5 *Diagnostic confusion* – when people did not make the connection between symptoms and health problems (e.g. breathlessness was attributed to lung problems and not the heart; pain was wrongly perceived to be arthritis).
> 6 *Lack of knowledge and awareness* – lack of knowledge about the causes, treatments and risk of heart disease and a low perception of the risk due to low visibility of the disease.

> ### Activity 12.7
>
> Suggest activities that could be instigated to address the issues in box 12.13 and increase uptake of health services by marginalized and socially excluded communities.

Reasons for unwillingness of staff in health facilities to carry out health promotion

- Health workers may feel that they are too busy with seeing patients and do not have the time for health promotion.
- Some feel that people who use well-person clinics are mainly the professional social classes, the worried well and people of lower risk.
- Some health workers do not believe that health promotion can actually change behaviour.
- Some are reluctant to advise patients to change their behaviour because they feel that it is a moral intrusion into people's lives.
- There are limited cash incentives for general practitioners to carry out health promotion.

> ### Activity 12.8
>
> Imagine you were working in a situation where the health-service staff were unwilling to become involved in health promotion for the above reasons. What could you do to address their concerns and convince them of the value of increasing their involvement?

Realizing the potential for health promotion within health services

Health promotion within health-care settings has a valuable role to play, but increasing its quality and quantity requires a planned systematic approach. This entails defining the contributions that health promotion can make; identifying any barriers and taking appropriate actions to overcome them; obtaining the involvement and participation of staff and patients; providing training opportunities and support for health-care staff; and changing services to make them more accessible and appropriate. A critical issue is the need to move from a medical model of health towards the expert patient concept, with its emphasis on partnership between heath-care staff and patients. This means challenging the traditional attitudes and assumptions of both health-care workers and patients/clients. Another barrier is the inevitable inertia that is experienced within any organization towards the introduction of change. We discuss the process of management of change within institutions in chapter 16.

Further reading

For a discussion of the role of health promotion for pharmacists, see:
- Blenkinsopp, A., Panton, R., and Anderson, C. (1999). *Health Promotion for Pharmacists*. Oxford: Oxford University Press.

For a detailed discussion of the role of health promotion in nursing, see:
- Maville, J. (2001). *Health Promotion in Nursing*. San Diego: Singular Press.

For a guide to patient education in a range of health-care settings, see:
- Webb, P. (ed.) (1997). *Health Promotion and Patient Education: A Professional's Guide*. Cheltenham: Nelson Thornes.

13 The Workplace Setting

Contents

CHAPTER 13 The Workplace Setting

Key issues within this chapter:

- Workplaces are important settings for health promotion.
- Workplace settings can be used to address both occupational health issues and general health promotion topics.
- Workplace health promotion involves health education directed at the workforce; service improvement, including introduction of occupational health services; and advocacy to implement policies on health issues.

By the end of this chapter you should be able to:

- critically assess the potential of the workplace as a setting for health promotion
- describe the role of health promotion in the workplace
- plan health promotion in a workplace setting.

The workplace is one of the most important – and under-utilized – settings for health promotion. We spend at least forty years of our lives, one-third of the day, five days a week and over forty weeks in the year in a workplace setting. Workplace injuries and workplace-related illness form a significant component of the disease burden in society. The workplace provides an opportunity for person-to-person promotion with large numbers of people. These people make up a community in their own right, with networks of staff that can provide support to each other and reinforce – both positively and negatively – health decisions.

What is a workplace?

A workplace in defined both by the physical environment in which the work takes place and by its social organization. Patterns of employment are constantly changing, with new kinds, such as call centres and computer-based home working, emerging and some kinds, such as mining, in decline. Workplaces can be classified according to:

- size – ranging from large firms employing thousands, such as local government, the National Health Service and private companies, down to small businesses employing a few, and individuals who are self-employed
- the kind of activity that takes place – factories manufacturing products, open-air work such as farming, building sites and road construction, offices, call centres, shops, mobile businesses, servicing and repairs
- the organization of the workspace – individual offices, open plan, shop floor, mobile services, working from outside locations and from home.

The influence of the workplace on health

The workplace influences health in many ways. While some instances, such as the presence or absence of harmful substances, are obvious, others are less so. For some people work may just be a way of earning money to make a living. However, for many, work has other important functions. Work can provide a sense of identity, self-esteem and self-respect. One of the first questions people ask in polite conversation is 'What do you do?' People take pride in being a 'breadwinner'. Work can provide structure to people's lives. Work provides a network of social relationships.

This link between work and self-esteem can have its negative side. Just as having a challenging, exciting job can boost one's self-esteem, so working in a boring, unfulfilling job can be soul destroying. When work is taken away through unemployment, redundancy, disability, ill health and retirement, this can have a devastating effect on a person's sense of health and wellbeing and the structure that holds his or her life together.

It is one of the anomalies of modern society that activities in factories, offices, etc., are considered work while other forms of work are devalued, especially the demanding tasks of staying at home caring for children, elderly parents, cleaning, cooking, washing. The heavy value placed on employment in the construction of personal identity leads many to attempt the difficult balancing act of juggling demands of home and work. Those that do take a decision to stay at home find themselves redefined as housewife or house husband and socially marginalized.

While the focus of this chapter is on health promotion in the workplace, it is important to put that workplace in context. There is a good argument to support the view that too much emphasis is placed on work and that one of the goals of mental-health promotion is to create a sensible balance between work and other aspects of life.

Activity 13.1

Take a workplace and make a list of all the ways in which that workplace affects the health – either positively or negatively – of the workers.

Box 13.1 The European Network for Workplace Health Promotion

The European Network for Workplace Health Promotion is an informal network of national occupational health and safety institutes, public health, health promotion and statutory social insurance institutions. Its vision statement states that:

Healthy work is the result of an interplay of various factors. The most important factors or workplace health determinants include:

- The values and policies of decision-makers within organisations (private sector companies, public administrations, health-care facilities, institutions

in the area of education etc) and outside at the level of social security and policy-making;
- The specific form of the culture of participation within and outside organisations;
- Leadership and management practices;
- The production concept and principles for daily work organisation;
- The provisions for job security;
- The quality of the working environment;
- Personal health practices and life style habits.

(www.enwhp.org)

Box 13.2 How to tell if your workplace is health promoting

- Is it a safe environment and free of hazards such as noise, chemicals, dust and unsafe equipment?
- Does it provide a healthy environment? Temperature, lighting, ventilation, enough space?
- Does it make realistic and fair demands on effort and time? Are there agreed job descriptions and fair expectations, and is there transparency in disciplinary proceedings?
- Is it free from sexual harassment and discrimination according to gender, race, disability and age?
- Does it promote self-esteem, including respect, recognition of worth, fair treatment and reward for good performance?
- Is it family friendly? Are there allowances for family

needs, including sick children and other family members?
- Are health and other support services provided? Are there occupational health services and counselling available?
- Is information provided on health matters, e.g. on notice boards, in the staff manual and on the company's intranet?
- Are there policies to cover specific health issues, e.g. HIV/AIDS, alcohol abuse, drugs?
- Are facilities health promoting, e.g. menus in canteens, facilities for exercise, sports?
- Is it used for general health promotion activities, e.g. screening, exercise promotion?

> **Activity 13.2**
>
> Assess the level of health promotion in a workplace with which you are familiar using the checklist in box 13.2. Are there any other criteria that you would like to add?

Health promotion debates and the workplace

Health and safety in the workplace provides an example of contrasting structuralist and individualistic approaches that formed one of the debates described in chapter 1. The individualistic 'careless worker' perspective sees injuries as a result of lack of attention to safety by employees and a failure to wear protective clothing and take adequate precautions. Health education targeted at the workforce is seen as the main response. In contrast, the structuralist 'work is dangerous for your health' perspective sees injuries as resulting from a dangerous work environment and considers it inherently a management responsibility to secure the safety of the workplace through protective measures. In practice, an effective approach should include a comprehensive strategy that addresses individual and structural elements of health promotion:

- **health education** to create a workforce that is aware of potential risks and rights under current workplace health and safety legislation, that uses the safety measures provided and that is adequately trained to work in any potentially hazardous situations
- **service improvement**, including hazard monitoring, training opportunities for management and trade union safety representatives on health issues, the availability of appropriate first aid and occupational health services, training for occupational health doctors and nurses, access to protective clothing and containment of hazardous substances
- **advocacy** to introduce/enforce health and safety at work policies, release staff for training, control/find substitutes for hazardous substances, fund research on safe alternatives, strengthen health and safety enforcement systems, and protect the rights of employees to refuse to work in hazardous situations.

Workplace health policies

A useful approach is to set up policies in a workplace that cover specific health topics, such as smoking, coronary heart disease, alcohol and HIV/AIDs, and the actions by management and workers to address those issues.

HIV/AIDS in the workplace

Workplaces throughout the world have responded to the threat of HIV/AIDS by setting up policies for HIV/AIDS. The World Health Organization, International

Labour Office and League of Red Cross and Red Crescent Societies have produced guidelines on HIV/AIDS in the workplace (UNAIDS, 1998; Hubley, 2002) which can be summarized as:

1 **HIV/AIDS screening** – Screening, whether direct or indirect, or in the form of asking questions about tests already taken, should not be required.
2 **Confidentiality** – Confidentiality regarding all medical information, including HIV/AIDS status, must be maintained.
3 **Informing the employer** – There should be no obligation for the employee to inform the employer regarding his or her HIV/AIDS status.
4 **Protection of employee** – Persons in the workplace affected, or perceived to be affected, by HIV/AIDS must be protected from stigmatization and discrimination by co-workers, unions, employers or clients. Information and education are essential to maintain the climate of mutual understanding necessary to ensure this protection.
5 **Access to services** – Employees and their families should have access to information and educational programmes on HIV/AIDS as well as to appropriate referral.
6 **Benefits** – HIV-infected employees should not be discriminated against, and should have access to standard social security benefits and occupationally related benefits.
7 **Reasonable changes in working arrangements** – HIV infection by itself is not associated with any limitation on fitness to work. If fitness to work is impaired by HIV-related illness, reasonable alternative working arrangements should be made.
8 **Continuation of employment** – HIV infection is not a cause for termination of employment. As is the case of persons with many other illnesses, those with HIV-related illnesses should be able to work as long as they are medically fit.
9 **First aid** – In any situation requiring first aid in the workplace, precautions need to be taken to reduce the risk of transmitting blood-borne infections, including hepatitis B. These standard precautions will be equally effective against HIV transmission.

Alcohol in the workplace

The Alcohol Harm Reduction Strategy for England (Cabinet Office, 2004) noted that up to 17 million working days are lost in the UK each year due to alcohol. A comprehensive review of alcohol in the workplace in Europe (Henderson and Hutcheson, 1996) found the following: heavy drinkers are at a higher risk for work absenteeism from hangovers, accidents or injury occurring at work or elsewhere, and from health problems associated with long-term drinking, including mental health problems such as depression and anxiety. Problem drinkers take between two to eight times as much sick leave as other employees. Heavy drinkers are less productive, and are responsible for greater costs in health services.

The Department of Health and the Health and Safety Executive recommend that all employers should have an alcohol policy setting out signs to look for and procedures to follow.

> **Activity 13.3**
>
> Suggest what you might include in a workplace policy for one of the following: mental health, alcohol, coronary heart disease, physical fitness.

What kinds of health promotion can be carried out in the workplace?

A systematic review of the effectiveness of workplace health promotion (Peersman et al., 1998) identified three types of programmes:

- **awareness programmes** which aim to increase workforce level of awareness in relation to specific health topics. Typical activities are health fairs; posters, newsletters, educational classes; and health screening.
- **lifestyle change programmes** aimed directly at changing employees' health behaviour through a variety of approaches such as skills training and self-help
- **supportive environment programmes** aimed at promoting a sustainable healthy lifestyle through creating a workplace environment that supports and encourages healthy practices, such as using the stairs rather than the lift and the provision of healthy food choices in the canteen.

The systematic review identified examples of workplace health promotion activities directed at cardiovascular health, weight reduction, alcohol abuse, prevention of osteoporosis and healthy eating. Many of the studies included in the review were from the United States, where employers' liability for payment of health-care benefits provides a strong incentive to set up workplace health promotion activities which might reduce expenditure on health care. A typical worksite health promotion programme follows a set pattern: (1) an initial health risk appraisal which involves an assessment of personal health habits and risk factors; (2) an estimation of the individual's future risk of death/adverse health outcomes; and (3) the provision of educational methods and counselling about ways to change personal risk factors. Some examples of workplace health promotion from this systematic review are quoted in box 13.3.

Box 13.3 Some examples of health promotion in workplace settings quoted in Peersman et al. (1998)

Walk in to work out

A pack was produced containing written interactive materials based on the stages of change model of behaviour change (see chapter 3 for more details of this model) to encourage people to walk or cycle to work. A randomized trial of 295 employees in three Glasgow workplaces found that the intervention was successful in increasing walking but not cycling, and concluded that more needed to be done to improve conditions for cycling.

Heartbeat award scheme in England

Adopted by many local authorities in England, the heartbeat award was originally developed by the Health Education Authority and the Department of Health and is endorsed by the Chartered Institute of Environmental Health. It is managed locally by environmental health officers, together with community dietitians and health promotion specialists. To qualify for the award a workplace has to meet standards in the following two areas:

- *good hygiene standards* – The premises must comply with the Food Safety (General Food Hygiene) Regulations, 1995, and with the Food Safety (Temperature Control) Regulations, 1995. By law the owner of a food business must ensure that all staff who handle food are supervised and instructed and/or trained in food hygiene matters.

- *healthier food choices* – By offering more 'healthier choices' (e.g. by offering potatoes as

alternatives to chips, lower fat, fruit-based desserts and different breads for sandwiches) and by adopting healthier food preparation, cooking and serving practices (e.g. by trimming fat from meat before cooking, reducing the amount of fat used in cooking and allowing customers to add their own salt).

Nottingham City Hospital blood-pressure initiative

An occupational health nurse carried out blood-pressure testing and offered health promotion advice on heart disease to men working in the Finance Department and Facilities and Nutrition Division of the city hospital. An evaluation found that convenience was a strong factor in ensuring uptake, with a 46-year-old male stating, 'In fact I am certain that I still wouldn't have had my blood pressure tested if it had not been done in the workplace.'

Smoke-free workplaces in the USA, the UK, Germany and Australia

Fichtenberg et al. (2002) carried out a systematic review of twenty-six smoke-free workplace policies. They found that the number of smokers decreased by 3.8 per cent and the continuing smokers cut the number of cigarettes consumed per day by 3.1 per cent. They concluded that not only did smoke-free workplaces protect non-smokers from the dangers of passive smoking, they also encourage smokers to quit or to reduce consumption.

(Cited in Peersman et al., 1998)

Teamwork in workplace health promotion

Depending on the size and organization of a workplace, there may be a number of helath-promotion personnel on the staff.

- **Health and safety officers** are employees with responsibility for health and safety, fire safety, etc.; these exist mainly in larger workplaces.
- **Occupational nurses and physicians** have a role in screening, assessing, and giving advice on reducing risks to health as well as in rehabilitation.
- **Occupational hygienists** have skills in assessing and in making specific technical recommendations on reducing risks from noise, gas, etc.
- **Ergonomists** advise on adaptations to the workplace to suit employees and tend to have particular expertise in issues of handling, workstation design, etc.
- **Occupational psychologists** are involved in advising on organizational structures and procedures and the wellbeing of workers and in giving advice on stress-related issues.
- **Trade union health and safety representatives** are often employed by large national trade union offices. Local branches of trade unions can have elected lay health and safety officers and individual workplaces have elected health and safety representatives. Recognition and rights of health and safety representatives are set out in the 1974 Health and Safety at Work Act and the Safety Representatives and Safety Committee Regulations (1977).

Box 13.4 Case study: Scotland's Health at Work

Scotland 's Health at Work is a national award programme which was set up in 1996 to reward employers who demonstrate commitment to improving the health and ultimately the performance of their workforce and to reducing sickness absence. Workforces are encouraged to set up an action plan with health promoting activities which can lead to bronze, silver and gold awards. Companies receiving awards are listed in a 'roll of honour' on the website (www.shaw.uk.com). A network of advisers provide support, guidance and training for companies wishing to participate.

Health services as a workplace

The National Health Service is the largest single employer in the United Kingdom, with more than a million employees. As part of the Framework Action for Primary Care, the health at work in primary-care project, the Health Development Agency proposed the tool in figure 13.1 for planning health promotion interventions within primary-care workplace settings (HDA, 2001). This follows a similar approach to the health promotion planning cycle we introduced in chapter 1 and identifies six key stages for planning workplace health promotion.

Figure 13.1 The workplace health good practice planning tool

1 **Set up support structures for workplace health** – This involves gaining commitment to workplace health from the employer and senior staff and assessing what resources in terms of time and finances are allocated to workplace health and what additional resources might be available in future.

2 **Gather information** – Key information required includes details of the work environment, sickness absence, staff turnover, ill health/early retirements,

referrals to occupational health, complaints, insurance claims and grievance procedures.

3 **Develop a strategic action plan** – This should include a statement of intent from the partners; the aims of the workplace health programme; resources to be allocated to the programme; details of who is responsible for carrying out specific areas of the programme; activities covered within the programme; scheduling, evaluation and review of the programme.

4 **Implement and monitor the plan –** This will depend on the specific actions involved but would be expected to include the carrying out of activities, the monitoring of progress against targets, the reporting of achievements and regular communication with staff and feedback about the changes being introduced.

5 **Evaluate the plan** – This entails the collection of information and the assessment of the impact of the programme.

6 **Review plan and support structures** – All staff should be involved in building up a picture of what worked well and which areas could be improved.

While it was developed for health promotion within primary-care workplaces, the model in figure 13.1 provides an excellent basis for planning health promotion within all workplace settings.

It is important to take into consideration the available resources in each workplace setting when planning a health promotion strategy. For example, an office in a multinational corporation will pose different challenges than a small, locally owned factory.

Challenges for health promotion in workplace settings

Despite their inconsiderable potential, workplaces in Europe have been disappointingly slow to become involved in health promotion. A review of programmes in Scotland found that larger firms in the public sector were more likely to be actively involved and that there was a need to persuade smaller companies to take up health promotion. That survey also found that most emphasis was placed on health and safety at work and on alcohol and tobacco, and less attention was given to exercise, mental-health promotion/stress reduction, drugs and nutrition (Docherty et al., 1999). An important challenge for the future is to strengthen advocacy for workplace health promotion.

Box 13.5 Benefits of workplace health promotion

The European regional office of the World Health Organization suggests the following reasons why workplace health promotion benefits both the employer and employee:

Benefits to the organization	Benefits to the employee
A well-managed health and safety programme	A safe and healthy work environment
A positive and caring image	Enhanced self-esteem
Improved staff morale	Reduced stress
Reduced staff turnover	Improved morale
Reduced absenteeism	Increased job satisfaction
Increased productivity	Increased skills for health protection
Reduced health-care costs	Improved health
Reduced risk of fines and litigation	Improved sense of wellbeing

---

Activity 13.4

Imagine you were visiting a small company employing 100 people, e.g. a call centre or a manufacturing business. The management is very concerned about costs and does not want to spend money unnecessarily. What arguments could you use to convince them to set up a workplace health promotion programme?

Further reading

The following texts provide further information on strategies for promotion of health in workplace settings:

- Kerr, J., Griffiths, A., and Cox, T. (eds.) (1996). *Workplace Health, Employee Fitness and Exercise*. London: Taylor & Francis.
- McPartland, P. A. (1991). *Promoting Health in the Workplace*. New York: Harwood Academic.
- O'Donnell, O. (2001). *Health Promotion in the Workplace*. Albany, NY: Delmar.

14 Settings Used by Children and Young People

Contents

14 Settings Used by Children and Young People

Key issues within this chapter:

- Nursery schools, schools, colleges, out-of-school clubs and higher education establishments are important settings for reaching children and young people.

- School health promotion involves actions to improve the school environment, school health education and school health services.

- School health promotion should use a child-centred approach appropriate to the age and ability of the children and the needs of the community.

- School and preschool health promotion should involve a wide range of people, including the pupils, teachers, health workers, parents and the community.

By the end of this chapter you should be able to:

- understand how health promotion can be incorporated into settings that reach out to preschool/school-age children and young people

- be able to describe the components of a health promoting school

- apply concepts of health promotion to the planning of health promotion strategies to reach children and young people.

Given that attendance at some form of educational establishment is compulsory up to the age of sixteen years, schools provide a way of ensuring that everyone has access to health promotion. In this chapter we build on discussions of the lifespan in chapter 4 to consider the role of health promotion in some of the settings shown in box 14.1.

> **Box 14.1 Key settings to reach young people**
> - Nursery schools, crèches attached to workplaces, playgroups
> - Primary schools/before- and after-school clubs/holiday play schemes
> - Secondary (high) schools
> - Further education colleges
> - Vocational training institutions
> - Universities
> - Other colleges (e.g. police, military)
> - Youth job-creation schemes/employment exchanges
> - Youth centres
> - Young offenders' institutions
> - Uniformed groups: scouts, guides, brownies, cubs, boys' brigade, girls' brigade

The contribution of schools to public health

Education and health are mutually reinforcing. Education and learning promote health literacy and an increased capacity to make informed decisions on health matters (St Leger, 2001). A healthy child has greater potential to benefit from education than one who has poor health and misses schooling. Health promotion in educational settings thus benefits public health in three ways:

- **benefiting directly the health of the child** through the learning and other support activities, such as the provision of school health services, free school meals, milk and fruit schemes
- **promoting future health** by providing the necessary understanding, skills, values and competencies that children use in their future lives – more specifically so they can:
  - develop patterns of lifelong learning that can be applied to health and other topics
  - effectively make health decisions and manage future transitions/life events
  - obtain employment and a standard of living that will enable them to meet their physical and material needs and be free from deprivation and social exclusion
- **benefiting the health of the community** through the transfer of knowledge, skills and values from the school to the home and the community.

There is widespread discussion and debate about the role of schools in society. Some people see this as preparation for future employment and for fostering healthy lifestyles. Others have a broader vision, encompassing the development of the capacity for decision-making and the achievement of potential, which is broadly equivalent to the concept of health literacy and self-efficacy that together make up health empowerment. Promoting health literacy involves providing young people with the conceptual tools and social skills required to make informed decisions about their health (St Leger, 2001). Promoting self-efficacy implies developing the self-esteem of young persons and the confidence that they can achieve the goals in life to which they aspire.

Preschool education

Preschool education benefits the health of the child and so of the future adult (see figure 14.1). It takes place through a range of state and private provision which caters for children for varying lengths of time, from a full working day, part of the working day or a whole week. Some nurseries are able to care for very young children from the first few months, while others do not take them until they are two or three years old. Operated by salaried staff and volunteers, among these facilities are:

- day care nurseries
- crèches
- nursery schools
- reception intakes of primary schools
- preschool play groups
- Sure Start preschool programmes
- parents' and toddlers' groups
- child minders working from home and child minder drop-in centres
- portage services – home visiting educational service for preschool children with additional support needs.

Additional back up is provided through a network of specialists, including health visitors, district nurses, speech and language therapists, and teachers of the visually and hearing impaired. While day care and nursery education have traditionally been considered distinct provisions, the current approach is to link them together within the broader concept of integrated care and education. The importance of the early years has already been discussed in chapter 4. A systematic review of research evidence on the under-six age group found that 'the impact of integrated care and education was beneficial for children and led to improved cognitive and socio-emotional outcomes' (Penn et al., 2004).

The National Curriculum and the preschool child

The foundation stage of the National Curriculum begins when children reach the age of three, and the last year of the foundation stage is often described as the reception year. The National Curriculum Authority (2000) suggests ten areas, summarized below, as critical for inclusion in the foundation stage:

> **Curriculum:** Everything children do, see, hear or feel in their setting, both planned and unplanned. (Qualifications and Curriculum Authority, 2000)

1 **Personal, social and emotional wellbeing** – including the development of a strong self-image and self-esteem
2 **Positive attitudes and dispositions towards learning** – in particular an enthusiasm for knowledge and learning and a confidence in the ability to be a successful learner
3 **Social skills** – in particular how to cooperate and work with others
4 **Attention skills and persistence** – in particular the capacity to concentrate on their own play or on group tasks
5 **Language and communication** – the ability to talk, listen and communicate using a range of vocabulary and communication skills in a range of situations
6 **Reading and writing** – in a broad range of contexts and materials
7 **Mathematics** – an understanding of number, measurement, pattern, shape and space
8 **Knowledge and understanding of the world** – including solving problems, making decisions, experimenting, predicting, planning and finding out about their environment
9 **Physical development** – the development and practice of motor skills and an increase in the understanding of how their bodies work and what they need to do to be healthy and safe
10 **Creative development** – the exploration and sharing of thoughts, ideas and feelings through art, design and technology, music, movement, dance, imagination and role-play activities.

Activity 14.1

For the ten areas listed above, suggest at least one way in which each can contribute to health.

Approaches to preschool education

Figure 14.1 Ways in which preschool provisions can improve child health and development

Preschool provisions improve child health and development through

- *enabling parents to work and so increase family income*

- *providing opportunities for reaching children with health and nutrition services, including screening, growth monitoring, immunization, feeding programmes*

- *educational opportunities (e.g. for social, emotional, language and intellectual development) for children from poor and deprived communities and laying the foundations for good performance at school*

- *specific health education activities which encourage healthy routines such as handwashing, care of teeth, nutrition*

- *providing opportunities to carry out non-formal education with parents on child health and development*

Activity 14.2

Spend twenty minutes each with a child that is three, four and five years old respectively. Play with them and talk to them about their bodies and health. Afterwards, list the most important lessons you have learnt from this experience about children's concepts of health.

The importance of play

One of the most important ways in which preschool children develop is through play. While playing, children learn many things, such as exploring movements by using hands and the body and balancing; developing powers of thinking; finding out how to express themselves and communicate; using imagination; and learning how to get on with others. Play is an activity that takes place naturally. Children are curious and interested in the world around them. In exploring their world, they involve the people around them in their play. Play is the best way of introducing ideas about health to the preschool child, since you can introduce basic health concepts through puzzles, stories, songs, acting, drawing and games.

Box 14.2 How to involve fathers in preschool activities

Most community-based programmes directed at preschool children have involved mothers, and the participation of fathers has been disappointingly low. An international meta-analysis suggests that early childhood interventions embracing fathers as well as mothers may be more effective in enhancing parental sensitivity and children's attachment (Bakermans-Kraneburg et al., 2003). Issues of parental consent and cooperation would need to be taken into account when involving fathers.

An evaluation of the role of fathers in the Sure Start programme (Lloyd et al., 2003) found that men took their fathering role seriously and welcomed more opportunities for participation but also identified barriers to involvement. Many fathers perceived the activities to be targeted at mothers and felt out of place among gatherings mainly of women. The evaluation generated the following suggestions.

- Plan activities to involve fathers right from the pre-natal period.

- Include images of fathers in any educational and publicity materials.
- Employ male workers and male volunteers.
- Explain to the preschool workers and mothers why it is important to involve fathers.
- Hold activities at times when fathers are available, e.g. at evenings and weekends.
- Use outdoor activities and 'fun days' to involve fathers (the Sure Start evaluation found that men preferred to become involved in activities rather than discussions).
- Recognize and cater for the different kinds of fathers that might exist in the community: lone fathers, sole carers, separated fathers, disabled fathers, fathers working shifts, fathers from minority ethnic and faith groups.
- Be sensitive to situations when it would not be appropriate to involve men, e.g. when working with groups of women who have been victims of domestic violence.

Schools and health promotion

Schools influence children in the three broad ways, shown in figure 14.2. This involves the school environment, school health services and school curriculum.

How schools promote health

School environment

- School buildings
- Meals
- Play facilities
- Safe surroundings
- Water/sanitation

Health education

- Classroom activities
- Out-of-school activities
- Community projects
- Hidden curriculum
- Values at school
- Example of teachers
- Parent involvement

School health services

- Screening
- First aid
- Counselling
- Treatment/referral
- Adolescent clinics

Figure 14.2 How schools promote health

Play is a healthy activity through which children learn about things like their own bodies and taking risks.

School health services

Depending on local needs, schools can be used for a wide range of important activities, such as:

- screening for growth (weight and height), hearing and eyesight
- immunizations against common childhood diseases, including measles and rubella
- screening for dental health; simple preventive dental services
- identification of hygiene problems and necessary action, e.g. head lice infestation
- counselling for children (and parents) with psycho-social problems and other needs, e.g. sexual health, bullying.

In the UK, the school nurse is the specialist public health nurse with a key role. This includes reviewing health and supporting the development of children, providing specific information to encourage a healthy lifestyle (alcohol and drugs, nutrition and physical activity, mental health and psychological wellbeing, sexual health and teenage pregnancy, safety and welfare) and working in partnership with other agencies to promote child-centred public health (Department of Health, 2004), so contributing to the target of raising the health of all children (Children and Young People's Plan) (Department for Education and Skills, 2003a). Figure 14.3 acknowledges the interdependence of the various roles along the continuum of community to individual, including the National Service Framework (NSF).

Young people make use of GPs for health care. In addition, there is a growing international movement calling for the establishment of 'youth friendly' clinics that provide tailor made and non-judgemental health care for young people (WHO, 2004b). An alternative approach is to locate health services within the context of broad-based information and support services for young people, and at the end of this chapter we provide an example of this kind of service in Bradford, Yorkshire.

Activity 14.3

What would you consider to be the characteristics of a 'youth friendly' clinic? Do you feel that this could be provided within the context of a GP service or is there a need for special 'youth friendly' clinics?

Figure 14.3 The role of the school nurse in public health (Department for Education and Skills/Department of Health, 2006)

Public health programmes at community level	Whole school and community	Group work	Health prevention and promotion with individual children, young people and their families
For example:	**For example:**	**For example:**	**For example:**
Health needs assessment and coordination of school health plans	School Health Plan	Personal social health education	Drop-in clinics
Contribution to the Children and Young People's Plan	*Healthy Schools* programme	Sex and relationship education	Individual health plans for children and young people with disability or long-term conditions
Inter-agency and local partnerships	School policy development, e.g. sex education, healthy school meals, availability of drinking water, physical activity	Cookery clubs	Use of new technology (email/text) to improve access to health information
Implementation of NSF	Extended schools provision	Listening groups	Safeguarding work immunization
		Circle time	
		Smoking cessation	
		Parenting groups	

The school environment

The environment of the school is important for the health of the schoolchild and covers:

- buildings, heating, lighting, ventilation and general appearance
- play areas (adequacy and safety), lack of hazards, protection from outside, provision of rubbish bins
- immediate surroundings of the school – especially traffic/road safety, crossing points
- toilets, water, cleanliness, soap, towels
- drinking water
- school meals – these can have an important role in the nutrition of the schoolchild, and food should be prepared in clean conditions by properly supervised cooks following national nutritional guidelines.

Box 14.3 How to improve the school health services and environment

Below is a shortened version of a list of suggested actions by the Department of Health (Department for Education and Skills/Department of Health, 2006). While prepared with the school nurse in mind, they involve all members of the school health team, including teachers, school governors, health workers and youth workers.

- Work with parents, local authority housing, schools, leisure and environmental health, police and fire services to promote safer school environments and play areas, speed restrictions, safe crossings, cycling proficiency and first aid training courses.
- Run groups and provide individual support/referral to specialist mental health services for children and young people involved in bullying and at risk from alcohol/drug-related harm, abuse or prostitution.
- Run groups and provide individual support to help children and parents to cope with managing behaviour problems and the effects of bereavement, transition stages at school and exams and other issues.

- Establish a school nutrition action group involving children, parents, caterers, school governors and school staff with other agencies to develop a 'whole school food and drink policy' and promote changes in school to help make healthy food choices easier (e.g. vending machines, tuck shops, school meals).
- Provide and promote confidential drop-ins/counselling services at school and community venues, ensuring they are linked to wider primary health care, family planning/emergency contraception, screening for sexually transmitted infections, and genito-urinary medicine (GUM) services.
- Provide sessions for parents that will support and prepare them in their central role as educators. Engage them in writing the school sex and relationship policy.
- Work with parenting groups to promote increased activity with their children. Examples could include lunchtime activities, street play schemes, play buses or an exercise-promoting environment with roller, skateboard or cycle tracks.

Health education component

Health education can be embedded within all subjects of the curriculum and also provided through personal, social and health education (PSHE).

Health education as part of other subjects

The advantages of including health within subjects such as English, maths and science are that these are considered 'core' subjects in the National Curriculum. The potential for incorporating health issues, such as exercise promotion, nutrition and the functions of the body, in the teaching of science, physical education and design and technology are obvious. Less clear cut but also relevant are subjects such as English and drama, history, geography and maths. Not only can these subjects be vehicles for introducing health concepts, but including examples from health can greatly enrich the teaching of these subjects. Box 14.4 gives a complete listing of the National Curriculum subjects. Specific details on the content of each subject and different key stages are provided on the National Curriculum internet website.

Box 14.4 Subjects in the National Curriculum

Art and design	Mathematics
Careers education	Modern foreign languages
Citizenship	Music
Design and technology	Personal, social and health education
English	Physical education
Geography	Religious education
History	Science
Information and communication technology	Work-related learning

---

Activity 14.4

Take one of the following health topics (or another of your own choice): nutrition, obesity, injury prevention, tobacco, sexual health. For each of the subjects in the National Curriculum listed in box 14.4 suggest an activity that fits and which could also be used to illustrate that health topic.

Personal, social and health education (PSHE):
PSHE provides pupils with the knowledge, understanding, skills and attitudes to make informed decisions about their lives. (Department for Education and Skills/Department of Health, 2006)

Health education as a subject area

Health education can be delivered as a subject in its own right. The advantage of this is that it is possible to include health education as a part of the curriculum, providing a comprehensive coverage of the topic over key stages 1 to 4. Health education is now part of the curriculum of personal, social and health education and citizenship, the objectives of which are summarised in box 14.5. The advantages of locating health education within a comprehensive curriculum need to be offset by the disadvantage of the lower status of PSHE, which is classified as non-statutory within the National Curriculum.

Box 14.5 Personal, social and health education (PSHE) in the National Curriculum

Key stage 1 – year groups 1 to 2 (5- to 7-year-olds)
Pupils learn about themselves as developing individuals and as members of their communities, building on their own experiences and on the early learning goals for personal, social and emotional development. They learn the basic rules and skills for keeping themselves healthy and safe and for behaving well. They have opportunities to show they can take some responsibility for themselves and their environment. They begin to find out about their own and other people's feelings and become aware of the views, needs and rights of other children and older people. As members of a class and school community, they acquire social skills such as how to share, take turns, play, help others, resolve simple arguments and resist bullying.

Key stage 2 – year groups 3 to 6 (7- to 11-year-olds)
Pupils learn about themselves as growing and changing individuals with their own experiences and ideas, and as members of their communities. They become more mature, independent and self-confident. They discover about the wider world and the interdependence of communities within it. They develop their sense of social justice and moral responsibility and begin to understand that their own choices and behaviour can affect local, national or global issues and political and social institutions. As they begin to develop into teenagers, they face the changes of puberty and transfer to secondary school with support and encouragement from their school. They learn how to make more confident and informed choices about their health and environment; to take more responsibility, individually and as a group, for their own learning; and to resist bullying.

Key stage 3 – year groups 7 to 9 (11- to 14-year-olds)
Pupils learn about themselves as growing and changing individuals and as members of their communities with more maturity, independence and power. They become more self-aware, and are capable of more sophisticated moral reasoning. They take more responsibility for themselves and become more aware of the views, needs and rights of people of all ages. They acquire new skills to help them make decisions and play an active part in their personal and social life. They learn how to plan and manage choices for their courses and career. They continue to develop and maintain a healthy lifestyle, coping well with their changing bodies and feelings. They also discover how to cope with changing relationships and understand how these can affect their health and wellbeing.

≫→

Key stage 4 – year groups 10 to 11 (14- to 16-year-olds)
Pupils develop the self-awareness and confidence needed for adult life, further learning and work. They have opportunities to show that they can take responsibility for their own learning and career choices by setting personal targets and planning to meet them. They develop their ability to weigh up alternative courses of action for health and wellbeing. They gain greater knowledge and understanding of spiritual, moral, social and cultural issues through increased moral reasoning, clarifying their opinions and attitudes in discussions with their peers and informed adults and considering the consequences of their decisions. They learn to understand and value relationships with a wide range of people and gain the knowledge and skills to seek advice about these and other personal issues. They also learn to respect the views, needs and rights of people of all ages.

(Summarized from Qualifications and Curriculum Authority, 2006)

Health education in schools is about more than providing facts. It is important to equip children with the skills and values for now and for the future.

Activity 14.5

Take one of the following health topics (or another of your own choice): personal relationships, obesity, exercise, violence and bullying, alcohol. For each of the key stages in the National PSHE Curriculum, suggest an activity or topic that could be used to develop understandings and skills relevant to that health topic.

Life skills: Abilities for adaptive and positive behaviour that enable individuals to deal effectively with the demands and challenges of everyday life. (WHO, 1993)

Learning methods for school health education

Many are critical of traditional teaching approaches in schools that over-emphasize the learning of facts and the passing of exams. In health education we want to do more than provide facts. We wish to equip children to make decisions, explore attitudes and values, and adopt healthy practices both now and in their future lives, using approaches such as those listed in box 14.6.

Box 14.6 Approaches in school health education

- *Child-centred approach* – placing the emphasis on meeting the needs of the child, starting with their perception of a healthy lifestyle, and recognizing that individuals learn at different rates. The ideas introduced at each level of primary and secondary schooling should reflect the social/emotional, physical and intellectual development of the child.
- *Active learning methods* that encourage exploration and discovery and relate the information presented to everyday life – bridging the gap between school, home and community.
- *Problem-solving or 'issue-based'* learning which organizes the learning around issues or problems rather than traditional subject disciplines. In this approach, students usually take a health topic and carry out a range of activities/projects in the classroom, at home and in the community. Their finished project might include songs, drawing, arithmetic, science experiments and story writing.
- *Decision-making methods* – role plays and exercises where children learn to take decisions. This might include a situation where a young person has opportunities to try out different responses to another person's attempt to persuade them to smoke a cigarette, take alcohol or have sex.
- *Life skills* – methods which promote decision-making and use a variety of active learning methods such as role play and case studies to help

young people respond to the challenges that they are facing now and will encounter in their future life.
- *Peer teaching methods* which encourage the use of older respected children as 'peer models'. For example, an older child might tell younger children that it is not particularly grown up to smoke cigarettes, and the information may have greater credibility than if it is given by an adult.
- *Drama and role play* – including activities in which young people act out situations (e.g. risky situations and different options for managing them); practise skills (e.g. how to refuse cigarettes without giving offence, how to say no to sex); and have an opportunity to reflect on what it is like to be in a specific situation (e.g. to be a teenage mother). By directly engaging at the level of emotions and feelings, this is a very powerful health promotion method. In 'theatre-in-education' approaches an external theatre group develops performances around health themes, performs in schools, and involves young audiences in discussing the characters and health issues.
- *Self-esteem enhancement* – involving educational approaches that help children develop confidence in themselves and their worth and reduce feelings of failure; children with high self-esteem are more likely to have the confidence to resist pressure from others to engage in risky behaviour.

The health promoting school

The World Health Organization has taken a leading international role in developing the concept of the health promoting school (see box 14.7). A key element of this is the establishment of criteria for schools to work towards in order to become designated as health promoting schools. They are encouraged to form networks to exchange experiences about health and pupils. The European Network of Health Promoting

Box 14.7　The health promoting school

The World Health Organization provides the following definition of a health promoting school: 'A health promoting school is one that constantly strengthens its capacity as a healthy setting for living, learning and working.'

A health promoting school:

- fosters health and learning with all the measures at its disposal
- engages health and education officials, teachers, teachers' unions, students, parents, health providers and community leaders in efforts to make the school a healthy place
- strives to provide a healthy environment, school health education, and school health services along with school/community projects and outreach, health promotion programmes for staff, nutrition and food safety programmes, opportunities for physical education and recreation, and programmes for counselling, social support and mental-health promotion
- implements policies and practices that respect an individual's wellbeing and dignity, provide multiple opportunities for success, and acknowledge good efforts and intentions as well as personal achievements
- strives to improve the health of school personnel, families and community members as well as pupils; and works with community leaders to help them understand how the community contributes to, or undermines, health and education.

Health promoting schools focus on:

- caring for oneself and others
- making healthy decisions and taking control over life's circumstances
- creating conditions that are conducive to health (through policies, services, physical/social conditions)
- building capacity for peace, shelter, education, food, income, a stable ecosystem, equity, social justice, sustainable development
- preventing leading causes of death, disease and disability, e.g. tobacco use, HIV/AIDS/sexually transmitted infections, sedentary lifestyle, drugs and alcohol, violence and injuries, unhealthy nutrition
- influencing health-related behaviours: knowledge, beliefs, skills, attitudes, values, support.

Schools (ENHPS) is a strategic programme in more than forty countries in the European region with the aim of promoting the concept of the health promoting school and integrating it into the wider health and education sectors. It is supported by the Council of Europe, the European Commission and the WHO regional office for Europe (Jensen and Simovska, 2002; Stewart-Brown, 2006).

Within the United Kingdom the concept of the health promoting school is advanced by the National Healthy Schools Programme of the Department of Health in England, the Scottish Health Promoting Schools Unit (SHPSU), the Welsh Network of Healthy School Schemes, and the Health Promotion Agency for Northern Ireland (1999).

Activity 14.6

Take the criteria outlined in box 14.7 and apply them to a school with which you are familiar. What improvements would be necessary in order for it to qualify for the status of a health promoting school? How would you go about making those improvements?

Violence in schools

Schools should be places where children are safe and protected from harm, and it is important that they have policies in place to address issues of violence – especially bullying. The values promoted by schools should be those of non-violence, tolerance and good relations with others, but the reality is often far from the case, with a wide range of violence directed against pupils, teachers and school property. This includes insults, ridicule, bullying by peers and gangs, vandalism, gang violence and violent incidences with knives and guns.

> **Bullying:** Persistent unwelcome behaviour, mostly using unwarranted or invalid criticism, nit-picking, fault-finding, also exclusion, isolation, being singled out and treated differently, being shouted at or humiliated, excessive monitoring, having verbal and written warnings imposed, and much more. Bullying is usually a series of incidents over time (unlike harassment or assault, which usually refer to a single incident). (Adapted from www.bullyonline.org)

Those on the receiving end of bullying include the overweight student, the disabled child, children who stammer, the social outsider, the minority child and the gay or lesbian adolescent. Violence in school affects health in three ways: through direct physical harm, psychological distress, and longer-term mental/physical ill health, even suicide. The psychological damage to a child of persistent verbal abuse, taunts, insults and other forms of emotional violence – including sexual violence – from teachers or peers can have a significant impact. In 1997–8 Due et al. (2005) carried out a survey of 123,227 students aged eleven, thirteen and fifteen from a sample of schools in twenty-eight countries in Europe and North America. They found that bullying was associated with both physical symptoms (headache, stomach ache, backache, dizziness) and psychological symptoms (bad temper, feeling nervous, feeling low, difficulties in getting to sleep, morning tiredness, feeling left out, loneliness, helplessness).

Reaching young people in out-of-school settings

School-based approaches should be complemented by other ways of reaching young people. We have already discussed the role of the mass media in chapter 7 and the increasingly important role of the internet in chapter 9.

Peer education with young people involves selecting individuals and providing training and support to carry out education among their peers in informal settings, such as school surroundings, cafes, bars and clubs. This approach has been widely used, especially to address sexual health, drugs and smoking, and builds on the respect and credibility that young people can have with their peers and the opportunities provided to reach them outside of the formal school setting. A systemic review by Harden et al. (1999) 'found some evidence to support the effectiveness of peer-delivered health promotion for young people'. A practical problem with peer education with adolescents is the high turnover, as they are at a period of their lives when they are in transition to work and higher education; therefore investment in effort and time is required in order to monitor and train new peer educators to replace those who have moved on.

Another useful approach with considerable potential is that of information shops. These provide health promotion on an informal 'drop-in' basis from accessible locations in high streets and communities (see box 14.8).

Box 14.8 The Bradford information shop for young people

This centre has been set up in Bradford to meet the needs of young people in the area. Services provided include:

- *details of jobs and employment opportunities* and help in the preparation of curriculum vitae
- *information* on rights, housing, sport facilities, leisure, training and education
- *free internet access*
- *a walk-in centre* three times a week to provide free and confidential advice on contraception and sexual health, including the provision of pills and emergency contraception, free condoms, pregnancy testing and general information
- *the 'lads' room'* – confidential information on any aspects of health for males provided twice-weekly by male workers
- *free condoms* for young people up to twenty-five years old
- *free confidential advice and testing for sexually transmitted infections*, with separate sessions for men and women each week.

Settings in higher education

Higher education settings cover a range of 'post-compulsory education' provision, including further education colleges, apprentice schemes, specialist colleges for the police and military, and universities. As discussed in chapter 4, the taking up of studies in higher education is an important transitionary stage for young people. It often involves leaving home and adopting a student lifestyle, taking up new ideas and challenging traditional authority. While this process of questioning values and dominant assumptions is a natural and important part of the student experience, it can lead to risk-taking which can have long-term health consequences.

As discussed in chapter 7, the media – television, radio and magazines – have an important influence on young people. A survey of first-year university undergraduates by MacFadyen et al. (2003) found that magazines – especially men's magazines such as Loaded, FHM, Maxim, Minx, etc. – were both widely read and a major source of pro-smoking images. In particular, the association of smoking with risky 'laddish' anti-establishment behaviour had a special appeal to the young reader. While highlighting these negative influences, the authors also point to the considerable potential of harnessing magazines to deliver balanced health promotion messages to young people.

Higher education institutions have invested heavily in information technology and online facilities, and students use these to access health information from internet websites and also through in-house intranet systems (see chapter 9). In 2003 the Health Education Board for Scotland (now known as NHS Scotland) carried out a trial of health promotion information placed on 600 computers in twelve higher education institutions in Scotland. An evaluation found that students were interested in the information provided, but more effort was needed as far as the presentation of the material was concerned in order to gain the attention and interest of students (Douglas et al., 2004).

The formal education provided at the higher level is focused on the specific academic and vocational demands of the chosen fields of study. Health promotion is provided mainly through student services such as health centres and counselling and through specific health campaigns provided by student unions and other agencies. There is considerable scope and potential for the development of health promotion in higher education settings.

Activity 14.7

Choose one of the following health topics (or a topic of your own choice): smoking, alcohol, sexually transmitted infections, exercise, healthy eating. Design a health promotion programme on your health topic to reach students in a university or further education setting.

Further reading

For further information on national policy for services for children in the United Kingdom, see:

- Department of Health (2004). *National Service Framework for Children, Young People and Maternity Services*: www.dh.gov.uk/en/Policyandguidance/ Healthandsocialcaretopics/Childrenservices/Childrenservicesinformation/ index.htm.

For a detailed review of the evidence base of the research literature on health promotion and young people, see the following report:

- Peersman, G. (1996). *A Descriptive Mapping of Health Promotion Studies in Young People*. London: EPPI-Centre, Institute of Education, University of London.

An international perspective on health promotion is provided by the following WHO report:

- WHO (1998). *Promoting Health through Schools: Report of a WHO Expert Committee on Comprehensive School Health Education and Promotion*. Geneva: World Health Organization.

CHAPTER **15** Institutional Settings

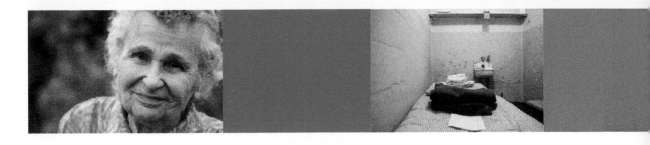

Contents

CHAPTER 15 Institutional Settings

Key issues within this chapter:

- Institutional settings provide valuable opportunities for health promotion with specific sections of the community, such as older people, persons with learning disabilities, abused children and offenders.

- People may make transitions between community and institution along a continuum of care.

- A common feature of many institutions is that the residents are not there by choice and often experience loss of control and freedom and feel that they are not able to make their own decisions.

- Health promotion involves health education targeted at residents, service improvements to change the nature of the institutions to improve the quality of provision and their responsiveness to the needs of residents, and advocacy for improvements and safeguards to protect persons in institutions.

By the end of this chapter you should be able to:

- understand the way the organization of institutions can affect the health of residents

- provide a justification for health promotion delivered through organizations

- be able to describe the characteristics of a health promoting institution, including the active involvement of residents in the operation of the institution, support during transitions from one form of provision to another, and active communication between the staff and residents

- discuss the particular needs of persons within prison settings

- explore the role of health promotion – health education, service improvement and advocacy – within each setting.

As we discussed in chapter 4, many aspects of care take place within family and community settings. However, a significant proportion of the population may spend some time within an institutional setting such as a care home, a children's home or a correctional institution (prison).

A common feature of these institutions is that they are residential and can be both permanent and transitional. An older person, for example, with deteriorating health, may progress from living independently in the community, through various care packages, to being a resident in a nursing home, or a young person may move from a care home to a foster home and then return to their family home.

In recent years media scandals about neglect and abuse in care homes and institutions have highlighted cases where those in charge have abused their power and found it convenient to keep residents in a passive, disempowered state, with over-reliance on medication. While these abuses are probably exceptional, they have heightened awareness of the need to ensure adequate regulation and monitoring to guarantee good quality care.

With the changing demographic profile in the UK towards an ageing population, this chapter will use the example of institutions for older people to illustrate many of the issues of health promotion within institutional settings. We will then consider other institutions catering for age- or client-specific groups, including prisons – an institutional setting that poses major challenges and opportunities for health promotion.

The health promoting institution

The characteristics of health promoting institutions are similar to those of other settings (box 15.1).

Box 15.1 How can I tell if an institution is health promoting?

All institutions offering services for vulnerable people should strive to be health promoting. Questions you can ask to assess the health promoting status of the institution and need for interventions include the following.

Does the institution:
- treat people with respect and dignity?
- protect people from physical, psychological and sexual abuse?
- provide access to the best possible heath and social care to maximize functioning?
- provide a stimulating environment with opportunities for self-development, learning opportunities and personal growth?
- provide social contact with other residents and the wider community?
- offer a diet which meets personal, cultural, religious and nutritional needs?
- offer a healthy and safe physical environment which includes accommodation?

- provide health education and encouragement to take as much responsibility for self-care as possible?
- involve residents in decision-making about the running of the organization, whenever possible?
- have explicit written policies and procedures (e.g. anti-discrimination) for staff and residents?
- have health and safety procedures for staff and residents?
- meet the national guidelines and standards of care applicable to the particular client group?
- prepare each individual for transition to the next stage of their life?

Transition – transfer between settings

In chapter 4 we discussed health promotion through the lifespan, identifying specific needs for different age groups. Most residents of institutions can be considered 'temporary', as they will move from the institution at some point in time. Therefore, besides 'the here and now', there is an opportunity to discuss and help individuals prepare for the next step or stage in their life course. There is much potential for health promotion to be utilized in making the transition as smooth and easy as possible. In the case of hospices and care homes for elderly and terminally ill people, the major transition is death and dying, and an important aim of palliative care is to make this process as comfortable and positive an experience as possible for the person and their family.

People must have the opportunity to verbalize their concerns, clarify the situation, gain information about practical issues and receive emotional support. Using the example of older people, we illustrate the potential for refocusing from treatment to active promotion of health in its broadest sense (see box 15.2).

Institutions for older people

Transition between settings is a key issue for older people, as is effective communication and meeting the needs of carers, which are discussed subsequently. The journey as illustrated in figure 15.1 is typical of many older people, who experience a series of illness episodes, resulting in medical interventions. When the main focus of care is on treatment, opportunities for promoting health are often neglected.

Activity 15.1

What different kinds of support does an older person and family need through the series of events shown in figure 15.1? What opportunities for health promotion are there?

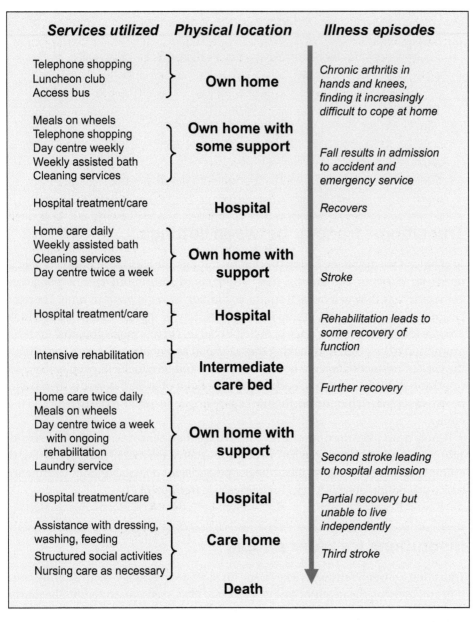

Figure 15.1
Transition lifeline – an individual journey illustrating some potential transitions for an older person

The *National Service Framework for Older People* (Department of Health, 2001c) highlighted four important issues to be addressed in providing services for older persons, which should be implicit and embedded within any health promotion. These are:

- **rooting out age discrimination**
- **providing person-centred care**
- **promoting older people's health and independence**
- fitting services around people's needs.

The role of health promotion involves:

- **health education** of the older person to provide the necessary understandings and skills to manage their lifestyle, live independently and make use of the services and benefits available. It is also important to provide the necessary understanding and skills for their carers within the family and community. Alongside this there is a need for health education directed at the public to counter the many myths and false assumptions that surround old age and lead to age discrimination.
- **service improvements** such as reorientation of health facilities to meet the needs of the older person and providing training so that hospital staff can identify and respond to these. Support services are required to help people remain in their own homes for as long as possible, **such as personal and nursing care, the former including food shopping, assistance with food preparation, delivery of cooked meals, cleaning and laundry services, and mechanisms to attend a luncheon club.** They also involve facilities to enable older people to be active and independent, for example specific times for older persons at leisure facilities such as gyms and swimming pools and accessible public transport routes.
- **advocacy**, such as the introduction of regulations to counter age discrimination, raising awareness of the need to channel more resources into provisions for older people, and the enactment/enforcement of legislation to ensure quality of care for older people. Older people should be fully involved in any discussions on provisions of services and other matters that affect them, and one approach to advocacy is to set up 'older people's champions'.

Box 15.2 Journey through transitions – health education and service improvements

Physical location	Health education – potential topics	Service improvements – potential facilities
Own home	Safety, including personal security and fire prevention Maintaining physical activity Preventing social isolation Coping with bereavement Access to financial advice Nutrition – cooking for one, shopping on a budget Self-management of chronic health conditions	Leisure services for older people Disabled car parking Cultural/religious activities Luncheon club Community centre Day centre Access bus – transport for those with restricted mobility Telephone/internet shopping Local support groups – Alzheimer's Society, Stroke Association Organized holidays

Box 15.2 *continued*

Physical location	Health Education – potential topics	Service Improvements – potential facilities
Own home with support	Overcoming isolation Safe use of medicines Continence advice Avoiding falls 'Easy to prepare' meals Preventing dehydration	Social services assessment Appropriate adaptations – hand rails Community meals (meals on wheels) Assistance with activities of daily living Laundry service Cleaning services District nurse Sitting services to enable carer to take a break
Sheltered accommodation	Coping with loss Encouraging independence	Warden control Short-term rapid-response health team
Respite care	Encouraging independence Assisting the carer to accept that it is OK to have a break	Reassessment of needs Short break (7 to 14 days) providing accommodation
Care home	Risk-taking opportunities Physical activities Links with wider community Involvement in decision-making	Residential accommodation with support for activities of daily living May require nursing care to treat health matters
Older person with dementia	Maintaining function and connection with reality Support for family and friends	Residential accommodation with support for activities of daily living May require nursing care

(Adapted from Copeman and Hyland, 2007)

Communicating with older persons

The second key issue is effective communication. This appreciation of difference will help in any interaction. Many older people are fit and active, and it could therefore appear condescending to automatically make some assumptions. However, a consultation with a chronically ill or frail older person may take longer, as time needs to be allowed to build trust, obtain accurate information and ensure that any advice is relevant, realistic, fully understood and acceptable. It is important with any consultation that the individual feels comfortable and valued and has sufficient time to ask questions. We have already discussed the importance of effective one-to-one communications in chapter 5.

Effective communication with older people requires understanding the individual's needs and abilities.

Box 15.3 How to communicate with older persons

The following are factors to consider when interviewing an older person.

General environment – Eliminate background noise and other distractions. Switch off the TV or radio, for example.

Seating – A firm chair with arms of the appropriate height may be better than an armchair. Sit in a position so that the person can clearly see you. Move the furniture if the light is inappropriate (e.g. sunlight falling across your face, making it difficult for someone to see what you are saying).

Privacy – Can you be overheard? Individuals whatever their age have a right to discuss personal manners in private. Respect issues of confidentiality.

Means of address – During the introduction, or prior to the meeting, establish how the individual wants to be addressed. Start formally, with 'Mr', 'Mrs' or 'Miss', unless you are given permission to be more informal.

Communication – Find out whether the older person has any difficulties in hearing or speaking and adjust your approach accordingly.

Reason for interview – Explain the reason for the interview (or referral). Does the older person agree?

Written material – Ensure that any material given is clearly written both in content and appearance (especially size of letters). Would an audio-cassette be more useful?

Giving advice – This needs to be relevant, realistic and of value to the older person. Are they able to follow your advice? Older people may take longer to assimilate new information and ask questions. However, once they are convinced of the benefits of action they are very likely to take action.

Communication with others – Do any other people need to be informed of any decisions? Who, why, how, when? Health and social-care professionals, carers or family? Remember confidentiality issues and ask permission from the older person when possible.

Box 15.4 Specialist provisions for older persons

Luncheon clubs/day centres

Luncheon clubs are coordinated by the voluntary sector, social services, church and other faith groups or interested individuals. They are primarily social settings where people of a similar age can meet to chat, share and eat together – a means of reducing social isolation. Many attendees rely on transport from volunteer drivers, an access bus or other arrangements to reach the luncheon club.

Day centres tend to provide a greater range of facilities for the more 'dependent' older person living in the community. Health and social needs can be assessed and support provided such as a weekly bath. The group setting enables common issues to be discussed, with information and advice sharing. Some day centres organize bulk shopping so that individuals can return home with their weekly shopping carried by the volunteer driver. This is increasingly popular since supermarket home services have minimum delivery charges.

Some examples of luncheon clubs and day centres

Tea Centre, St John's Centre, Leeds

This facility provides snacks and drinks to a range of customers, predominantly older people who are shopping in Leeds and 'fancy a cup of tea and chat'. Retired people, acting as volunteers, serve the refreshments. A free legal service is provided twice a week.

Age Concern Luncheon Club in Acton High Street, London

The premises host a pop-in cafe, hairdresser, library, art, tai chi, bingo, dancing, quizzes, bowls, whist, outings, holidays, chiropody, audiology, advice and an Asian club.

Age Concern Southall Day Centre, London

This centre offers a tea club, language classes, seaside excursions, keep-fit, lectures, discussion groups, poetry and library service. Summer outings and holidays are arranged.

Sheltered accommodation

Local authorities, housing associations, the voluntary sector or private landlords provide sheltered accommodation. These are warden-controlled flats where older people can live with their own possessions, but in an emergency an intercom link means that support can be provided quickly.

Assistance with activities of daily living or nursing care is not given, though in the short term home care organized by social services or district nurses can be initiated. Many of these purpose-built blocks have adapted facilities, including a shared lounge for residents to meet. This supportive environment enables some independence to be maintained in a safe environment.

Care homes for older people

In the UK, 5 per cent of older people live in long-term residential care homes. These individuals are generally frail, with chronic illnesses, unable to continue to live at home even with complex packages of social support. Moving into a residential care home can be traumatic, entailing the loss of control and decision-making about many daily activities. One of the roles of health promotion is to ensure that the residents are treated with respect and dignity and are encouraged to be as independent as possible within their capabilities.

The health promotion goals for frail older people are to maintain as much independence as possible and to encourage quality of life. Often care homes employ someone with specific responsibilities to coordinate resident activities, including meal provision, social activities, visits, quizzes, games and physical activities.

Activity 15.2

Suggest health promotion activities that could be carried out with older people attending a day centre. How could you persuade the day centre manager of the value of health promotion for the clients? Design a programme of activities to meet some of the potential social needs of the clients.

Activity 15.3

How could a residents' committee be mobilized to maximize health promotion opportunities in a sheltered housing complex or in a residential care home? Can you suggest five activities that you could undertake to enhance the sense of control and wellbeing among the residents?

Meeting the health promotion needs of carers

About 6 million people in the UK act as informal carers. It is estimated that over half of all carers look after someone aged over seventy-five years. In chapter 5 we discussed 'burnout' and identified the need to support people working with vulnerable adults. The national strategy for carers introduced by the Department of Health (1999) presented the findings of research on the needs of carers:

- the freedom of the carer to have a life of their own
- the importance of the carer maintaining their own health
- the importance of building up confidence in services
- the right to have a say in service provision.

Box 15.5 How to support a carer

- Spend time with them.
- Listen to their concerns and fears.
- Provide reassurance and help them deal with feelings of guilt.
- Address their own heath issues.
- Make sure they have some time for themselves.

Provide:
- advice about financial matters, including benefit entitlements and assistance with form filling
- emotional support – on a group and an individual basis
- training about how to cope with particular needs, such as assisting with feeding

- help to acknowledge and obtain support to meet their own health needs
- information about a carers' network (and if necessary set up a network in your locality)
- information about any newsletters or special events
- support when any conflict arises between the needs of the patient and those of the carer
- written information in an appropriate language, layout and typeface
- opportunities for day care and home support so that the carer can have time for their personal needs.

The needs of carers should not be overlooked, but carers can often be invisible and hard to reach as a group.

Institutions for children

At any one time, around 60,000 vulnerable children in the UK are 'looked after' in care. Two-thirds live in foster care and one in ten in children's homes. In 2001–2, 41 per cent of children in care were aged ten years or under. Most children – 80 per cent – enter care because of abuse or neglect or for family reasons (Social Exclusion Unit, 2003). An analysis of the 1970 British birth cohort children at the ages of five, ten, sixteen and thirty found that children in care are more likely to achieve poorer education qualifications, spend time in prison, be homeless, have psychiatric morbidity and have poorer general health (Viner and Taylor, 2005).

A case control study of 142 children aged five to sixteen in local authority care concluded that the overall heath care of those who had been in care for more than six months was significantly worse than that of children living in their own homes, especially with regard to emotional and behavioural health. They were more likely to have had discontinuities in GP care, have incomplete immunizations, receive inadequate dental care, suffer from anxieties and difficulties in interpersonal relationships, wet the bed, smoke, use illegal drugs and have been charged with a criminal offence (Williams et al., 2001).

Considerable concern has been expressed for the mental health of children in care. A needs assessment study of forty-eight children and young people in foster homes and residential care in one local authority found 56 per cent to have significant psychiatric morbidity (Blower et al., 2004).

Children's homes

Social services are tasked with the responsibility to provide:

- individual support to the child and their family, identifying and responding to needs
- child protection
- opportunities for training and employment for young people
- support when a young person is leaving care
- training and support to carers
- selection of and training for foster parents
- monitoring and evaluating the services
- access to appropriate health services
- access to education.

Health promotion with children in institutional care involves a mixture of:

- **health education** to introduce life skills and to build awareness of their rights and of mechanisms for seeking help, to improve self-esteem and self-respect, and to learn anger management, respect for others and control of bullying
- **service improvement** to strengthen children's support services, the quality of educational provision, and opportunities for children to draw attention to abuses and seek help, to develop community-based care, to improve inspection and to train staff
- **advocacy** to strengthen rights of children and child protection regulations and to channel resources into improving institutional and community-based care and links with the community.

Institutions for persons with learning disabilities

People with learning disabilities are one of the most vulnerable groups in society and have been the subject of various government reports (e.g. Department of Health, 2001a). More than half of adults with learning disabilities live at home and are cared for by their parents (Department of Health, 2005). In the first instance a priority is to support these carers but, as these carers themselves age, a challenge arises to identify alternative forms of provision outside the family. During the 1980s, as part of the 'Care in the Community' approach, there was a move to close many large institutions where people with mental health issues had lived for a long time. Some adults with learning disabilities live in the community alone or in shared accommodation, with or without regular residential support.

The role of health promotion should be **to help people with learning disabilities to lead rich and fulfilling lives** and to maximize their autonomy in a safe environment. This involves:

- **health education** directed at persons with learning disabilities to provide life skills such as personal hygiene, home safety, self-care, nutrition, managing a home, shopping, cooking, etc. A challenging area is that of the provision of sex education and advice on contraception. Health education with persons with learning disabilities needs to be tailored to their individual needs, in particular taking into account their developmental rather than their chronological age and also the use of appropriate communication methods (box 15.6). An important aspect is education directed at the general public to dispel myths about people with learning disabilities and to counter fear and opposition to care in the community.

- **service improvements**, including the participation of councils, voluntary organizations and private agencies in the provision of appropriate care and support, the setting up of self-help and carer groups, the arrangement of specialist health services, such as regular health monitoring, and the training of health workers, staff in residential homes, wardens in sheltered accommodation and volunteers.

- **advocacy** is needed to raise awareness of the needs of this neglected group, the importance of providing adequate community-based provisions and the enactment of protective legislation, including protection from discrimination.

Box 15.6 How to communicate with a person with learning disabilities

It is important to establish a two-way conversation with the person with the learning disability and not just talk with their carer. When communicating with such people you will need to adapt your approach to meet their specific needs.

A person with learning disabilities may:

- be unable to speak clearly
- not be able to express themselves
- have difficulty understanding what has been said by others
- have a visual or hearing impairment
- have limited physical movement
- have difficulties sitting, standing or walking
- be a wheelchair user
- have psychological or social issues that impact on their ability to relate to another individual
- have specific behaviour problems
- have additional physical health needs
- have additional mental health needs
- have severe learning disabilities with complex needs
- have a particular cultural, ethnic or religious background.

> ### Activity 15.4
>
> You have been invited to take a group of older teenagers with mild learning disabilities on an activity weekend. What specific health promotion goals might you aim to fulfil? Would you need any special preparation and, if so, what and why?

Prisons and young offender institutions

With their rising population, prisons form a setting which has been receiving increased attention in recent years. Health promotion in prisons is important for two reasons: firstly, because many behaviours that have a high risk to health take place within prisons (e.g. substance abuse, drug injection and sexual abuse) and, secondly, it provides an opportunity to address many aspects of health that will benefit the prisoner in his or her future life outside of prison. Typically prisoners have had a poor education and very little support from family and friends.

A comprehensive review of prison health by Watson et al. (2004) found that the main issues in prison heath care are mental health, substance abuse, especially alcohol and drugs, and communicable diseases such as HIV/AIDS and tuberculosis. It is estimated that one-fifth of male prisoners and two-fifths of women prisoners in England and Wales have attempted suicide, with most making an initial attempt before being admitted to prison. That same review found that the rate of suicide among men in prisons was five times that of the general male population. Particularly disturbing was the high rate of suicide among boys aged fifteen to seventeen, which was a staggering eighteen times the rate of that among boys in the general population (Fazel et al., 2005). Many of these individuals have a background of violence and abuse, or mental disorders such as schizophrenia.

As there is a strong link between social deprivation, limited education, mental ill health and imprisonment, health promotion needs to include both better screening and treatment of mental illness, and education to facilitate employment opportunities on release. This needs to be multi-agency and to support the ex-offender to integrate into the community. Furthermore the prison population needs to be separated into groups with clear and distinct needs, i.e. young offenders, men, women and older people, each of which will require tailored approaches.

A comprehensive health promotion approach will involve all three elements:

- **health education** directed at increasing understanding of health issues, the promotion of life skills and the building of self-esteem. The peer education approach (see chapter 11), through which a group of prisoners are trained and used to reach other prisoners, has been found to be of particular value in prison settings.
- **service improvements** such as screening for health problems and mental illness, suicide watches, the provision of treatment/rehabilitation services for alcohol

Health promotion in a prison setting poses particular challenges. For example, the suicide rate among boys aged fifteen to seventeen in young offender institutions is eighteen times higher than that among boys of the same age in the general population.

and substance abuse, the establishment of needle-exchange programmes for injecting drug users and the supply of condoms.

- **advocacy** for prison reforms, putting more resources into health promotion activities within prison settings.

Box 15.7 Why health promotion in prison

People in prison have poorer health than the population at large and many of them have unhealthy lifestyles. Many will have had little or no regular contact with health services before coming into prison, and prison populations reveal strong evidence of health inequalities and social exclusion.

- The majority of prisoners are young and male.
- 60 to 70 per cent of them were using drugs before imprisonment and over 70 per cent suffer from at least two mental disorders.
- It is estimated that at least 80 per cent of prisoners smoke.

- 66 per cent of all injecting drug mis-users in the community have been in prison at some time, of whom half had been in prison before they started injecting.
- Male prisoners are much more sexually active in the community than the general population, all age groups having more lifetime sexual partners, and more partners in the year before entry to prison, than would be expected from the general population. They are also six times more likely to have been a young father.

(Department of Health, 2004)

Box 15.8 How to assess whether a prison is health promoting

A health promoting prison should have:

- a reasonable balance between a punitive and a rehabilitative role
- screening for mental illness and treatment where needed
- mental health promotion and counselling
- rehabilitation
- a healthy diet
- opportunities for exercise/physical activity
- access to information on health
- voluntary counselling and testing for HIV and other STIs that is confidential and non-discriminatory
- a harm reduction strategy, including needle-exchange for drug injectors and the provision of condoms
- a comprehensive health service, e.g. treatment for HIV, TB
- a health education programme, e.g. using peer education
- educational opportunities
- follow-up after release, with support to reintegrate the ex-offender into the community.

Activity 15.5

Imagine that you were having a conversation with some people who believed that the main purpose of prisons was the protection of society and punishment of the offender. What arguments could you use to convince them of the importance of the role of rehabilitation and health promotion?

Inevitably consideration of the role of health promotion in prisons becomes part of the debate on the purpose of prisons especially the balance between punishment of the offender, protection of society and rehabilitation of the offender. Of these three roles, the rehabilitation of the offender and preparation for a future life without crime has been given less profile. A neglected dimension has been the needs of spouses and children of prisoners who share in the punishment through the disruption of family life.

Further reading

- Chambers, H., Howell, S., and Madge, N. (2002). *Healthy Care: The Evidence Base for Promoting the Health of Looked-After Children*. London: National Children's Bureau.

For a multi-disciplinary review with case studies of the needs of looked-after children and young people, see:

- Dunnett, K., White, S., Butterfield, J., and Callowhill, I. (2006). *Health of Looked After Children and Young People*. Lyme Regis: Russell House Publishing.

For a detailed discussion of sexual health of looked-after children, see:

- Mackie, S. (2003). *Let's Make it Happen: Training on Sex, Relationships, Pregnancy and Parenthood for Those Working with Looked After Children and Young People*. London: Family Planning Association.

A textbook directed at health workers, which covers the role of health promotion and gerontologic health care together with a discussion of normal aging and disorders common to elderly:

- O'Neill, P. (2001). *Caring for the Older Adult: A Health Promotion Perspective*. London: W. B. Saunders.

PART IV

Implementation, Evaluation and Reflection

CHAPTER 16

Planning and Management of Health Promotion

Contents

16 Planning and Management of Health Promotion

Key issues within this chapter:

- Successful health promotion involves the planning, management and evaluation of activities, the improvement of services and the bringing about of change.
- Management involves planning, setting targets, and organizing people, resources and time.
- A range of useful management skills and tools can be applied in health promotion.
- As your career in health promotion develops, you may find yourself in a management role with responsibilities for supporting and supervising a team.

By the end of this chapter you should be able to:

- understand the importance of planning and management in health promotion
- consider your own present and future role as a manager
- identifiy a range of skills that you can use in your health promotion work.

Change – whether the introduction of new activities or the reforming of existing ones – is always challenging and needs to be planned carefully to overcome inertia and resistance. In this chapter we will explore change within organizations, suggest approaches that can be used to influence your workplace, and review the management skills needed to plan, implement, monitor and evaluate health promotion.

There is a vast literature on management principles and theory applied to a wide range of health-service settings. In selecting what to include in this chapter we have drawn mainly on our own experiences and suggest practical strategies that we have found useful within the specific context of health promotion activities.

What is a manager?

In any group of people there are various roles that individuals adopt – the leader, the follower, the organizer, the joker, the fixer, the individual who always says 'it isn't possible', the negotiator, the person 'who can always find a way' ...

- The **change agent** is often the individual who sees the potential for change, the innovator who wants to try something new.
- The **facilitator** is the enabler, the person who will negotiate with others to demonstrate that the idea or project is feasible.
- The **manager** is the organizer, the practical operations person.

In essence the work of a manager is to 'decide what needs to be done' and then to 'get other people to do it'. This process can be divided into four sequential stages:

- to plan and set objectives
- to analyse and organize resources to meet the plan
- to measure and control the use of resources towards meeting the objectives
- to motivate, develop and train staff at all levels to meet the changing situation in order to fulfil the plans.

Box 16.1 How to be a good manager

The resources available to the manager generally fall into four categories – people with skills, knowledge, experience and motivation; money; materials and equipment; and time. A flexible manager will be able to utilize all the available resources to achieve the agreed objectives.

A good manager, therefore,

- has people skills – is a good listener and communicator
- promotes teamwork to get the maximum from the people they manage
- pays attention to motivating those around them and provides encouragement and praise
- makes decisions:
  - gets the information to make decisions
  - thinks ahead – anticipates consequences of actions and plans accordingly
  - considers alternatives
  - will take appropriate advice
  - accepts the responsibility for the decision
- pays attention to detail – never assumes that planned activities will happen and checks to make sure things get done
- learns from mistakes.

Good managers need a range of skills, including the ability to promote teamwork and motivate those around them by providing encouragement and praise.

Management and health promotion planning

In figure 1.9 we set out the health promotion planning cycle with its four stages: needs/situation analysis; define health promotion strategy; implement; evaluate/reflect. Management skills are important at each stage of this cycle.

> **Activity 16.1**
>
> Refer to the health promotion planning cycle in figure 1.9. Which of the skills in box 16.1 are needed at each of the four stages?

Leadership

An effective manager needs skills in organization and leadership.

- **Leadership** involves providing vision, establishing direction, motivating and inspiring others, and encouraging the best performances from others.
- **Organizational/management skills** include organization and staffing, planning and budgeting and problem-solving.

Leadership may come naturally to some people through their personal characteristics. However, for most of us, leadership is a skill that needs to be learnt through attending training courses and through practice. We will return to the issue of leadership later in this chapter when we consider the role and functioning of groups and committees in organizations.

Activity 16.2

Identify someone who is a good leader. Make a list of the reasons why that person is a good leader. Identify someone who is a good manager. Make a list of reasons why that person is a good manager. Can you think of examples of leaders who are not good managers or managers who are not good leaders?

Key management skills

Skills for Health (the UK-wide sector skills council for health) is developing a comprehensive package of National Occupational Standards (NOS) and National Workforce Competences (NWC) for use within the health sector. These competencies can be used by individuals and organizations for personal and professional development. In box 16.2 we present a list of the skills required for level 3, Senior Healthcare Assistants/Technicians.

Box 16.2 Management and leadership personal competencies expected at level 3 KSF (Knowledge Skills Framework)

Personal competencies	Descriptors – In performing effectively you will show that you:
Acting assertively	<ul><li>take personal responsibility for making things happen</li><li>can say no to unreasonable requests</li></ul>
Building teams	<ul><li>actively build relationships with others</li><li>make time available to support others</li><li>provide feedback designed to improve people's future performance</li><li>show respect for the views and actions of others</li><li>keep others informed about plans and progress</li></ul>
Communication	<ul><li>listen actively</li><li>identify the information needs of listeners</li><li>encourage listeners to ask questions or rephrase statements to clarify their understanding</li><li>modify communication in response to feedback from listeners</li><li>adopt communication styles and approaches to listeners and situations, including selecting an appropriate time and place</li></ul>

Personal competencies	Descriptors – In performing effectively you will show that you:
Focusing on objectives	• maintain a focus on objectives • tackle problems and take advantage of opportunities as they arise • prioritize objectives and schedule work to make best use of time and resources
Managing self	• take responsibility for meeting your own learning and development needs • seek feedback on performance to identify strengths and weaknesses • accept personal comments or criticism without becoming defensive • remain calm in difficult or uncertain situations • learn from your own mistakes and those of others • change behaviour when needed as a result of feedback • handle others' emotions without becoming personally involved in them
Thinking and taking decisions	• break processes down into tasks and activities • identify implications, consequences or causal relationships in a situation • produce a variety of solutions before making a decision • take decisions which are realistic for the situation • reconcile and make use of a variety of perspectives when making sense of a situation • focus on facts, problems and solutions when handling an emotional situation.

Setting aims and objectives

Aims are general statements of what the programme is trying to achieve, such as:

Aims: These are general statements of intent that indicate overall priorities and purposes without going into specific details.

- reduce inequalities in health
- promote mental health in the community
- reduce teenage pregnancies.

It is increasingly common for organizations to express their aims as 'mission statements' or 'vision statements'. These are general statements of intent and not expressed in a measurable way. A useful team-building activity is to bring people together to discuss and agree on shared aims and a common purpose.

However, more specific statements are needed when planning programmes. An 'objective' – also called a target – is a statement of proposed change over a fixed time period. An objective should be *measurable*. Setting measurable objectives will enable you to let others know exactly what you are planning, make decisions about its implementation, and evaluate the programme, e.g:

> *Between February and August the percentage of cyclists on the four main roads going out of Bridgetown wearing cycle helmets will increase from 30 per cent to 50 per cent as measured by a spot check observation street survey.*

You can set objectives for the intended *outcomes* of the programme, e.g. health status, behaviour change and health empowerment, and it is also useful to set them for any activities required to achieve the desired outcome, such as completion of a training course, production of a leaflet, etc. These latter objectives sometimes called operational or process, objectives, can be put on a workplan and time chart and used to monitor a programme.

Vision statements:
These are similar to aims and state what the overall end purpose of an activity, group or organization is.

Mission statements:
These are similar to vision statements but refer specifically to the aims and purpose of an organization.

Objectives – also called targets: These are very precise measurable statements of what is to be achieved by an activity.

Box 16.3 How to write a measurable objective/target

Define a measurable indicator for what you want to achieve (e.g. acquire facts, develop a decision-making ability, change beliefs, change behaviour, learn a practical skill, change a service, establish a new policy; (see chapters 2 and 17 for a discussion of indicators). The indicator should be relevant and it should be clear how it will be measured.

Specify :

- the *amount of change* above the initial baseline level, e.g. the percentage of the community with smoke alarms in their homes should increase from 10 per cent to 50 per cent
- *who* is to change (including where they live) – often called the 'target audience' (e.g. residents in Tower Hills Estate, men aged sixteen to nineteen in Leeds, catering managers in schools, etc.)
- the *timescale* over which the desired change should take place (e.g. over the next twelve months)
- changes that are *relevant* and *realistic*.

One way of remembering the characteristics of good objectives is the use the word SMART: *S*pecific, *M*easurable, *A*chievable, *R*elevant, *T*ime bound.

Figure 16.1 Turning an indicator into an objective/target

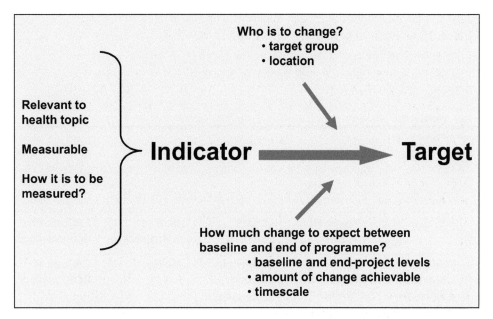

Activity 16.3

Write a SMART target for the achievement of one of the following (or a health promotion topic of your own choice): reduction in teenage pregnancy, setting up of youth-friendly clinics, take-up of a community exercise programme for the over fifties, increase in use of sun block on beaches.

Strategic decision-making

Planning health promotion programmes involves deciding the best strategy for achieving your objectives and breaking down that strategy into a set of activities that can be expressed in a workplan. Thus the basic building block of a plan is an activity – e.g. a home visit, a training course, the broadcast of a radio programme, the setting up of an exhibition, the holding of a meeting, the completion of a survey, etc.

Activity: The basic unit in planning. A programme is made up of a set of activities.

Strategy: A set of activities that, when implemented, are intended to achieve the objective/target.

Box 16.4 How to prepare a workplan

Decide the best strategy for achieving your objectives.
Break down the strategy into a set of discrete activities.
For each activity specify:

- when it will be done
- who will be responsible
- who else will be involved
- what indicator you can use to tell you when the activity is successfully completed.

Put the information into a table (figure 16.2) and time chart (figure 16.4).

Activity	Responsible person	Others involved	Date for completion	Indicator for achievement	Cost
Design, pre-test and print 2,000 copies of leaflet on breastfeeding	Graphic designer at city Health Development Agency	Community dietitian Community midwife National childbirth coordinator	March	Delivery of 2,000 leaflets	£750
Community radio phone-in programme on breastfeeding	National childbirth coordinator	Director of public health Community radio producer	April	Broadcast of phone-in programme	£150

Figure 16.2 Example of a workplan

Defining roles and responsibilities

An important planning task is to specify the responsibilities of the different persons involved in implementation; these are often set out in a workplan (see figure 16. 2). It is also helpful to stipulate the detailed roles/job descriptions of each key person. This involves consulting all interested groups, including management, field staff, and the community, to ensure that the proposed functions are acceptable and realistic and fit in with existing workloads.

Job descriptions are required for:
- the educators operating at the community level (e.g. health trainers, peer educators, volunteers)
- field staff involved in delivering essential services (e.g. patient education)

- persons carrying out a supervisory role
- the key person managing the health promotion programme

in order to:

- ensure that the responsibilities for important tasks are defined
- make sure that everyone is clear about their roles
- prevent overlap of activities as well as gaps
- define lines of authority and supervision
- determine whether training will be required to provide additional skills.

Delegation and supervision

Delegation: The process of devolving responsibilities for carrying out tasks to others.

An important role of management is delegation and passing on responsibilities to others. Delegation frees up your own time to concentrate on management and coordination and spreads the workload. It also taps the initiative of others, who are given an increased involvement in activities and greater responsibility and motivation.

Supervision: The process by which you monitor progress and ensure that staff are fulfilling their tasks. It also provides an opportunity to give support and training as well as to identify and solve any problems that they are facing.

Supervision is the process of keeping track of the activities of members of your team, providing support and dealing with any difficulties that may have arisen. Effective supervision can improve staff interest and performance, boost confidence in their own abilities, and encourage staff morale and sense of wellbeing.

Box 16.5 How to delegate

To delegate successfully you must:

- clearly define in your own mind the task, related authority and responsibility to be delegated
- choose a person willing and capable of accepting responsibility and carrying out the task
- provide the person to whom you are delegating with sufficient authority and time to obtain the results
- give clear instructions on what you are asking them to do and check they have understood them
- inform others of the tasks that you have delegated
- monitor their performance and provide supervision and support.

Giving and receiving criticism

Both giving and receiving criticism pose challenges. As a manager you need to ensure that tasks are carried out by others to the highest standard possible and that any faults are corrected and prevented from recurring. It is also important to respond to any criticism of your own performance in a positive way. If handled constructively, criticism can be an opportunity to learn and improve one's performance. If handled insensitively, it can be a destructive force leading to denial, defensive behaviour, blame and recrimination. Constructive criticism should focus on the achievement or non-achievement of previously agreed responsibilities and not attack or blame individuals.

Box 16.6 How to create a motivating environment

Creating a motivating environment is one of the most important ways in which a manager can get the best out of others.

- Have clear expectations of self and others and communicate these.
- Be consistent in dealings with all members of the team.
- Develop the concept of teamwork.
- Integrate the needs and wants of the team members with the overall purpose of the organization.
- Provide experiences for staff members that challenges and broaden their knowledge.
- Request participation and input from all staff.
- Be a firm decision-maker using agreed processes.
- Ensure all staff understand the reasons behind decisions and actions.
- Allow others to exercise individual judgement as much as possible.
- Recognize and reward good performance and behaviour.
- Create a trusting and helping relationship.
- Arbitrate fairly and consistently.
- Do not show favouritism.
- Be supportive of staff, encouraging individual growth and development.
- Know the strengths and weaknesses of each person.

Activity 16.4

From the list of motivating factors in box 16.6, choose five that are the most important to you. Compare your five with the choices of other people.

Coordination and effective communication

Coordination prevents overlap and confusion and ensures that everyone is working towards the same objectives. It is achieved through effective communication, which can be realized by establishing an appropriate organizational structure, making certain that everyone can express ideas freely, and providing clear lines of communication and responsibilities. Principles of one-to-one and group communication and group dynamics introduced in chapters 5 and 6 also apply to working within organizations (see boxes 16.10 and 16.11).

Meetings

Meetings – either one-off or of ongoing committees, working groups and task forces – are an essential part of working in organizations. If well managed, meetings can:

- bring together a wide pool of skills and experience to consider the problem and ensure that as many different aspects as possible are considered when reaching decisions
- provide a participatory framework for planning and decision-making that involves all stakeholders. Decisions that are reached as a result of real group discussion are more likely to have the commitment of the whole group than those imposed from higher authority.
- provide a mechanism for partnership and intersectoral collaboration
- enable a manager to obtain instant feedback about how the rest of a group feels about a particular issue or proposal.

Meetings have a wide variety of functions. For example, they provide an opportunity to involve stakeholders in planning and decision-making.

Many people are critical of meetings and argue that they take up too much time, are poorly carried out, and lead to delays and frustration. In our discussion of group dynamics in chapter 6 we discussed some of the obstacles to group functioning and decision-making. In boxes 16.7 and 16.8 we provide practical guidelines on managing meetings and group leadership.

Box 16.7 How to manage meetings

For meetings to be effective they must have a purpose and be planned and organized. Too many meetings occur that have no clear rationale and consequently little is achieved. If you are unsure of the reason for a meeting it might be better to cancel it rather than waste people's time.

Advanced preparation
- Notification – Ensure that everyone who is invited knows the date, time and venue of the meeting.
- Apologies – Is there a process for people who cannot attend to contribute?
- Agenda – Establish a regular format and circulate in advance.
- Clarity – Be clear about the need for advanced reading or other preparation.
- Date of next meeting – Agree a date at the end of the previous meeting. Is it possible to set a regular series of dates?
- Guests – Are any special speakers invited?

Running the meeting
- At the first meeting it is useful to ask everyone present to introduce themselves and explain in what capacity they are attending.
- Present the agenda – sometimes it is helpful to set a time limit for a particular item for discussion.
- Keep the meeting going at a good pace and do not get bogged down.
- Confirm any agreed actions before closing the meeting.
- The role of the chairperson is to facilitate the meeting so that everyone present feels that they have contributed and their opinion has been valued.

Activity 16.5

Think back to a meeting that you have attended. How well was it run? List three actions that could have been taken to make that meeting run more effectively.

Box 16.8 Leadership and effective group functioning

How well a group performs depends a great deal on leadership. Studies of group dynamics point to a wide range of approaches to leadership. These fall along a spectrum ranging from a *laissez-faire* ('leave it to the members') approach through to a top-down *authoritarian* ('I am in charge') approach.

Authoritarian		Democratic		Laissez faire
Leader orders group	Leader persuades group	Leader consults group	Leader shares decisions with group	Leader leaves decision-making to group

The authoritarian approach can reduce creativity and ideas from the members and limit the output of the group, while a laissez-faire attitude can result in chaos and muddles. The best approach is one where the leader acts as *facilitator* and helps everyone to work together, but when necessary can provide some strong pressure on the group members as a stimulus to action if the meeting has become bogged down and is failing to reach a decision.

It is helpful to separate out the role of the group leader into two broad areas.

Task maintenance

Task maintenance functions are those activities which help to get the group's task done:

- *setting the agenda*
  'Today our priority is to plan next year's programme.'
- *introducing new information*
  'Funds are available for a leaflet.'
- *asking for further information*
  'How much will this cost?'
- *making things clear*
  'I think what Jim means is ...'
- *summarizing present position*
  'We are now agreed on setting up a drama project.'
- *inviting suggestions from members*
  'Does anyone have any suggestions for how we can ...?'
- *prodding*
  'There's ten minutes left to make a decision on this.'
- *trying to find new ways around a problem*
  'Let's think again how we can solve this.'
- *reviewing objectives*
  'Let's remind ourselves that our main aim is to find a way of reaching men with our safe-sex message.'
- *introducing brainstorms, buzz groups*
  'Let's try a brainstorm to see if we can get some new ideas.'

Group maintenance
The *group maintenance functions* of a leader are those dealing with the 'wellbeing' of the group. This might involve:

- dealing with difficult group members
- encouraging quieter members to participate
- dealing with conflicts
- seeking consensus
- lightening the tension
- expressing group feelings.

Setting up a task force

When instigating a new health promotion action, a common strategy is to set up a committee – often called a task force, action group or working group – to plan and implement it. Committees often go through the following evolutionary stages.

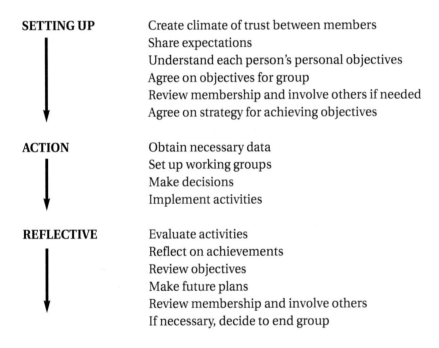

SETTING UP Create climate of trust between members
Share expectations
Understand each person's personal objectives
Agree on objectives for group
Review membership and involve others if needed
Agree on strategy for achieving objectives

ACTION Obtain necessary data
Set up working groups
Make decisions
Implement activities

REFLECTIVE Evaluate activities
Reflect on achievements
Review objectives
Make future plans
Review membership and involve others
If necessary, decide to end group

In the setting up stage it is essential to create a climate of trust. Everyone should feel free to give their opinion, share ideas and be prepared to work together to achieve the objectives. You have to look out for people who have hidden reasons for attending. Others may have come only because they have been told to attend by their employers but are really not very interested. Have you left out anyone important from the membership?

Achievements during the action stage depend heavily on the quality of leadership in the group. The reflective stage can be a period for expansion. However, it is also a time when a group can become fixed in its ways and inward looking. The challenge at this point is to find ways of keeping the enthusiasm and energy of members and, if appropriate, have the courage to take the decision to wind down the group and move on.

Training

Setting up health promotion activities and reorientating services usually involves learning new skills. As a manager you may find yourself in a position where you have to train others in your team. This might take place informally through practical on-the-job demonstrations or more formally through a planned learning experience that is an accredited part of continuing professional development. We have already presented some basic principles of learning and teaching in chapter 6. The competency-based approach to training (figure 16.3) builds on these general principles of learning by asking the following questions:

- What actions are you wanting the person to do – that is, what is their role/job description in your health promotion activity (e.g. to run a peer education programme, make home visits, hold group meetings)?
- What knowledge, skills (communication, decision-making and practical) and attitudes will they need to carry out these actions – that is, what learning?
- What do they know already and what needs to be provided through training?
- What is the best way to provide the necessary training?

Key decisions in planning training programmes are summarized in box 16.9.

Figure 16.3 A competency-based approach to planning training

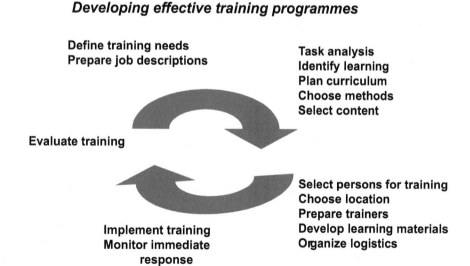

Developing effective training programmes

Define training needs
Prepare job descriptions

Task analysis
Identify learning
Plan curriculum
Choose methods
Select content

Evaluate training

Select persons for training
Choose location
Prepare trainers
Develop learning materials
Organize logistics

Implement training
Monitor immediate response

Training can take place informally, for example while 'on the job', or in a more formal, individual or group setting.

Box 16.9 How to plan a training programme

Components of training	Procedures/factors to be considered
Objectives	The starting point for planning training is defining the job descriptions/functions of key persons in the proposed implementation. The objectives for the training should enable participants to acquire those specific competencies. The content of the training is to deliver the specific competencies (and necessary knowledge, skills and attitudes) that the persons require to undertake their role in intervention.
Selection of participants	It is often useful to have a multi-disciplinary mix of participants (e.g. teachers, health workers and community workers) to encourage sharing of understandings. When training volunteers the community should be involved in the selection process.
Organization of training	The length of the training will be dependent on the objectives (e.g. an afternoon, a day, a few days or weeks, etc.). It is often a good idea to spread training out in blocks (e.g. weekly or monthly) so that participants can carry out reading and exercises in between the sessions. Pressure of work may severely restrict the time that people can spend away on training. You have to use sessions to cover what is really essential and consider including distance learning methods that the participants can follow from their workplace.

Box 16.9 *continued*

Components of training	Procedures/factors to be considered
Location of training	Choose a location that is convenient and accessible to the intended audience.
	Ensure the location meets the specific needs of the training. Possible requirements might be a room for group discussion sessions, a microphone/public address system, photocopiers for group reports, projectors, space for drama and role-play activities, catering facilities, secure storage of personal belongings, car parking, etc.
Selection of teaching methods	Educational methods should be appropriate to the learning objectives, especially for communication and for manual and decision-making skills.
	There should be opportunities for participants to practise skills with each other and to receive feedback.
	Training can be enhanced with inputs from resource persons, partner organizations and community members.
	Try to get a good mix of formal inputs and participatory learning activities, including exercises, games and problem-solving exercises.
Evaluation of training	*Short-term evaluation* can be achieved through observation/feedback questionnaires immediately after the course – e.g. have the participants acquired the knowledge or skills that were taught in the course?
	Long-term evaluation should take place through follow-up visits and supervisors' reports three to six months afterwards – are they putting into practice what they learnt during the training?

Managing time

Time is a precious resource. Poor time managers have one or more problems:

- relying on 'mythical' time – assuming that time is available when it does not really exist
- underestimating demands on time, including how long it takes to carry out activities
- an inability to say 'no'
- task hopping – jumping from one activity to another
- not knowing their own capabilities and how long it will take to complete activities.

> **Activity 16.6**
>
> Identify your top time-wasters. Share your list with a friend and think of some techniques to save time.

Box 16.10 How to control your use of time

- Establish what you need to carry out.
- Eliminate unnecessary and inappropriate activities – delegate as much as possible.
- Eliminate or reduce as many distractions as possible.
- Plan and schedule the use of your time (weekly and daily); make allowances for unexpected events and optimum use of your peak energy time.
- Set effective targets for your work that specify what you want to achieve and when you expect to finish each activity.
- A useful tool is a time chart – also called a timeline or Gantt chart – which sets out your planned activities in a visual format (see figure 16.4).

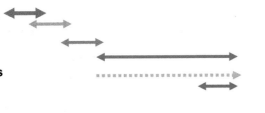

Baseline survey
Design/print materials
Train peer educators
Peer education activities
Weekly supervision visits
Evaluation survey
End of project report

Jan Feb Mar Apr May Jun Jul Aug Sep

Figure 16.4
Example of a time chart (Gantt chart) for a peer education programme

Activity 16.7

Choose a health promotion strategy such as setting up a community campaign or a patient education programme in a clinic. Separate the strategy into its different activities and put them onto a time chart.

Monitoring and evaluation

The purpose of monitoring – sometimes called formative evaluation – is to find out if the planned activities have been carried out, if the programme is on track and whether any changes are needed. Thus monitoring involves measurement of completion of activities (e.g. persons receiving training, numbers of people covered by health promotion activities, the production and distribution of educational materials, the completion of workshops).

In setting up monitoring systems the emphasis is on a 'management information system', using simple data collection methods that can be carried out quickly to give the required information (e.g. records, staff reports, supervisory meetings, community visits and qualitative methods such as focus-group activities). Monitoring activities are also specified in the workplan (see figure 16.2).

Monitoring: A continuous review of a programme to identify and solve problems so that activities can be implemented effectively.

The purpose of evaluation is to measure the impact the programme has on the community. Evaluation is discussed in chapter 17.

Assessing resource needs and resource mobilization

> **Resource mobilization:**
> The process of obtaining the resources you need to implement your planned activities.

What you can achieve will depend on the resources at your disposal. Health promotion involves the following three kinds of resources:

- human – people to carry out the work
- technical – equipment and specialist skills
- financial – money.

Resource mobilization involves assessing what is needed to carry out your planned activities and identifying any shortfall that has to be made up from inside or outside your own organization. Three sources that we suggest you consider are:

- **forming partnerships** – Are there other organizations operating locally that might be willing to work with you and share resources? (The role of partnerships, coalitions and intersectoral collaboration is discussed in chapter 11.)
- **community fundraising** – Could you run fundraising activities in the community? The starting point is to prepare an inventory of resources in the community, including persons, community groups, faith-based groups, voluntary sector organizations working in the community. (For more information on community fundraising, see chapter 11.)
- **fundraising from resource providers at a local, regional or national level** – Are there sources of funds that you can identify at a local level (e.g. from companies, businesses, churches and other faith groups)? Are there resource providers whom you might approach for funds, such as national charities, donor organizations and foundations?

Box 16.11 How to prepare a budget

Preparing a budget involves specifying anticipated costs of planned inputs and activities, principally:

- *capital costs*, which take place once during the life of a project, such as the purchase of equipment, the construction of buildings
- *recurrent costs*, which take place regularly. Examples of recurrent costs are the purchase of consumables such as leaflets and batteries, the printing of educational materials, travel expenses, costs of attending courses, salaries and catering.

Costs should allow for inflation and include a general contingency fund to cover unexpected expenses. When preparing a budget as part of an application for funding, it will be necessary to offer some justification for expenditures and explain why you need particular equipment, staffing, training, etc.

Introducing change

Introducing change within your organization and community poses challenges. Change can be a threatening process – especially when its benefits are not immediate but promised for the future.

It is important at the outset to consult all individuals involved to identify any possible concerns or fears. Communication of innovations theory, introduced in chapter 3, provides useful insights into what factors make changes more likely to be adopted. The theory predicts that innovations are more likely to be taken up if they are compatible with existing activities, are simple to carry out, can be tried out, and produce benefits that can be directly observed in the short term. It also predicts that an innovation is more quickly adopted when the idea for it came from the members of the organization rather than from outside. The theory highlights the usefulness of involving trusted/respected members of the organization (opinion leaders) in promoting the new ideas to their colleagues.

> **Resource provider:**
> An organization who might be able to provide you with financial resources.
> Each potential funder will have its special interests and criteria for offering grants or loans.

Many of the problems of introducing change originate from autocratic 'macho-management', imposing reform from above. When there is a lack of trust between management and staff, it is not surprising that any new initiative is received with suspicion and examined for possible hidden agendas. We advocate a participatory approach to change in which members of the organization/colleagues and community are involved in examining needs and finding solutions. In box 16.12 we set out a process for the introduction of change.

Box 16.12 How to facilitate change

Faciliating change involves asking the following questions:

What do you wish to change?
Why do you want to make this change?
How are you going to implement the change?
What alternative ways are there to implement the change?
Where is the change to be implemented?
When is the change to be implemented?
Which resources will you require?
Who else should you involve?

Who is going to implement the change?
Do they have sufficient skills or will additional training be required?
Who will benefit from the change?
What resistance can you expect?
How can you reduce the likelihood of resistance?
How are you going to evaluate the success of the change?
What criteria will you use to measure success?
How will you communicate the results of the change?

> **Box 16.13 How to prepare an action plan**
>
> An action plan is a short document which contains the following:
>
> - an explanation why the action has been required
> - a list of planned activities set out in a time chart/workplan
> - details of any training activities
> - an outline of any anticipated difficulties and how you propose to overcome them
> - specification of the roles and responsibilities of key persons
> - targets for the achievement of activities
> - mechanisms for coordination: meetings/consultations/supervisory activities
> - a budget.

Concluding remarks

Putting health promotion into practice involves setting out action plans (box 16.13), changing the style of services, and transforming ideas and theories into concrete actions. In this chapter we have provided some of the tools you need to take health promotion into the real world and to make a difference. One of the recurrent themes in this book is that health promotion is an iterative process in which we learn by doing, reflecting on the outcomes, learning from mistakes and putting the lessons into practice in our future activities. We will take up the theme of evaluation in the concluding chapter.

Further reading

For a review of the complexities of health organizations and a guide to the process of bringing about improvements in service provision, see the following:

- Skinner, H. (2002). *Promoting Health through Organizational Change.* San Francisco: Benjamin Cummings.

A comprehensive and detailed text on the principles of management, organizational systems, organizational change and leadership:

- Mullins, L. J. (2005). *Management and Organisational Behaviour.* Harlow: Prentice-Hall.

A practical guide to project management, including managing stakeholders, managing risks, specifying project components, time planning and tracking progress:

- Young, T. L. (2006). *Successful Project Management.* London: Kogan Page.

CHAPTER
17 Evaluation and Reflection

Contents

17 Evaluation and Reflection

Key issues within this chapter:

- A reflective practitioner is one who continually re-evaluates his or her practice and learns from experience.

- Evaluation is critical to assess the impact of health promotion activities.

- Health promotion is an evolving area of work and it is important to be familiar with new developments.

- Many sources of information on health promotion exist, including conferences, attending courses, peer-reviewed journals, publications from organizations (in-house or external reports) and magazines.

By the end of this chapter you should be able to:

- consider how you can apply the concept of reflective practitioner in your own work and plan your future learning in health promotion

- understand the concepts involved with evaluation and apply them in critically assessing reports of health promotion activities

- be familiar with sources of information on health promotion that you can draw upon in your work.

The reflective practitioner

This chapter provides an introduction to evaluation and reflection, which is the final stage of the planning cycle for health promotion that we introduced in chapter 1.

The concepts, theories and tools we have presented in this book are only guides and do not guarantee success. Health promotion is an ongoing 'iterative' process. That means that you need to be a 'reflective practitioner' and try out new ideas, evaluate your impact, learn from experience, try again in an improved form, evaluate once more, learn from experience, etc. In this way you can build up a body of knowledge of what works in your own situation.

Box 17.1 How to be a reflective practitioner

A reflective practitioner is someone who 'reflects' on what they do and then tries to improve on it. This involves:

- evaluating the impact of what you do and taking steps to improve your practice
- applying the concept of evidence-based practice
- taking note of what other practitioners are doing and learning from them
- keeping up to date with developments in a changing world
- making decisions about your own future learning needs
- preparing a plan for your personal development.

Evaluation

We evaluate communication and health education programmes for many reasons. The most important of these is to learn from our experiences and to improve our methods.

But there are other important reasons: you may need to evaluate your programmes to show that you are doing your job properly; you may need to justify the money you have received from a funding body; people around you may not believe that health promotion works and you may need to convince them to give you their support. You will need to decide at the outset *why* you are evaluating your programme and for *whom* the evaluation is intended. Some important terms used in evaluation are given below.

- **Effectiveness** – whether or not a programme achieves its stated objectives, i.e. did it work?
- **Efficiency** – the amount of effort in terms of time, human resources and money required to reach the objectives, i.e. was it worth the effort?
- **Formative evaluation** (sometimes called process evaluation) – 'monitoring' progress during the programme involving measurement of intermediate objectives, i.e. what have we achieved so far?

Evaluation: A systematic way of learning from experience and using the lessons learnt to improve current activities and promote better planning by careful selection of alternatives for future action. This involves a critical analysis of different aspects of the development and implementation of a programme and the activities that constitute it, its relevance, its formulation, its efficiency and effectiveness, its costs and its acceptance by all parties involved. (WHO, 1981)

Health promotion evaluation: An assessment of the extent to which health promotion actions achieve a 'valued' outcome. (WHO, 1998)

High attendance at a new programme or activity could be one example of a positive health promotion outcome.

- **Summative evaluation** (sometimes called outcome or impact evaluation) – measurement of impact or change at the end of the programme, i.e. have we achieved our objectives?

Evaluation involves showing that:

- **change** has taken place in the intended target group for the health promotion
- the change took place as a **result** of the programme
- the amount of **effort** required to produce the change was worthwhile.

Other considerations that need to be applied in evaluation are the issues of:

- **sustainability** – the extent to which the activity is able to continue after the external inputs have been withdrawn
- **equity** – the extent to which the programme has benefited the most disadvantaged and led to a reduction in inequalities in health.

Health promotion outcomes:
Changes to personal characteristics and skills, and/or social norms and actions, and/or organizational practices and public policies which are attributable to a *health promotion* activity.
(WHO, 1998)

Showing change has taken place and health promotion debates

Decisions about what changes to measure and how to measure them are really decisions about what your objectives/targets should be, which we discussed in chapter 16. They also depend on your approach to health promotion, especially in relation to the debates discussed in chapter 1 on the use of medical and social models, individualistic and structuralistic approaches, and the coercion–persuasion–health empowerment continuum (see box 17.2).

You should be realistic over what changes to look for in your evaluation. Changes in knowledge, understanding, awareness and belief might take place soon after the communication. However, changes in behaviour and health usually take longer to achieve. It is a good idea to carry out a *short-term evaluation* fairly soon after the activity and a *follow-up evaluation* afterwards to look for long-term changes.

Box 17.2 Indicators for evaluation – strengths and weaknesses

Type of change	Indicators	Strengths and weaknesses as an indicator for evaluation
Changes in health	Mortality (death rates) Morbidity (sickness rates, workplace absenteeism through ill health) Injury rates Notifiable diseases Quality of life indicators	Mortality rates are good for convincing policy-makers of the benefits of health promotion. However, it is difficult to achieve changes in health within a period of less than five years. Mortality is unsuitable for small-scale programmes because numbers are too small to make statistical comparisons with control communities.
Changes in behaviour	Lifestyle changes (diet, exercise, alcohol consumption) Uptake of services (e.g. immunization, screening) Adherence to prescribed courses of medicines	Behaviour changes are more suitable than changes in health/disease status for evaluation of health promotion because improvements in health can take a long time. However, changes in behaviours are more appropriate to programmes based on persuasion models rather than on empowerment.
Health empowerment	Self-efficacy scales Health literacy	This would be more suitable for community development and empowerment approaches.
Knowledge/ awareness/ attitudes	Knowledge of symptoms, causes, preventive measures for particular health conditions Perceived importance and susceptibility	Knowledge and attitudes can be measured using scales and are good indicators for measuring short-term impact. But change in knowledge or attitude does not necessarily imply changing behaviour, so these indicators are insufficient on their own.
Skills	Ability to perform specific skills (e.g. communication, decision-making)	For some programmes this is a useful indicator, but it is important to measure not only whether people have acquired the skills but also whether they are actually using them in their own lives.

Box 17.2 *continued*

Type of change	Indicators	Strengths and weaknesses as an indicator for evaluation
Advocacy	Enactment of legislation/policy Implementation of policies Media coverage of issues	These kinds of objectives are appropriate for advocacy components of programmes.
Service improvement	Training of staff Numbers of health promotion sessions delivered Uptake of new services Contacts between service providers and service users Quality/satisfaction indicators	Improving services is an important goal of health promotion. It is also important to establish that those services are being used by those in greatest need.

Activity 17.1

Imagine you were planning a health promotion activity on one of the following issues (or a topic of your own choice): prevention of teenage pregnancy, tobacco smoking among teenagers, prevention of cycling injuries, prevention of heart disease. Identify at least one indicator in each of the categories in box 17.2 that could be used to evaluate the health promotion activity. Which indicators do you think would be best? Give your reasons.

Showing whether change has taken place as a result of your programme

Most people would agree that it is important in evaluation to show whether change has occurred or not and, if so, to what extent. Evaluating whether any change took place as a result of your programme is less obvious. Consider the following situations where external factors had an influence on a programme:

1 During your breast cancer screening programme a well-known TV figure is diagnosed with breast cancer, and this leads to an increased uptake of screening.
2 During your local radio community-based 'five a day' nutrition campaign a new shop opens on the housing estate offering cheap vegetables.
3 Accident rates drop during your road safety campaign. But a new road system has been put into place during that same period, and this could have been the main reason for the reduction in accidents.

Does it really matter that these other factors helped your programme? Perhaps not, but what if your programme was an experimental pilot project testing out a new approach that you want to repeat elsewhere? You would have to make certain that the improvements made really had come about because of your methods and not for other reasons, otherwise money and effort would be wasted.

There are three ways of showing that change was caused by your intervention (this is called 'attributing causality'), which are shown in figure 17.1.

The strongest design, or 'gold standard', is the randomized trial study that we introduced in chapter 2. This involves measuring the impact of the programme on the intended beneficiaries (e.g. patients, parents, the community) and comparing it with the impact on another group, the members of which act as a 'control' and do not receive the health promotion. If the impact on the intervention group is significantly higher statistically than that of the control group, we can conclude that the programme has had an impact.

In practice, randomization is quite difficult to achieve for communities, so the other standard design is the 'quasi-intervention' study, in which subjects and controls are matched as closely as possible for social characteristics such as age, education, income and ethnicity.

It is not always possible to set up control groups, in which case a 'before and after study' evaluation design is used without controls. With no comparison group, the only way to attribute the change unambiguously to the intervention is to ask the test community why they changed – e.g. they might say that it was because they had attended the health promotion session or seen the television advertisement. In interpreting before and after studies without controls, you have to ask the question 'Could there be any other explanation, apart from the campaign that could account for the programme's success?'

In chapter 7 we showed how mass-media programmes are often evaluated by obtaining additional information showing that the people who changed were more likely to have seen and been influenced by the broadcasts. Another approach is to take

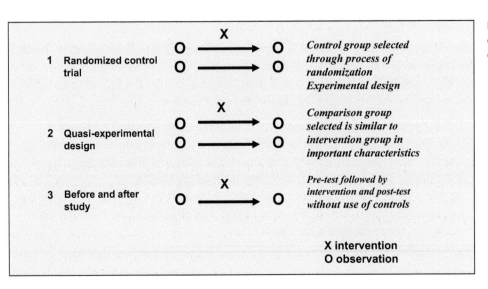

Figure 17.1 Three common evaluation designs

repeated measurements over time. If, immediately after your campaign, there is a surge in uptake of your campaign objective (e.g. family planning services, chlamydia testing, the purchase of smoke alarms, the return of expired prescription medicines) – and no other campaign on that same issue has been operating during that period – this can be taken as reasonable evidence that it is your campaign that has been responsible for the success.

Internal and external validity

Internal validity: The demonstration that an intervention was effective in the test community.

External validity: The extent to which the same success could be repeated in other communities.

A health promotion intervention might have been successful in one context, but the same success might not be achieved in another, where the local community may have a different culture/ethnic background or there are other differences (e.g. the presence or absence of a strong community identity or active local organizations and faith-based groups). When looking at an evaluation report of a health promotion intervention you need to consider whether there were any special features in that community that contributed to its success and, if so, whether the same success could be achieved if the approach was repeated elsewhere.

Process and participatory evaluation

This term is used for approaches to evaluation which place strong emphasis on the process of the programme. Process evaluations look for changes such as how well the field workers performed, the quality of the partnership between different organizations, the degree of involvement of community organizations, and overall the amount of follow-up activities in the community. Some people see process evaluation as a part of the monitoring process. Others see it as distinct from monitoring and especially appropriate for community-based interventions, where objectives are not fixed but evolve during the course of the programme.

Participatory evaluation – described in chapter 11 – is a form of process evaluation which emphasizes the involvement of communities and draws on the adult education theories of Paulo Freire (1972). Evaluation becomes a learning process in which the community is able to reflect on its experiences and plan future activities.

Common problems in evaluation

While most people agree on the importance of evaluation, it is often done poorly or even omitted. Reasons for this include the low priority given to evaluation, the fear of possible negative findings, the unwillingness of funding agencies to provide the necessary resources, and a lack of expertise in evaluation design.

We have drawn many times in this book on systematic reviews which seek to gain conclusions by critically examining evaluation studies. A common experience is that interesting studies have to be excluded from reviews because the methods used did not reach acceptable standards for drawing conclusions about effectiveness. The following are some common problems in evaluations.

- No objectives/targets were set at the beginning, so it was not clear what the purpose of the programme was.
- The objectives/targets are not measurable because they were set out in terms that were too general (e.g. increase exercise, increase awareness, empower people).
- No baseline study was carried out, so it is not possible to demonstrate any improvement as a result of the health promotion activity.
- Unanticipated benefits or negative outcomes are not picked up. The evaluation was focused only on the achievement or non-achievement of the objectives, so other changes were not noticed.
- A lack of impact is demonstrated, but reasons for failure are not known because insufficient supporting information was collected.
- An impact is demonstrated, but it could be for reasons other than the programme. A lack of controls or supporting information make it difficult to prove that the change observed was a result of the health promotion.
- The benefits of the health promotion are seen only after the end of the programme and are not noticed in the evaluation (sleeper effect).
- Improvements in the community are not sustained and the situation reverts back to the original state (backsliding).

In reviewing evaluations, you need to recognize that in the real world nothing is ever perfect. Evaluation is not easy and most assessments have flaws of some kind. You should take a positive approach and not dismiss an evaluation out of hand just because it contains some weaknesses. The challenge is to understand the limitations of an evaluation, learn what you can from it, but take care not to draw conclusions that are not supported by the findings.

Box 17.3 How to assess a health promotion activity

When reading a report of a health promotion activity, there are some questions that you should ask to assess what it has achieved.

- Which section or sections of the population are intended to benefit from the programme?
- What was the programme trying to achieve? Were any targets/objectives produced?
- Who initiated the programme?
- Why was the programme set up?
- Was a needs assessment carried out? If so, how was this carried out and by whom?
- How was the programme funded?
- How long did the programme last?
- What were the health education components of the programme?

- What were the service improvement components of the programme?
- What were the efforts directed at influencing policy components (advocacy)?
- Who are the people doing the work? How were they selected? Did they receive special training for the work? If so, what was the training?
- What was the involvement of the government, the community and voluntary organizations?
- Was the balance of health education, service improvements and advocacy adequate to achieve the objectives? If not, where were the shortfalls?
- Were there any other important features of the programme in addition to health education, service improvement and advocacy?
- Has an evaluation been conducted? Who carried out the evaluation? Were there baselines and controls? How was the data collected and analysed? Was there a good mix of quantitative and qualitative data collected? Were statistical significance tests used?
- What was the impact of the programme in the short and longer term? Which sections of the community benefited from the programme? What was the impact on inequalities in health?
- Were any problems encountered in the programme? If so, what steps were taken to overcome them?
- Did activities continue after the end of the project (sustainable)?
- What were the features that contributed to the success or failure of the programme in this community? Would a similar effect be achieved in other locations?

Activity 17.2

Look at a report of a health promotion activity and apply the checklist in box 17.3.

Managing your personal development

In this book we have provided an introduction to the rich and evolving discipline of health promotion. For some of you this will only be the start of a process of learning that will continue as your health promotion work develops. In this chapter we suggest ways in which you can take your studies in health promotion further, map out your future learning needs, and manage your own personal development in health promotion.

Box 17.4 How to map out my own future development in health promotion

Here are some of the questions you will need to consider:

- *How are my needs likely to change in the future?*
- *What skills will I need in my future work?*
- *Where can I find out more about health promotion practice?*
- *How can I take charge of my own learning?*
- *How can I evaluate my own health promotion?*
- *How can I evaluate other people's experiences in health promotion?*
- *How can I share my experiences with others?*

Activity 17.3

Make a visual chart of your own personal development needs in health promotion using the questions in box 17.4.

Learning about health promotion

In box 17.5 we list some of the different sources of information about health promotion. Some people may be happy just to learn from written materials. Others enjoy the opportunity to attend conferences and courses where they can meet and discuss issues with their peers.

Box 17.5 How to find out about health promotion activities/evidence

Paper-based
- Books
- Grey literature
- Newsletters/professional magazines
- Peer-reviewed journals
- Reports and systematic reviews

Internet-based
- Internet web sites
- Email newsletters
- Discussion groups

Meetings and courses
- Networking forums with colleagues in and outside your community
- Short courses
- Conferences and workshops
- Longer courses, e.g. postgraduate courses in health promotion and public health

Health promotion literature

Health promotion literature can be found in four main formats.

Books – There are many books on health promotion, including both general texts and books that deal with specific aspects, such as research, evaluation, mental health, men's health, etc. We have made suggestions for some of these in the further reading sections of our chapters. Inevitably some of the material in a book becomes out of date. Some books try to minimize this by providing a website with updated reading lists and web links (see details of our own website at the end of this chapter).

Grey literature – This is the vast body of literature that is produced mainly as in-house reports distributed by individuals and organizations, found on websites and informally distributed by colleagues. The richness and diversity of such material needs to be balanced against the difficulties finding out about and getting hold of it. While grey literature from well-known and trusted organizations is usually reliable, this is not the case when the sources are unknown, as there are no controls on the quality of the research or the accuracy and honesty of the information provided.

Newsletters/professional magazines – Many organizations send out newsletters on their activities by post or via email. Another source of information and news is magazines targeted at professionals, such as *Health and Social Service Journal* and *Community Care*. Newsletters are good ways of finding out about recent developments. A disadvantage is that case studies of health promotion activities are often presented as short 'newsy' articles without any peer reviews or research data to help you judge the quality of the evidence.

Peer-reviewed journals – These are the most reliable source of research and evaluation of health promotion. At least two independent researchers in the field will have looked at each paper to ensure that it adequately covers the subject and that the conclusions are supported by the data provided. It can take a year and sometimes longer from submission of a manuscript until its appearance in a journal, so the information is not as timely as that in magazines and newsletters.

In box 17.6 we suggest a core group of peer-reviewed journals that specifically focus on health promotion and health education, as well as some journals that consistently include material relevant to health promotion. However, you will need to look well beyond these journals, as information on health education, service improvement and advocacy is presented in a very wide range of journals from the field of medicine, epidemiology, health services, health professions (e.g. nursing and social science) and specific health topics (e.g. tobacco control, hypertension, etc.).

Some useful formats for research papers are:

- **evaluations of programmes** that provide evidence of effectiveness
- **case studies** which provide a detailed description of particular programmes
- **general reviews** of the research findings on health promotion topics

- **systematic reviews** (see chapter 2 for discussions of systematic reviews) of the current 'state of the art' for tackling health promotion issues, using particular methods
- **research studies** on the needs of target audiences
- **discussion papers** that challenge existing practice and present new ideas and theories.

One of the best ways of looking for health-related papers in peer-reviewed journals is the search through Pubmed (also called Medline) – the journals database of the National Library of Medicine in the United States, which is available to anyone on an open-access basis via the internet. This is a good source for finding papers on health-related journals, but it is useful to supplement this with searches using other literature databases, such as Psychological Literature, Sociological Literature, CINAHL (health and social services literature) and ERIC (education literature). For detailed assistance in using these databases you should consult our website or your nearest university or NHS Trust library.

Box 17.6 Some peer-reviewed journals for health promotion

American Journal of Health Promotion
Health Education
Health Education and Behaviour (formerly *Health Education Quarterly*)
Health Education Journal
Health Education Research – Theory and Practice
Health Promotion Practice
International Journal of Health Promotion
International Journal of Health Promotion and Education
International Quarterly of Community Health Education
Journal of Health Communication
Patient Education and Counselling
Promotion and Education

Journals not specifically on health promotion but which often include health promotion issues:

Public Health
Social Science and Medicine
Sociology of Health and Illness
Bulletin of the World Health Organization

Internet websites

Many internet web sites provide valuable resources for health promotion. One of the problems with the internet is that anyone can set up a site and there is no control on the information provided, which might be biased and incorrect. The NHS Executive Research and Development Programme funded the DISCERN project to provide guidelines on assessing health information on the internet, which have been published on a website (www.discern.org.uk) and as a short manual (Charnock, 1998). Health on the Net is a non-profit foundation which awards a seal of approval to web sites dealing with health issues that conform to its eight-point code of conduct for quality. In box 17.7 we provide some suggestions as to how you can decide whether the information on a site is reliable and accurate.

Box 17.7 How to tell if the information on an internet website can be trusted

- Who has produced the web site? Is it an authoritative source from a well-known and respected organization? Beware of sites that have similar addresses to well-known organizations but are not connected.
- Are there any obvious biases in the presentation of the information? Are there vested interests or hidden agendas for the organization producing the site? Is it a commercial company selling a product? Does it present both sides of the issues, including any areas of uncertainty?
- Is it clear where the information used in the website comes from and when it was collected? Are sources (e.g. peer-reviewed journals) given for the information provided?
- If it provides unpublished data, does it explain how it was collected, and was an appropriate method used to collect and analyse the data?
- If the website refers to specific medical treatments, does it present all the options, including alternatives to medicines; explain how treatment works; explain the benefits and risks, including any impact on quality of life; explain what would happen if no treatment was taken?
- Do 'respectable' websites, such as those of the World Health Organization (www.who.int) or the UK Department of Health (www.doh.gov.uk), give a link to the site? If so, it is probably genuine.
- Does it have the Health on the Net seal of approval (www.hon.ch)?

Professional networking through discussion groups

The internet provides opportunities for networking and exchanging ideas and information with others involved in health promotion, through email, membership of email list serves, and online discussion groups. A list serve is an electronic discussion group. You subscribe by sending an email to the list serve address. Once you are in the group, any email you send is automatically copied to all of the members, and you also receive any emails that others send out. When individual members send out comments, others respond, and thus a dialogue is created.

Professional associations

The **International Union for Health Education and Promotion** is the leading global network for health promotion, with international headquarters in Paris and regional offices in Europe and other parts of the world. Among its activities are the hosting of an international health promotion conference every three years, annual regional meetings and the producion of a newsletter, *Promotion and Education.*

The **Society of Public Health Education** is the main organization for health promotion in the United States and has been in existence for more than fifty years. It runs annual and regional conferences and a range of other activities which are described in a very comprehensive internet website.

The **Institute of Health Education** serves as a focal point for heath promotion in the United Kingdom. It organizes conferences and produces the *International Journal of Health Education and Health Promotion.*

The **Society for Health Education and Promotion Specialists** is the focal point for health promotion specialists, and its website provides information on health promotion, details of its network of membership, and advice on health promotion careers.

The **Faculty of Public Health** is the focal point for public health in the United Kingdom.

Closing remarks

In this final chapter we have provided some basic tools on evaluation, assessing evidence, and opportunities for networking and learning to help you become a reflective practitioner. We wish you every success in applying this work. You can contribute to the evolution of health promotion as a discipline by sharing the results of your activities with others. Good luck!

Further reading

For a useful brief review of evaluation methods for health promotion, see:
- Nutbeam, D. (2006). *Evaluating Health Promotion in a Nutshell.* New York: McGraw-Hill.

For more extended discussion of the concepts and methods in evaluation of health promotion, see:
- Valente, T. W. (2002). *Evaluating Health Promotion Programs.* Oxford: Oxford University Press.
- Thorogood, M., and Coombes, Y. (eds) (2004). *Evaluating Health Promotion: Practice and Methods.* Oxford: Oxford University Press.

References

Acheson, D. (1988). *Public Health in England: The Report of the Committee of Inquiry into the Future Development of the Public Health Function.* London: HMSO.

Acheson, D. (1998). *Independent Inquiry into Inequalities in Health Report.* London: HMSO.

Ad Hoc Committee on Health Literacy for the Council on Scientific Affairs, American Medical Association (1999). Health literacy: report of the Council on Scientific Affairs. *Journal of the American Medical Association,* 281: 552–7.

Allsop, J., Jones, K., and Baggott, R. (2004). Health consumer groups in the UK: a new social movement? *Sociology of Health and Illnesses,* 26: 737–56.

Anderson, C. (2000). Health promotion in a community pharmacy: the UK situation. *Patient Education and Counseling,* 39: 285–91.

Arnstein, S. R. (1969). A ladder of citizen participation. *American Institute of Planners Journal,* 35: 216–24.

Ashton, J., and Seymour, H. (1988). *The New Public Health.* Milton Keynes: Open University Press.

Baggott, R. (1995). *Pressure Groups Today.* Manchester: Manchester University Press.

Baggott, R., Allsop, J., and Jones, K. (2005). *Speaking for Patients and Carers: Health Consumer Groups and the Policy Process.* Basingstoke: Palgrave.

Bakermans-Kraneburg, M. J., Van Ijzendoorn, M. H., and Juffer, F. (2003). Less is more: meta-analyses of sensitivity and attachment interventions in early childhood. *Psychological Bulletin,* 129: 195–215.

Bandura, A. (1986). *Social Foundations of Thought and Action: A Social Cognitive Theory.* Englewood Cliffs, NJ: Prentice-Hall.

Barlow, J. H., Sturt, J., and Hearnshaw, H. (2002). Self-management interventions for people with chronic conditions in primary care: examples from arthritis, asthma and diabetes. *Health Education Journal,* 61: 365–78.

Barlow, J. H., Turner, A. P., and Wright, C. C. (2000). A randomized controlled study of the arthritis self-management programme in the UK. *Health Education Research,* 15: 665–80.

Barr, A., and Hashagen, S. (2000). *ABCD Handbook: A Framework for Evaluating Community Development.* London: CDF Publications.

Bass, S. B., Ruzek, S. B., Gordon, T. F., Fleisher, L., McKeown-Conn, N., and Moore, D. (2006). Relationship of internet health information use with patient behavior and self-efficacy: experiences of newly diagnosed cancer patients who contact the National Cancer Institute's cancer information service. *Journal of Health Communication,* 11: 219–36.

Batten, T. T., and Batten, M. (1967). *Nondirective Approach in Group and Community Work*. Oxford: Oxford University Press.

Beauchamp, T. L., and Childress, I. F. (1994). *Principles in Biomedical Ethics*. 4th edn, New York: Oxford University Press.

Beaver, K., and Luker, K. (1997). Readability of patient information booklets for women with breast cancer. *Patient Education and Counseling*, 31: 95–102.

Berkman, L. F., and Syme, S. L. (1979). Social networks, host resistance, and mortality: a nine-year follow-up study of Almeda county residents. *American Journal of Epidemiology*, 109: 186–204.

Berkman, L. F. Leo-Summers, F., and Horvitz, R. I. (1992). Emotional support and survival after myocardial infarction: a prospective, population-based study of the elderly. *Annals of Internal Medicine*, 117: 1003–9.

Bhatt, A. (1997). *Many Voices, One Message: Guidance for the Development and Translation of Health Information*. London: Health Education Authority.

Black, D. (1980). *Inequalities in Health: Report of a Working Group*. London: Department of Health and Social Security; Harmondsworth: Penguin, 1982.

Blower, A., Addo, A., Hodgson, J., Lamington, L., and Towlson, K. (2004). Mental health of 'looked after' children: a needs assessment. *Clinical Child Psychology and Psychiatry*, 9: 117–29.

BMA (2000). *Eating Disorders, Body Image and the Media*. London: British Medical Association.

Bowers, H., Secker, J., Llanes, M., and Webb, D. (2003). *The Gap Years: Rediscovering Midlife as the Route to Healthy Active Ageing*. London: Health Development Agency.

Bradford-Hill, A. (1965). The environment and disease: assocation or causation? *Proceedings of the Royal Society of Medicine*, 58: 295–300.

Broadfoot, M., Britten, J., Tappin, D. M., and MacKenzie, J. M. (2005). The baby friendly hospital initiative and breast feeding rates in Scotland. *Archives of Diseases in Children*, 90: F114–F116.

Brown, P., Zavestoski, S., McCormick, S., Mayer, B., Morello-Frosch, R., and Gasior, A. R. (2004). Embodied health movements: new approaches to social movements in health. *Sociology of Health and Illness*, 26: 50–80.

Brug, J., Glanz, K., van Assema, P., Kok, G., and van Breukelen, G. J. (1998). The impact of computer-tailored feedback and iterative feedback on fat, fruit, and vegetable intake. *Health Education and Behavior*, 25: 517–31.

Bull, J., McCormick, G., Swann, C., and Mulvihill, C. (2004). *Ante- and Post-Natal Home-Visiting Programmes: A Review of Reviews*. London: Health Development Authority.

Cabinet Office (2004). *Alcohol Harm Reduction Strategy for England*. London: Cabinet Office Strategy Unit.

Cabinet Office (2005). *eAccessibility of Public Sector Services in the European Union*. London: Cabinet Office.

Campbell, C., Wood, R., and Kelly, M. (1999). The relevance of social capital to health promotion. In *Social Capital and Health*. London: Health Education Agency.

Campbell, N. C., Thain, J., Deans, H. G., Ritchie, L. D., Rawles, J. M., and Squair, J. L. (1998). Secondary prevention clinics for coronary heart disease: randomized trial of effect on health. *British Medical Journal*, 316: 1434–7.

Chapman, S. (1996). Civil disobedience and tobacco control: the case of BUGA UP: Billboard Utilising Graffitists Against Unhealthy Promotions. *Tobacco Control*, 5: 179–85.

Charnock, D. (1998). *The DISCERN Handbook Quality Criteria for Consumer Health Information on Treatment Choices*. Oxford: Radcliffe Press.

Christmann, S. (2005). *Health Literacy and the Internet: Recommendations to Promote Health Literacy by Means of the Internet*. Brussels: EuroHealthNet.

Cochrane, A. L. (1972). *Effectiveness and Efficiency: Random Reflections on Health Services*. London: Nuffield Provincial Hospitals Trust.

Copeman, J., and Hyland, K. (2007). Older adults. In B. Thomas (ed.), *Manual of Dietetic Practice*. Oxford: Blackwell Science.

Corkrey, R., Parkinson, L., and Bates, L. (2005). Pressing the key pad: trial of a novel approach to health promotion advice. *Preventive Medicine*, 41: 657–66.

Dahlgren, G., and Whitehead, M. (1991). *Policies and Strategies to Promote Social Equity in Health*. **Stockholm: Institute of Future Studies.**

Davies, J. K., and Kelly, M. (eds) (1993). *Healthy Cities: Research and Practice*. London: Routledge.

Davis, T. C., Dolan, N. C., Ferreira, M. R., Tomori, C., Green, K. W., Sipler, A. M., and Bennett, C. L. (2001). The role of inadequate health literacy skills in colorectal cancer screening. *Cancer Investigation*, 19: 193–200.

Dearing, J. W., and Rogers, E. M. (1996). *Agenda-Setting*. Thousand Oaks, CA: Sage.

Della Porta, D., and Diani, M. (1999). *Social Movements: An Introduction*. Oxford: Blackwell.

Department for Education and Skills (2003a). *Every Child Matters*. London: HMSO.

Department for Education and Skills (2003b). *Skills for Life: The National Strategy for Improving Adult Literacy and Numeracy Skills: Focus on Delivery to 2007*. London: Department for Education and Skills.

Department for Education and Skills/Department of Health **(2006).** *School Nurse: Practice Development Resource Pack: Specialist Community Public Health Nurse.* **London: Department for Education and Skills/Department of Health.**

Department of Health (1998a). *Our Healthier Nation: A Contract for Health*. London: HMSO [Green Paper].

Department of Health (1998b). *Healthy Living Centres: Report of a Seminar*. London: Department of Health.

Department of Health (1999). *Saving Lives: Our Healthier Nation*. **London: HMSO.**

Department of Health (2001a). *Valuing People*. London: Department of Health.

Department of Health (2001b). *The Expert Patient: A New Approach to Chronic Disease Management for the 21st Century*. London: Department of Health.

Department of Health (2001c). *National Service Framework for Older People*. London: Department of Health.

Department of Health (2004). *Choosing Health: Making Healthier Choices Easier*. London: Department of Health.

Department of Health (2005). *Health Needs Assessment: A Practical Guide*. London: Department of Health.

Department of Health and Social Security (1976). *Prevention and Health: Everybody's Business*. London: HMSO.

Department of Health and Social Security (1992). *The Health of the Nation: A Strategy for Health in England*. London: HMSO.

Dixon-Woods, M. (2000). The production of printed consumer health information: order from chaos? *Health Education Journal*, 59: 108–15.

Dixon-Woods, M. (2001). Writing wrongs? An analysis of published discourses about the use of patient information leaflets. *Social Science and Medicine*, 52: 1417–32.

Docherty, G., Fraser, E., and Hardin, J. (1999). Health promotion in the Scottish workplace: a case for moving the goalposts. *Health Education Research*, 14: 565–73.

Doll, R., and Hill, A. B. (1954). The mortality of doctors in relation to their smoking habits: a preliminary report. *British Medical Journal*, 1: 1451–5.

Douglas, F., Brindle, S., van Teijlingen, E., Fearn, P., and MacKinnon, D. (2004). An exploratory study of computer screen-based health promotion messages aimed at students. *International Journal of Health Promotion & Education*, 42: 118–26.

Drentea, P., and Moren-Cross, J. L. (2005). Social capital and social support on the web: the case of an internet mother site. *Sociology of Health and Illness*, 27: 920–43.

Due, P., Holstein, B. E., Lynch, J., Diderichsen, F., Gabhain, S. N., Scheidt, P., Currie, C., and the Health Behaviour in School-Aged Children Bullying Working Group (2005). Bullying and symptoms among school-aged children: international comparative cross-sectional study in 28 countries. *European Journal of Public Health*, 15: 128–32.

Durkheim, E. (1952). *Suicide: A Study in Sociology*. London: Routledge & Kegan Paul [first pubd 1897].

European Opinion Research Group (2003). Eurobarometer 58.0: European Union citizens and sources of information about health. Brussels: European Opinion Research Group.

Farquhar, J. W., Fortmann, S. P., Maccoby, N., Haskell, W. L., Williams, P. T., Flora, J. A., Taylor, C. B., Brown, B. W., Jr., Solomon, D. S., and Hulley, S. B. (1985). The Stanford five-city project: design and methods. *American Journal of Epidemiology*, 122: 323–34.

Farrington, J., and Tsouros, A. (2006). *Healthy Cities in Europe*. London: Routledge.

Fazel, S., Benning, R., and Danesh, J. (2005). Suicides in male prisoners in England and Wales, 1978–2003. *The Lancet*, 366: 1301–2.

Federal, Provincial and Territorial Advisory Committee on Population Health (1999). *Toward a Healthy Future: Second Report on the Health of Canadians*. Ottawa: Ministry of Works and Public Services.

Festinger, L. (1957). *A Theory of Cognitive Dissonance*. Stanford, CA: Stanford University Press.

Fichtenberg, C. M., Stanton, A., and Glantz, S. A. (2002). Effect of smoke-free workplaces on smoking behaviour: systematic review. *British Medical Journal*, 325: 188.

Fishbein, M., and Ajzen, I. (1975). *Belief, Attitude, Intention and Behavior: An Introduction to Theory and Research*. Reading, MA: Addison-Wesley.

Fox, S., and Rainie, L. (2001). *Vital Decisions: How Internet Users Decide What Information to Trust when They or their Loved Ones are Sick*. Pew Internet & American Life Project: **www.pewinternet.org/**.

Fraser, C., and Restrepo-Estrada, S. (1998). The quick and the dead: a tale of two educational radio programmes. In *Communicating for Development*. London and New York: I. B.Tauris, pp. 130–44.

Freidson, E. (1970). *Professional Dominance*. Chicago: Aldine.

Freire, P. (1972). *Pedagogy of the Oppressed*. Harmondsworth: Penguin.

French, J. (2004). *Components of Successful Media Campaigns*. London: Health Development Agency.

Furnham, A., Ingle, H., Gunter, B., and McClelland, A. (1997). A content analysis of alcohol portrayal and drinking in British television soap operas. *Health Education Research*, 12: 519–29.

Future Skills Wales Steering Group (2003). *Future Skills Wales 2003 Generic Skills Survey*. Caerphilly: Future Skills Wales Unit.

Gagnon, A. J. (2000). Individual or group antenatal education for childbirth/parenthood. *Cochrane Database of Systematic Reviews*, CD002869.

Galabuzi, G. (2002). Social exclusion. Paper given at the Social Determinants of Health across the Life-Span conference, Toronto, November.

Gray, N. J., Klein, J. D., Cantrill, J. A., and Noyce, P. R. (2002). Adolescent girls' use of the internet for health information: issues beyond access. *Journal of Medical Systems*, 26: 545–53.

Gray, N. J., Klein, J. D., Noyce, P. R., Sesselberg, T. S., and Cantrill, J. A. (2005a). Health information-seeking behaviour in adolescence: the place of the internet. *Social Science and Medicine*, 60: 1467–78.

Gray, N. J., Klein, J. D., Noyce, P. R., Sesselberg, T. S., and Cantrill, J. A. (2005b). The internet: a window on adolescent health literacy. *Journal of Adolescent Health*, 37: 243.e1–243.e7.

Green, E. C., and Witte, K. (2006). Can fear arousal in public health campaigns contribute to the decline of HIV prevalence? *Journal of Health Communication*, 11: 245–59.

Green, L. W., Gottlieb, N. H., and Parcel, G. S. (1987). Diffusion theory extended and applied. In W. B. Ward (ed.), *Advances in Health Education and Promotion*. Greenwich, CT: JAI Press.

Grey, A., Owen, L., Bowling, K., Ryan, H., and McVey, D. (2000). *A Breath of Fresh Air: Tackling Smoking through the Media*. **London: Health Development Agency.**

Griffiths, C. J., Motlib, A., Azad, J., Ramsay, S., Eldridge, G., Feder, R., Khanam, R., Munni, M., Garrett, M., Turner, A., and Barlow, J. (2005). Randomised controlled trial of a lay-led self-management programme for Bangladeshi patients with chronic disease. *British Journal of General Practice*, 55: 831–7.

Haddock, J., and Burrows, C. (1997). The role of the nurse in health promotion: an evaluation of a smoking cessation programme in surgical pre-admission clinics. *Journal of Advanced Nursing*, 26: 1098–110.

Harden, A., Weston, R., and Oakley, A. (1999). *A Review of the Effectiveness and Appropriateness of Peer Delivered Health Promotion Interventions for Young People*. London: **EPPI-Centre, Institute of Education, University of London.**

Hardyman, R., Hardy, P., Brodie, J., and Stephens, R. (2005). It's good to talk: comparison of a telephone helpline and website for cancer information. *Patient Education and Counseling*, 57: 315–20.

Hariri, S., Goodyer, L. I., Meyer, J., and Anderson, C. (2000). Assessment of a touch-screen health promotion system in independent community pharmacies. *Health Education Journal*, 59: 99–107.

Harvey, H. D., and Fleming, P. (2003). The readability and audience acceptance of printed health promotion materials used by environmental health departments. *Journal of Environmental Health*, 65: 22–8.

Hastings, G. B., and Haywood, A. J. (1994). Social marketing: a critical response. *Health Promotion International*, 9: 59–63.

Hastings, G., and MacFadyen, L. (2002). Controversies in tobacco control: the limitations of fear messages. *Tobacco Control*, 11: 73–5.

Hastings, G. B., Smith, C. S., and Lowry, R. J. (1994). Fluoridation: a time for hope, a time for action. *British Dental Journal*, May: 273–4.

Hastings, G., Stead, M., and MacKintosh, A. M. (2002). Rethinking drugs prevention: radical thoughts from social marketing. *Health Education Journal*, 61: 347–64.

Hastings, G. B., Stead, M., Whitehead, M., Lowry, R., MacFadyen, L., McVey, D., Owen, L., and Tones, K. (1998). Using the media to tackle the health divide: future directions. *Social Marketing Quarterly*, 4: 42–67.

HDA (2000a). *Improving Health through Community Participation*. London: Health Development Agency.

HDA (2000b). *Art for Health: A Review of Good Practice in Community-Based Arts Projects and Initiatives which Impact on Health and Wellbeing*. London: Health Development Agency.

HDA (2001). *Workplace Health is Good Practice*. London: Health Development Agency.

HDA (2003). *Making the Case: Improving the Health and Wellbeing of People in Mid-Life and Beyond*. London: Health Development Agency.

HDA (2004a). *Lessons from Health Action Zones*. London: Health Development Agency.

HDA (2004b). *The Effectiveness of Public Health Campaigns*. London: Health Development Agency.

Health Education Board for Scotland (2002). *Young People, Health and the Internet: A Needs Assessment*. Edinburgh: Health Education Board for Scotland.

Health Promotion Agency for Northern Ireland (1999). *The European Network of Health Promoting Schools in Northern Ireland: The Health Promoting School: A Self-Assessment Guide to Assist Planning for School Development*. Belfast: Health Promotion Agency for Northern Ireland.

Heaney, D., Wyke, S., Wilson, P., Elton, R., and Rutledge, P. (2001). Assessment of impact of information booklets on use of healthcare services: randomised controlled trial. *British Medical Journal*, 322: 1218–21.

Helman, C. G. (2000). *Culture, Health and Illness*. London: Arnold.

Henderson, M., and Hutcheson, G. (1996). *Alcohol and the Workplace*. Copenhagen: World Health Organization Regional Office for Europe.

Henderson, P., and Thomas, D. N. (2002). *Skills in Neighbourhood Work*. London: Routledge.

Henderson, P., Summer, S., You, C., and Raj, T. (2004). *Developing Healthier Communities: An Introductory Course for People using Community Development Approaches to Improve Health and Tackle Health Inequalities*. London: Health Development Agency.

Hill, D., Chapman, S., and Donovan, R. (1998). The return of scare tactics. *Tobacco Control*, 7: 5–8.

Holmes, T. H., and Rahe, R. H. (1967). Holmes–Rahe life changes scale. *Journal of Psychosomatic Research*, 11: 213–18.

Hope, A., and Timmel, S. (1995). *Training for Transformation*, vols 1–3. London: Intermediate Technology Publications.

House, J. S., Landis, K. R., and Umberston, D. (1988). Social relationships and health. *Science*, 241: 540–5.

Houston, F. S., and Gassenheimer, J. B. (1987). Marketing and exchange. *Journal of Marketing*, 51: 3–18.

Howe, A., Owen-Smith, V., and Richardson, J. (2002). The impact of a television soap opera on the NHS cervical screening programme in the North West of England. *Journal of Public Health Medicine*, 24: 299–304.

Hubley, J. H. (1983). Poverty and health in Scotland. In G. Brown and R. Cook (eds), *Scotland, the Real Divide*. Edinburgh: Mainstream.

Hubley, J. (1995). AIDS and STDs: a guide to planning training programmes. *AIDS Letter*, no. 49, 1–2.

Hubley, J. H. (2002). *The AIDS Handbook Revised*. Basingstoke: Macmillan.

Hubley, J. (2003). *Communicating Health: An Action Guide to Health Education and Health Promotion*. Basingstoke: Macmillan.

Hubley, J. (2005). Promoting health in low and middle income countries: achievements and challenges. In A. Scriven and S. Garman (eds), *Promoting Health: Global Perspectives*. Basingstoke: Palgrave Macmillan.

Hunt, S. (2005). *The Life Course: A Sociological Introduction*. Basingstoke: Palgrave Macmillan.

Illich I. (1976). *Medical Nemesis: The Expropriation of Health*. New York: Pantheon Books.

INTRAH (1987). *Teaching and Learning with Visual Aids*. Chapel Hill, NC: INTRAH.

Jackson, M., and Peters, J. (2003). Introducing touchscreens to black and ethnic minority groups: a report of processes and issues in the three cities project. *Health Information Library Journal*, 20: 143–9.

Janz, N. K., and Becker, M. H. (1984). The health belief model: a decade later. *Health Education Quarterly*, 11: 1–47.

Jensen, B., and Simovska, V. (2002). **Models of Health Promoting Schools in Europe**. Copenhagen: European Network of Health Promoting Schools.

Jones, C. (1997). *The Context of PRA: Participatory Appraisal Pack*. Hull: University of Hull, Department of Public Health and Primary Care.

Jones, R., Pearson, J., McGregor, S., Cawsey, A. J., Barrett, A., Craig, N., Atkinson, J. M., Gilmour, W. H., and McEwen, J. (1999). Randomised trial of personalised computer based information for cancer patients. *British Medical Journal*, 319: 1241–7.

Kaduskar, S., Boaz, A., Dowler, E., Meyrick, J., Rayner, M., and Dixon-Woods, M. (1999). Evaluating the work of a community cafe in a town in the south east of England: reflections on methods, process and results. *Health Education Journal*, 58: 341–54.

Kawachi, I. (1997). Social capital, income inequality and mortality. *American Journal of Public Health*, 87: 1491–8.

Kerr, J., Eves, F., and Carroll, D. (2000). Posters can prompt less active people to use the stairs. *Journal of Epidemiology and Community Health*, 54: 942–3.

Kotler, P., and Zaltman, G. (1971). Social marketing: an approach to planned social change. ***Journal of Marketing*, 35: 3–12.**

Kreuter, M., and Strecher, V. J. (1996). Do tailored behavior change messages enhance the effectiveness of health risk appraisal? Results from a randomized trial. *Health Education Research*, 11: 97–105.

Kreuter, M., Farrell, D., Olevitch, L., and Brennan, L. (1999). *Tailored Health Messages:*

Customizing Communication with Computer Technology. Mahwah, NJ: Lawrence Erlbaum.

Lalonde, M. (1973). *A New Perspective on the Health of Canadians.* Ottawa: Department of Health.

Last, J. M., Spasoff, R. A., and Harris, S. S. (2000). *A Dictionary of Epidemiology.* New York: Oxford University Press.

Lee, R. G., and Garvin, T. (2003). Moving from information transfer to information exchange in health and health care. *Social Science and Medicine*, 56: 449–64.

Lefebvre, R. C., Lancaster, T. M., Carleton, R. A., and Peterson, G. (1987). Theory and delivery of health programming in the community: the Pawtucket heart health program. *Preventive Medicine*, 16: 80–95.

Leidig, M. (2006). Becker promotes condom use in Germany. *British Medical Journal*, 332: 812.

Leiner, M., Handal, G., and Williams, D. (2004). Patient communication: a multidisciplinary approach using animated cartoons. *Health Education Research*, 19: 591–5.

Lewin, K. (1948). *Resolving Social Conflicts: Selected Papers on Group Dynamics.* New York: Harper.

Ling, J. C., Franklin, B. A. K., Lindsteadt, J. F., and Gearion, S. A. N. (1992). Social marketing: its place in public health. *Annual Review of Public Health*, 13: 341–62.

Lipkus, I. M., Rimer, B. K., Halabi, S., and Strigo, T. S. (2000). Can tailored interventions increase mammography use among HMO women? *American Journal of Preventive Medicine*, 18: 1–10.

Little, P., Griffin, S., Kelly, J., Dickson, N., and Sadler, C. (1998). Effect of educational leaflets and questions on knowledge of contraception in women taking the combined contraceptive pill: randomised controlled trial. *British Medical Journal*, 316: 1948–52.

Lloyd, N., O'Brien, M., and Lewis, C. (2003). *Fathers in Sure Start Local Programmes.* London: Department for Education and Skills.

Lusk, S. L., Ronis, D. L., Kazanis, A. S., Eakin, B. L., Hong, O., and Raymond, D. M. (2003). Effectiveness of a tailored intervention to increase factory workers' use of hearing protection. *Nursing Research*, 52: 289–95.

Lynch, B. M., and Dunn, J. (2003). Scoreboard advertising at sporting events as a health promotion medium. *Health Education Research*, 18: 488–92.

McDermott, L. J., Dobson, A., and Owen, N. (2006). From partying to parenthood: young women's perceptions of cigarette smoking across life transitions. *Health Education Research*, 21: 428–39.

McElroy K. (1988). An ecological perspective on health promotion programs. *Health Education Quarterly*, 15: **351–77.**

MacFadyen, L., Amos, A., Hastings, G., and Parkes, E. (2003). 'They look like my kind of people': perceptions of smoking images in youth magazines. *Social Science and Medicine*, 56: 491–9.

McKeown, T. (1965). *Medicine in Modern Society.* London: Allen & Unwin.

McKinlay, J. B. (1981). A case for refocussing upstream: the political economy of illness. In P. Conrad and R. Kern (eds), *The Sociology of Health and Illness: Critical Perspectives.* New York: St Martin's Press.

McLaughlin, G. H. (1969). SMOG grading: a new readability formula. *Journal of Reading*, 12: 639–46.

MacMahon, B., Yen, S., Trichopoulos, D., Warren, K., and Nardi, G. (1981). Coffee and cancer of the pancreas. *New England Journal of Medicine*, 304: 630–3.

Maslow, A. (1943). A theory of human motivation. *Psychological Review*, 50: 370–96.

Massett, H. A. (1996). Appropriateness of Hispanic print materials: a content analysis. *Health Education Research*, 11: 231–42.

Mayor, S. (2003). Arsenal helps publicise testicular cancer website. *British Medical Journal*, 326: 1282.

Meric, F., Bernstam, E. V., Mirza, N. Q., Hunt, K. K., Ames, F. C., Ross, M. I., Kuerer, H. M., Pollock, R. E., Musen, M. A., and Singletary, S. E. (2002). Breast cancer on the world wide web: cross sectional survey of quality of information and popularity of websites. *British Medical Journal*, 324: 577–81.

Midha, A., and Sullivan, M. (1998). The need to redefine the practice of health promotion in the United Kingdom. *Health Policy*, 44: 19–30.

Miller, C. (1998). *Joint Action on Health Inequalities: The Policy Drivers for the Health Service and for Local Authorities*. London: Health Education Agency.

Mitchell, K. (1997). Encouraging young women to exercise: can teenage magazines play a role? *Health Education Journal*, 56: 264–73.

Montazeri, A., and McEwen, J. (1997). Effective communication: perception of two anti-smoking advertisements. *Patient Education and Counseling*, 30: 29–35.

Morgen, S. (2002). *In our own Hands: The Women's Health Movement in the United States 1969–1990*. New Brunswick, NJ: Rutgers University Press.

MORI (2003). *Patient Choice*. Worcester: MORI.

Murray, G. G., and Douglas, R. R. (1988). Social marketing in the alcohol policy arena. *British Journal of Addiction*, 83, 505–11.

Murray, S. A., Tapson, J., Turnbull, L., McCallum, J., and Little, A. (1994). Listening to local voices: adapting rapid appraisal to assess health and social needs in general practice. *British Medical Journal*, 308: 698–700.

National Cancer Institute (1998). *How the Public Perceives, Processes, and Interprets Risk Information: Findings from Focus Group Research with the General Public*. Bethesda, MD: National Cancer Institute.

National Literacy Trust and National Association of Head Teachers (2001). *Early Language Survey of Headteachers*. London: National Literacy Trust.

Neighbourhood Renewal Unit (2002). *Factsheet 1: What is Neighbourhood Renewal?* London: Office of the Deputy Prime Minister.

New, B. (1998). *Public Health and Public Values*. London: King's Fund.

Norton, B. L., McLeroy, K. R., Burdine, J. N., Felix, M. R. J., and Dorsey, A. M. (2002). Community capacity: concept, theory and methods. In R. J. DiClemente, R. A. Crosby and M. C. Kegler (eds), *Emerging Theories in Health Promotion Practice and Research*. San Francisco: Jossey-Bass, pp. 194–227.

Oenema, A., Brug, J., and Lechner, L. (2001). Web-based tailored nutrition education: results of a randomized controlled trial. *Health Education Research*, 16: 647–60.

Office for National Statistics (2003). *Social Capital: Measuring Networks and Shared Values*. London: Office of National Statistics.

Ong, B. N., Humphris, G., Annett, H., and Rifkin, S. (1991). Rapid appraisal in an urban setting: an example from the developed world. *Social Science and Medicine*, 32: 909–15.

Opportunity Age (2005). London: HMSO.

Parsons, T. (1951). *The Social System*. New York: Free Press.

Peersman, G., Harden, A., and Oliver, S. (1998). *Effectiveness of Health Promotion Interventions in the Workplace: A Review*. London: Health Education Authority.

Penn, H., Barreau, S., Butterworth, L., Lloyd, E., Moyles, J., Potter, S., and Sayeed, R. (2004). *What is the Impact of Out-of-Home Integrated Care and Education Settings on Children aged 0–6 and their Parents?* London: EPPI-Centre, Institute of Education, University of London.

Pringle, A., and Sayers, P. (2004). It's a goal! Basing a community psychiatric nursing service in a local football stadium. *Journal of the Royal Society of Health*, 124: 234–8.

Prochaska, J. O., and DiClemente, C. C. (1982). Transtheoretical therapy toward a more integrative model of change. *Psychotherapy: Theory, Research and Practice*, 19: 276–87.

Putnam, R. B. (1995). Bowling alone: America's declining social capital. *Journal of Democracy*, **6: 65–78.**

Qualifications and Curriculum Authority (2000). *Curriculum Guidance for the Foundation Stage*. London: Qualifications and Curriculum Authority/Department for Education and Employment.

Qualifications and Curriculum Authority (2006). *Personal, Social and Health Education Guidelines for National Curriculum*. www.nc.uk.net **[accessed August 2006].**

Rifkin, S. B., and Pridmore, P. (2001). *Partners in Planning*. London: Macmillan.

Rifkin, S. B., Muller, F., and Bichmann, W. (1988). Primary health care: on measuring participation. *Social Science and Medicine*, 26: 931–40.

Ritchie, D., Parry, O., Gnich, W., and Platt, S. (2004). Issues of participation, ownership and empowerment in a community development programme: tackling smoking in a low-income area in Scotland. *Health Promotion International*, 19: 51–9.

Robinson, S. E., and Roberts, M. M. (1985). A women's health shop: a unique experiment. *British Medical Journal*, 291: 255–6.

Rogers, E. M., and Shoemaker, F. F. (1983). *Diffusion of Innovations*. 3rd edn, New York: Free Press.

Ross, H., and Mico, P. (1997). *Theory and Practice in Health Education*. Palo Alto, CA: **Maryfield.**

St Leger, L. (2001). Schools, health literacy and public health: possibilities and challenges. *Health Promotion International*, 16: 197–205.

Schein, E. H. (1980). *Organizational Psychology*. Englewood Cliffs, NJ: Prentice-Hall.

Schillinger, D., Grumbach, K., Piette, J., Wang, F., Osmond, D., Daher, C., Palacios, J., Sullivan, G. D., and Bindman, A. B. (2002). Association of health literacy with diabetes outcomes. *Journal of the American Medical Association*, 288: 475–82.

Schou, L. (1987). Use of mass-media and active involvement in a national dental health campaign in Scotland. *Community Dental and Oral Epidemiology*, 15: 14–18.

Scottish Executive (2003). *Improving Health in Scotland: The Challenge*. Edinburgh: Scottish Parliament.

Scottish Office (1999). *Towards a Healthier Scotland: A White Paper on Health*. London: HMSO.

Seale, C., Ziebland, S., and Charteris-Black, J. (2006). Gender, cancer experience and internet use: a comparative keyword analysis of interviews and online cancer support groups. *Social Science and Medicine*, 62: 2577–90.

Sharma, S., and Anderson, C. (1998). The impact of using pharmacy window space for health promotion about emergency contraception. *Health Education Journal*, 57: 42–50.

Sinclair, H., Bond, C., Scott Lennox, A., Silcock, J., and Winfield, A. (1997). An evaluation of a training workshop for pharmacists based on the stages of change model of smoking cessation. *Health Education Journal*, 56: 296–312.

Sinclair, H. K., Bond, C. M., Lennox, A. S., Silcock, J., Winfield, A. J., and Donnan, P. T. (1998). Training pharmacists and pharmacy assistants in the stage-of-change model of smoking cessation: a randomised controlled trial in Scotland. *Tobacco Control*, 7: 253–61.

Social Exclusion Unit (2001). *A New Commitment to Neighbourhood Renewal: National Strategy Action Plan.* London: HMSO.

Social Exclusion Unit (2003). *A Better Education for Children in Care.* London: Office of the Deputy Prime Minister.

Stead, M., Tagg, S., MacKintosh, A. M., and Eadie, D. (2005). Development and evaluation of a mass media theory of planned behaviour intervention to reduce speeding. *Health Education Research*, 20: 36–50.

Steinberg, L. (1990). Autonomy, conflict, and harmony in the family relationship. In S. S. Feldman and G. R. Elliot (eds), *At the Threshold: The Developing Adolescent.* Cambridge, MA: Harvard University Press.

Stewart-Brown, S. (2006). *What is the Evidence on School Health Promotion in Improving Health or Preventing Disease and, Specifically, What is the Effectiveness of the Health Promoting Schools Approach?* Copenhagen: WHO Regional Office for Europe Health Evidence Network.

Strecher, V. J., and Rosenstock, I. (1997). The health belief model. In K. Glanz, F. M. Lewis and B. K. Rimer (eds), *Health Behavior and Health Education: Theory, Research, and Practice.* 2nd edn, San Francisco: Jossey-Bass.

Strecher, V. J., Shiffman, S., and West, R. (2005). Randomized controlled trial of a web-based computer-tailored smoking cessation program as a supplement to nicotine patch therapy. *Addiction*, 100: 682–8.

Tod, A. M., Read, C., Lacey, A., and Abbott, J. (2001). Barriers to uptake of services for coronary heart disease: qualitative study. *British Medical Journal*, 323: 214.

Tones, K., and Tilford, S. (2001). *Health Promotion, Effectiveness, Efficiency and Equity.* London: Nelson Thornes.

Tönnies, F. (1957). *Community and Society*, trans. and ed. Charles P. Loomis. East Lansing: Michigan State University Press.

Tudor Hart, J. (1971). The inverse care law. *The Lancet*, 29: 405–12.

UNAIDS (1998). *HIV/AIDS and the Workplace: Forging Innovative Business Responses.* Geneva: UNAIDS.

Van Gennep, A. (1977). *The Rites of Passage.* London: Routledge & Kegan Paul [first pubd 1908].

Vernon, D., and Brewin, M. (1998). Doorsteps walks: an evaluation of the impact of a low cost intervention to assist primary health care teams in promoting physical activity. *Health Education Journal*, 57: 224–31.

Viner, R. M., and Taylor, B. (2005). Adult health and social outcomes of children who have been in public care: population-based study. *Pediatrics*, 115: 894–9.

Voracek, M., and Fisher, M. L. (2002). Shapely centrefolds? Temporal change in body measures: trend analysis. *British Medical Journal*, 325: 1447–8.

Walker, K., MacBride, A., and Vachon, M. (1977). Social support networks and the crisis of bereavement. *Social Science and Medicine*, 11: 35–41.

Walker, Z., Townsend, J., Oakley, L., Donovan, C., Smith, H., Hurst, Z., Bell, J., and Marshall, S. (2002). Health promotion for adolescents in primary care: randomized controlled trial. *British Medical Journal*, 325: 524.

Wallack, L., Dorfman, L., Jernigan, D., and Thema, M. (1993). *Media Advocacy and Public Health: Power for Prevention.* **Newbury Park, CA: Sage.**

Watson, R., Stimpson, A., and Hostick, T. (2004). Prison health care: a review of the literature. *International Journal of Nursing Studies*, 41: 119–28.

Weiss, B. D. (2003). *Health Literacy: A Manual for Clinicians.* Chicago: American Medical Association Foundation and American Medical Association.

Welsh Office (1998). *Better Health: Better Wales.* London: HMSO.

Werner, D., and Bower, B. (1982). *Helping Health Workers Learn.* Palo Alto, CA: Hesperian Foundation.

Whiteley, P. F., and Winyard, S. J. (1987). *Pressure for the Poor: The Poverty Lobby and Policy-Making.* London: Methuen.

WHO (1981). *Health Programme Evaluation: Guiding Principles.* Geneva: World Health Organization.

WHO (1986). *Ottawa Charter for Health Promotion: First International Conference on Health Promotion.* Geneva: World Health Organization.

WHO (1993). *Life Skills Education in Schools.* Geneva: World Health Organization.

WHO (1995). *Report of the Inter-Agency Meeting on Advocacy Strategies for Health and Development: Development Communication in Action.* Geneva: World Health Organization.

WHO (1996). *Equity in Health and Health Care. WHO/ARA/96.1.* Geneva: World Health Organization.

WHO (1998). *Health Promotion Glossary.* Geneva: World Health Organization.

WHO (2004a). *Standards for Health Promotion in Hospitals.* Copenhagen: World Health Organization.

WHO (2004b). Youth friendly health services in Europe. *Entre Nous: The European Magazine for Sexual and Reproductive Health*, no. 58, 1–32 [special issue].

WHO (2005). *Chronic Diseases: A Vital Investment.* Geneva: World Health Organization.

Williams, J., Jackson, S., Maddocks, A., Cheung, W. Y., Love, A., and Hutchings, H. (2001). Case-control study of the health of those looked after by local authorities. *Archives of Diseases in Childhood*, 85: 280–5.

Young, J. T. (2004). Illness behaviour: a selective review and synthesis. *Sociology of Health and Illness*, 26: 1–31.

Younghusband, E. (1968). *Community Work and Social Change.* London: Calouste Gulbenkian Foundation.

Index

Page numbers in *italics* refer to boxes, figures and plates.